LIFE & TRADITION
in the
LAKE DISTRICT

by
WILLIAM ROLLINSON

Foreword by Melvyn Bragg
Drawings by David Kirk

Dalesman Books
1987

The Dalesman Publishing Company Ltd., Clapham, via Lancaster LA2 8EB
First published by J. M. Dent & Sons Ltd., 1974
First paperback edition (re-set with minor corrections) 1981
Second edition 1987
© Text, William Rollinson, 1974, 1987

ISBN: 0 85206 885 9

Printed by Fretwell & Cox Ltd., Healey Works, Goulbourne Street, Keighley, West Yorkshire

CONTENTS

Acknowledgments 13

Foreword (by Melvyn Bragg) 15

Introduction 17

1. Farms and Farm Buildings 19

2. Hearth and Home—Some Farmhouse Equipment 32

3. Cumbrian Fare and Folk Dress 44

4. Some Customs and Traditions 67

5. Folk Medicine 73

6. Early Veterinary Practice 81

7. Mountain Sheep 87

8. Some Agricultural Tools and Techniques 113

9. Weather Lore 124

10. Dry-stone Walls 127

11. The Woodland Craft Industries 141

12. Slate Quarrying and Mining 151

13. Cockfighting and Foxhunting 166

14. Sports, Pastimes and Entertainments 176

15. Lakeland Transport 193

Glossary 221

Notes 223

Bibliography 229

Index 233

PLATES

Pages 49 to 64

1 Glencoyne Farm, Ullswater
2 The old farmhouse at High Yew-dale, near Coniston
3 Low House, Troutbeck
4 Stickle Barn near Broughton Mills
5 Barn at Field Head Farm, Hawks-head
6 Barn at Wall End, Great Langdale
7 A bank barn at Holme Ground, near Tilberthwaite
8 A 'spinning gallery' at Thorn House, Low Hartsop
9 Yew Tree Farm, near Coniston
10 Inscribed date stone, 1581, at Hewthwaite Hall, near Cocker-mouth
11 Date stone, 1683, at Askham
12 A dated lintel stone, 1592, Mill-beck, near Keswick
13 Dated wooden lintel in the barn at Townend, Troutbeck
14 A curious date stone at Hutton Moor End, near Threlkeld
15 Blacksmith's sign built into a wall at Oxen Park, High Furness
16 Lintel stone at Randle How, Esk-dale Green
17 Date stone, 1738, on a barn in Far Easedale
18 The fireplace at Glencoyne Farm about 1903
19 An Eskdale interior, Brotherilkeld Farm, *c.* 1890
20 An unusual view of the fireplace hood at High Birk House, Little Langdale
21 An eighteenth-century spice cup-board at Rydal Mount
22 A Longsleddale spice cupboard, 1662, now in the church vestry
23 The interior of a Tilberthwaite farmhouse, 1972
24 Carving on a bread cupboard, 1646.
25 A carved oak bread cupboard typical of Cumbrian farmhouses, in the Museum of Lakeland Life and Industry, Kendal
26 An outstanding example of a carved oak bread cupboard, dated 1660, at Lanehead, Patterdale
27 An eighteenth-century cast-iron range, Townend, Troutbeck
28 A seventeenth-century char dish
29 An iron frying-pan with bow handle, and a circular girdle
30 A bakstone formerly at Spring Gardens, Spark Bridge
31 A seventeenth-century carved oak bedhead at Townend
32 A 'candle bark' at Hare Hall, near Broughton-in-Furness
33–37 Candlesticks and rushlight holders
38 A Wasdale classroom, *c.* 1894
39 A rush-bearing procession at Warcop
40 Carrying a 'burden' at the rush-bearing
41 Part of the annual rush-bearing celebrations at Ambleside

42 Members of the Furness Morris Men perform the ancient Pace Egging Play
43 A deer's foot and a horseshoe nailed to the door of a byre, Askham

Pages 97 to 112

44 The late Isaac Cookson of Gill-head, Bampton
45 A nineteenth-century fell farmer
46 Mr A. E. Irving of Bridge End Farm, Boot, after 'laiting' his flock
47 Hand feeding in winter
48 Digging out a ewe from a snow-drift near Windermere
49 The spring-time return to the 'heaf'
50 Sheep at Glencoyne Farm
51 Sheep in All Hallows Lane, Kendal
52 Pages from *The Shepherd's Guide*, 1817
53 A Herdwick with a key-bitted lug mark
54 Mr J. Hudson marking a Rough Fell shearling
55 A fine group of rams at Steel End Farm, Wythburn
56 Horn branding
57 Dosing a yearling sheep
58 Sheep-dipping at Mearness Farm, Cartmel
59 An apprehensive-looking flock waits to be dipped
60 In the nineteenth century it was common to wash sheep before shearing
61 Shearing at Thorn House, Low Hartsop, about 1880
62 Clipping day in Eskdale, *c.* 1895
63 A Kentmere shearing
64 Rolling fleeces
65 Rough Fell Sheep with and without fleeces

66 After shearing the sheep are 'popped' with 'ruddle'
67 Mr J. Hudson shears by hand
68 Mr William Birkett shearing Herdwicks at Tilberthwaite
69 Mr and Mrs J. Hudson rolling fleeces, 1972
70 An eighteenth-century plough team in Eskdale
71 Horse-ploughing near Lowes-water
72 High-level ploughing
73 Horse-harrowing at Syke Farm, Buttermere
74 Broadcasting seed in the Great Langdale valley
75 Sowing with a 'fiddle', Cartmel
76 Reapers at Raisthwaite, Wood-land, High Furness, *c.* 1890
77 Horse-reaping in south-west Cumberland, *c.* 1920
78 A flail in use in the Lyth Valley
79 A steam threshing machine and farm-hands, *c.* 1920
80 Haymaking in High Furness, *c.* 1890
81 Horse-mowing on the shores of Grasmere
82 Haymaking with a horse and sled
83 Loading baled hay, Cartmel
84 Leading the hay through the medieval gatehouse, Cartmel
85 Mr Joe Youdell using a reaping hook and 'gebbie'
86 Mr Mitchell of Rawfold, Dunnerdale, scythes bracken
87 Peat-cutting at Witherslack
88 Stacking peat in 'winrows' to dry

Pages 129 to 136

89 The interior of a wheelwright's workshop, Museum of Lakeland Life and Industry, Kendal
90 Wheel hooping

91 A partly finished wheel made by Mr R. Dewhurst of Hawkshead

92 Wall at the side of the Garburn Road, Troutbeck

93 Where the Brathay Flags outcrop, fences of interlocking flags are found

94 Wall on Low Pike, near Ambleside

95 Eskdale: pink crystalline rock used for wall building

96 Water-worn seashore boulders used for wall building

97 Hexagonal columnar rhyolite provides unusual material to bridge a beck

98 A well-constructed wall in Borrowdale Volcanic rock

99 Wallers repairing a stone wall on the high fells

100 Repairing a dry-stone wall in limestone country

101 A stone mosaic at Wasdale Head

102 One of the Troutbeck 'painable' walls

103–5 Some Lakeland hogg-holes

106 A wall head near Coniston

107 An initialled and dated gatepost near Rosthwaite, Borrowdale

108 A 'Cyclopean' wall near Ulpha, Dunnerdale

109 A Wasdale Head wall, many feet thick

110–11 Two Cumbrian blacksmiths

Pages 153 to 160

112 Coppice woodland in the Furness Fells

113 The floor of an abandoned pit-stead in Woundale

114–21 Stages in the making of charcoal, near Hawkshead, *c.* 1900

122 A group of 'colliers' and their huts, around 1905

123 Charcoal burners at Kirkby Park about 1905

124 Bark peeling

125 Finishing bobbins at the Stott Park Bobbin Mill

126 Hoop-making at Hawkshead Field, *c.* 1910

127 Trimming 'smarts' for hoop-making

128–9 Mr Charlie Airey of Storth splitting oak timber into 'smarts', and shaving smarts with a two-handled knife

130 A swiller's tools

131 Using a 'set-horse' to make an ash 'bool'

132 Mr Hartley repairing a swill in his workshop at Eskdale Green

133 Mr Myles Newton, swiller, of Lowick Green

134 A Furness swiller and a partly finished basket

135 The Black Hog of Stricklandgate, Kendal

136–7 A rural woollen industry

Pages 177 to 184

138 The stone-breaker in a Cumberland quarry, *c.* 1895

139 Circular saw at work on Lakeland greenslate

140 Sledging slate with a trail barrow, Honister

141 Mr Rex Barrow riving a 'clog' of greenslate

142 A river's tools

143 Splitting slabs of greenslate by hand

144 The slate-dressing floor at Tilberthwaite, *c.* 1880

145 Prize money for fighting cocks competing at Troutbeck, 1771

146 The cockpit on the green at Stainton-in-Furness

147 A Penrith cockfight poster, 1787

148 A fine 'goose bield' overlooking Levers Water

149 West Cumberland foxhounds on the pack-horse bridge, Wasdale Head
150 The hunter—and the hunted
151 John Peel's Day celebrated at the Oddfellows Arms, Caldbeck
152 Tommy Dobson's gravestone, Eskdale
153 Sheepdog trials at Wasdale Head
154 The start of the hound trail at Rydal 'dog day'

Pages 201 to 216

155 A poster for Ulverston Fair, October 1809
156 Kendal Hiring Fair, 1899
157 Bowness musicians about to celebrate Queen Victoria's Diamond Jubilee
158 A High Furness sports day, *c.* 1895
159 Mr T. Thomas 'gurning through a braffin'
160 Skating on Windermere, 1895
161 The senior guides' race at Grasmere Sports
162 'Tekin' hod' at Grasmere Sports
163 What the best-dressed wrestlers wear
164–9 Handbills from Kendal and Ulverston for visiting theatrical companies
170–1 Two nineteenth-century social gatherings

172–3 Walking geese to market . . . or taking them on horseback
174 Packmen regularly visited Lakeland farms
175 Horse-power at Caldbeck, *c.* 1900
176 Fruit and vegetable delivery in south-west Cumberland, *c.* 1920
177 Mr E. Quirk's 1904 Darracq
178 The badly eroded, unsurfaced Garburn Road
179 The Kirkstone Pass Inn, *c.* 1860
180 A steep section on the 'Buttermere Round' *c.* 1890
181 Four-horse charabancs descending Kirkstone Pass, *c.* 1900
182 The Ullswater coach at Pooley Bridge, *c.* 1890
183 Coaches at Thirlspot, Thirlmere, *c.* 1890
184 A light trap, *c.* 1920s
185 A charabanc poster, 1895
186 The Ullswater (Royal Mail) Motor Coach, 1915
187 Crossing the sands of Morecambe Bay (Turner)
188 Modern cross-bay travellers fording the Leven
189 The first *Swan* at Waterhead, Windermere, *c.* 1895
190 The *Gondola* at the head of Coniston Water
191 The Boot Express
192 The Windermere steam ferry
193 The present Windermere ferry

DRAWINGS

Map, p. 18

Fig. 1 Tarn Hows Farm House; section and plan, 20

Fig. 2 Far Orrest, Windermere; elevation and plan, 21

Fig. 3 The Statesman plan, 23

Fig. 4 Glencoyne Farm; elevation and plan, 25

Fig. 5 Derwent Farm, Grange-in-Borrowdale; elevation and plan, 26

Fig. 6 Old Farm, High Yewdale; plan and elevation, 27

Fig. 7 Corn-drying kiln, Low Hartsop
A Lakeland bank barn, 29

Fig. 8 The kitchen hearth, 33

Fig. 9 A bakstone in a farm at Ayside, 35

Fig. 10 Carved chair from Townend, Troutbeck, 36

Fig. 11 Household illumination, 39

Fig. 12 Panel on a kist at Townend, 40

Fig. 13 Dairy equipment, 42

Fig. 14 Handbill of Mr Davis, optician, 75

Fig. 15 Handbill of Mr Summers, dentist, 76

Fig. 16 Handbill of Mr Ross, midwife, 77

Fig. 17 Handbill of Mr Charnock, surgeon, 78

Fig. 18 Some veterinary implements, 85

Fig. 19 Lakeland lug marks, 89

Fig. 20 Sheep-stealing handbill, 90

Fig. 21 Mountain sheep, 93

Fig. 22 Sheep band used for tethering, 95

Fig. 23 A bracken sled
A Cumbrian farm cart, 114

Fig. 24 Spades and push-ploughs, 117

Fig. 25 Ploughs, scythes and sickles, 119

Fig. 26 Threshing machine handbill, 121

Fig. 27 Part of the Troutbeck Painable Fence Book, 136

Fig. 28 Stages in the construction of a dry-stone wall
A rabbit 'smoot', 138

Fig. 29 Part of a wage receipt 1841, 140

Fig. 30 Announcement of sale of coppice wood, 143

Fig. 31 Account for woodland industries, 1770, 144

Fig. 32 Woodland industries, 147

Fig. 33 Handbill advertising blue slate, 1773, 162

Fig. 34 Stainton cockpit, plan and section
Steel cockspurs, 168

Fig. 35 Cross section of a 'goose bield'
Fox screws from Great Langdale, 173

Fig. 36 Pack-horse bell from Kendal, 194

Fig. 37 A carrier's handbill, 1811, 196

Fig. 38 Cross-sands coach poster, 197

Fig. 39 Handbill for Askew's Keswick-Borrowdale coach, 1909, 198

Thanks are due to the following for permission to reproduce illustrations:

Barrow Public Library, pls 19, 30, 38, 58, 62, 76, 80, 155, 160, 175, 189, 190, 191; Mr K. Benson of Ulverston, pls 122, 123; Mr Geoffrey Berry, Kendal, pl 193; Mr J. Fleming, pls 114–21; Mr D. W. Jones, Grange-over-Sands, pl 125; Kendal Public Library, pls 111, 124, 126, 140, 144, 156, 180, 181; Mr G. Lowe, Windlesham, Surrey, pl 18; Mr W. R. Mitchell, pls 39, 40, 85, 128, 129, 130; Museum of Lakeland Life and Industry, Kendal, pls 45, 47, 60, 61, 89, 90, 150, 157, 172, 173, 192; and from the Hardman Collection, pls 41, 44, 48, 49, 50, 51, 56, 59, 63, 64, 65, 66, 71, 72, 73, 74, 75, 78, 81, 82, 83, 84, 87, 88, 99, 127, 149, 151, 153; National Monuments Records, pls 20, 26; *North Western Evening Mail*, pls 42, 133; Mr R. Sankey, pl 174; Alice E. Smith and the late R. C. Cross, pls 4, 5, 6; Mrs J. H. Smith Collection, pls 77, 79, 110, 136, 137, 138, 176, 184; University of Reading Museum of English Rural Life, pl 134; *West Cumberland Times & Star and the Whitehaven News*, pl 159; *Westmorland Gazette*, pl 154; Westmorland Record Office, pls 145, 147, 164.

Other photographs are by the author.

ACKNOWLEDGMENTS

The names of the people who have helped in the production of this book would occupy many pages, but I must single out for particular thanks Mr F. Barnes of Barrow-in-Furness, who first stimulated my interest in Cumbrian folk culture; Miss S. MacPherson and Mr B. C. Jones, County Archivists of Cumberland and Westmorland; Mr J. Smith, Director of the Barrow-in-Furness Public Library; Mr R. Smith, Keeper of the Furness Local Collection, and his assistant, Miss M. Jones; and Mr J. Foster of the Kendal Public Library. Mr J. Anstee, Curator of the Museum of Lakeland Life and Industry, has patiently answered my many queries concerning agricultural equipment; Mr A. Frearson of Ayside, Cartmel, offered valuable advice on local architecture; and Mr P. Boyle of Dalston corrected my veterinary misconceptions. I am indebted to Mrs J. H. Smith of Broughton-in-Furness; Mr and Mrs J. Fleming of Hare Hall, Broughton; Mrs A. E. Smith of Grange-over-Sands; Mr K. Benson of Ulverston; Mrs H. Harrison, Mr W. Abbott and Miss Askew of Patterdale; Mr W. R. Mitchell of Settle and Mr R. Sankey of Barrow for allowing me to use photographs from their private collections. In addition, I must thank the following for assistance and information: Mr and Mrs Delmar Banner, Mr G. Bott, Dr R. W. Brunskill, Mrs Ada Flynn, The Leconfield Estate Co., Mr J. Melville, Mr and Mrs W. Moss, The National Trust and Mr C. H. D. Acland, Mr R. G. Plint, Mr B. L. Thompson, Mr A. J. Trohear, the Research Committee of the University of Liverpool and all those who allowed me to take photographs. Mr Douglas Birch and Mr George Dimmock of the Photographic Section of the Liverpool University Geography Department processed my photographic attempts and Mr A. G. Hodgkiss, the Department's Chief Cartographer, drew the map. Finally, my sincere thanks must go to Mr David Kirk, who spent many hours producing the line drawings, to Mrs E. I. Horne who typed the manuscript, and to my University Extension classes in Furness and North Lancashire for their helpful comments and discussion. I can honestly say that without the assistance and encouragement of all these people this book could not have been written.

William Rollinson, University of Liverpool, 1974

In preparing this second edition, I have taken the opportunity to correct some minor errors and to up-date material where necessary. I have not, however, attempted to eradicate the names of the former counties of Cumberland and Westmorland for I feel that where folk life is concerned, these traditional names should be retained. Once again I must thank all those people who kindly allowed me to use their photographs. I am particularly indebted to David Joy and the Dalesman Publishing Company Ltd. for their assistance and encouragement in the production of this edition, to David and Nina Kirk and Christine Denmead for valuable help with proof reading, and to my fellow Cumbrian, Melvyn Bragg, for his foreword.

February, 1981
William Rollinson, Barrow-in-Furness

FOREWORD

THIS book will delight everyone interested in the Lake District. William Rollinson's achievement is to have harvested great swathes of fresh information from the heartland of this unique region. His own enthusiasm is constantly on the surface making easy reading of careful scholarship. 'Life and Tradition in the Lake District' is both entertaining and authoritative—an essential complement to the great books of poetry and history which the place has inspired.

The strength of the book lies in the newness of so much of the material. William Rollinson is passionately interested in the way in which people lived their lives inside this natural fortress. He wants to know about the houses they built, the clothes they wore, the medicines and tools they had, the crafts they practised, their food and sport and work. Wordsworth drew great and intense poetry from the area: Collingwood saw it as a vivid stage for the panorama of British History: Rollinson sees it as home. A home to be lovingly noted down and cherished. Everything human intrigues him and like the born teacher he is, he can pass on his passion to the rest of us.

Here you can find out how butter and cheese were made; see examples of spinning galleries and carved oak bread cupboards; a simple rushlight holder will occupy him as devotedly as customs such as Bidden Weddings and Barring-Out. There's a chapter on folk medicine which is both amusing and instructive—they would live, you can see, where we would perish. All aspects of sheep-lore are displayed—from the lug marks to the shearing, the horn-branding to the dipping. The photographs—often his own—are full of the Cumbrian faces he so greatly admires. And so it goes on—swill-making, brush-making, slate-quarrying, hunting, cock-fighting, stone-breaking: the breadth of his interest is matched by the precision of his research: nothing, we feel sure, is skimped or twisted.

The romance and sympathy in William Rollinson is seen at its finest in his piece on dry stone walling. How exactly he differentiates between one sort of walling and another: how patiently he explores the history of that massive configuration of stone thrown down on the hills like a stone net from an ancient god: and how he teaches us to appreciate what those gangs of anonymous, ill paid men did up alone on the heights in all weathers laying out those countless marching columns.

There are few places as rich in so many ways as Cumbria. Not the least of its treasures is its literature. 'Life and Tradition in the Lake District' takes its place as one of the best books ever written about the place—telling us what its author has devoted himself to—the extraordinary history of so called ordinary men.

Melvyn Bragg

*In memory of
my mother and father*

INTRODUCTION

In common with most of the upland areas of Britain, the Lake District was once an area where the pace of life was slow, where changes and innovations were greeted with suspicion and where tradition and folk lore died hard. This innate conservatism was in part a response to the isolation of the region; while the wars, battles and revolutions of English history raged in the more prosperous areas of the country, here in the Cumbrian dales barely a whisper of discord disturbed the steady pattern of life determined by seedtime and harvest, by lambing and shearing. But such is no longer the case. The railways in the nineteenth century and the motorways in the twentieth have shattered the isolation of the Lake District; the mechanization of farming and the application of technology to a rural economy have wrought a second agricultural revolution, with the consequent decline of age-old farming practices. Yet these changes, though great in magnitude, are so recent that there are those alive today who remember a more self-sufficient economy, when peats were 'graved' for fuel and bracken was sledged down the fellsides on wooden sleds, when butter and cheese were made in farmhouse dairies and when haver bread was baked on a girdle over farmhouse fires. Although sadly reduced in numbers, there are still Lakeland craftsmen who know the art of building a dry-stone wall, who can fashion a swill basket, construct a cartwheel, or 'rive' a 'clog' of greenstone into wafer-thin slates. Fell farmers continue to rely as much on traditional weather signs and portents as on the Meteorological Office forecasts, and there are still dalesfolk who prefer to trust the well-tried folk medicine and hedgerow cures of their great grandparents rather than the pharmaceutical preparations of the twentieth century.

This book is an attempt to record some of the facets of folk life and culture in the Lake District; it is partly a story of a world we have lost—and one which is vanishing.

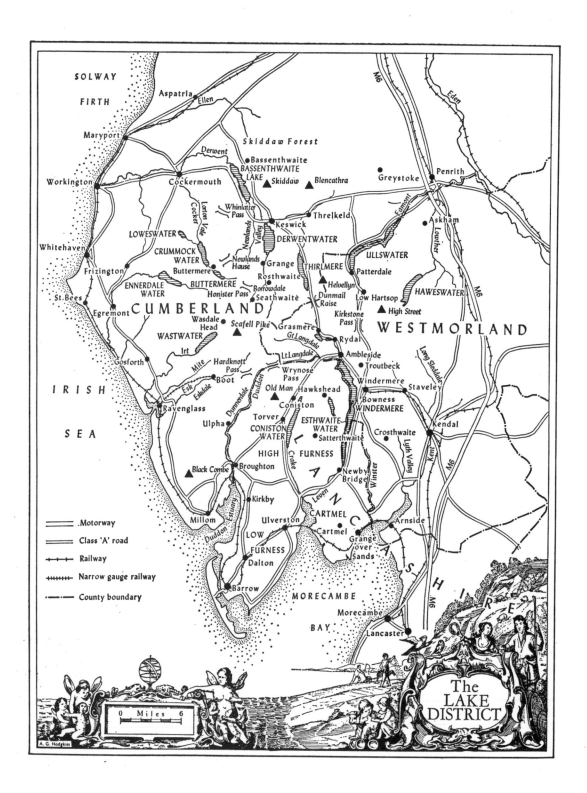

The
LAKE
DISTRICT

1 FARMS AND FARM BUILDINGS

FARMHOUSES

Little is known of the small Lakeland farm before the seventeenth century, for none has survived intact. From various literary references, however, it seems probable that most of these older farmhouses were built around a 'cruck' frame. Pairs of naturally arched 'cruck' timbers or 'siles', pegged together at the apex, were raised to support a ridge beam and a series of rough-hewn rafters; on this skeleton, which had a remarkable likeness to the frame of an inverted ship, the roof was fixed. The low walls of these buildings, which often hid the crucks, carried no load. Although there are several examples of barns in the Lake District built in this ancient manner (see p. 28) there are very few houses. However, those which do remain are typified by two examples, one at Far Orrest, near Windermere, and the other at Tarn Hows Farm near Coniston.[1]

At Tarn Hows the remains of an older cruck-built farm adjoin a larger, eighteenth-century stone-built farm, but from the surviving crucks it seems that the original farm here was a simple two-bay house (fig. 1). At Far Orrest Farm, although somewhat modified, it is possible to outline a detailed plan (fig. 2); in this case it is impossible to identify the remaining pair of cruck-trusses from outside the building. Because so few examples of cruck-built farms have survived in Cumbria, the dating of such buildings presents certain problems; basically, this is a medieval building style and it seems likely that in both these examples the original fireplace was an open hearth in the centre of the house. The change-over from this arrangement to the gable-end fireplace occurred about the first half of the sixteenth century, so that both the original farm at Tarn Hows and that at Orrest could date from the beginning of that century.

By the mid seventeenth century domestic architecture began to change, and for the next hundred years, until about 1750, most of the farms in the Lake District were rebuilt or drastically altered. Indeed, this period has come to be known as the era of 'the Great Rebuilding'.[2] Throughout much of England the rebuilding took place in the seventy years following 1570, but in the remote mountain fastness of Cumbria improvements and innovations in building patterns were slow to arrive. The reasons are not difficult to see; until the seventeenth century the Lake District fells afforded a harsh, uncompromising environment of small subsistence farms where capital for rebuilding was hard to come by. By the second half of that century, however, the troublesome Scottish border question[3] had been solved and the border counties began to enjoy a period of peace, stability and prosperity based on the woollen industry. Not surprisingly this newly acquired wealth found expression in the rebuilding of many farms, and this impetus lasted until the mid eighteenth century, when it subsided with the fortunes of the woollen trade.[4] By the beginning of the seventeenth century the so-called 'statesmen', small free-holders or customary tenants, had emerged as the most

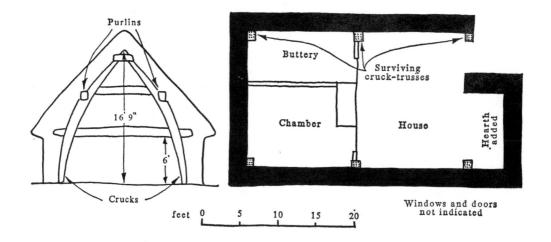

Purlins

16' 9"

6'

Crucks

feet 0 5 10 15 20

Buttery

Surviving
cruck-trusses

Chamber

House

Hearth
added

Windows and doors
not indicated

Fig. 1. TARN HOWS FARM HOUSE—ORIGINALLY A TWO-BAY HOUSE

powerful social group within Cumbria, and these yeomen farmers were at the forefront of the unprecedented wave of rebuilding.

After 1650 there seems to have been a minor architectural revolution; timber-framed houses were no longer built, and in their place load-bearing masonry was universally adopted for building purposes. In these pre-railway days, building materials were those which were locally available, and consequently they closely reflected the local geology; in West Cumberland, the Eden valley, and in parts of Low Furness the pink and rust-brown sandstones provided good freestone; in Cartmel, much of the Furness peninsula and the Kendal area, the silver-grey limestones were used, while along the Cumbrian coasts the rounded 'cobbles' of the seashore were readily available, giving a mottled appearance to the sturdily built homesteads. However, within the Lake District fells the grey, blue and sea-green slates and the rough, craggy, volcanic rocks were used in the absence of other, more easily worked freestone.

From this time a common type of plan emerged, which Dr R. W. Brunskill has called the 'statesman plan',[5] after the independent dalesmen who adopted it. One of the characteristic features of this plan was the 'hallan', or passage, which ran from the front to the back of the house, dividing it into two, one part being the 'down-house', or service area, the other the 'fire-house', or simply 'house'—the living accommodation. Although there were variations, depending on the wealth and status of the family, nevertheless this basic pattern is a common one and is worth investigating in detail (fig. 3).

The front door of the farm, leading into the 'hallan', was often low, but in addition an oak beam, four or five inches high, known as the 'threshwood',* was let into the floor and secured to the walls on either side of the door, so that entering the house necessitated

---

*In the Grasmere and Rydal area the threshwood was known as a 'sole' or 'sole-foot'. In 1713 Brathay Hall had 'neither Door Cheeks, Leafes, nor Soles about ye house but wanted repairing'. See Armitt, 1916, p. 306.

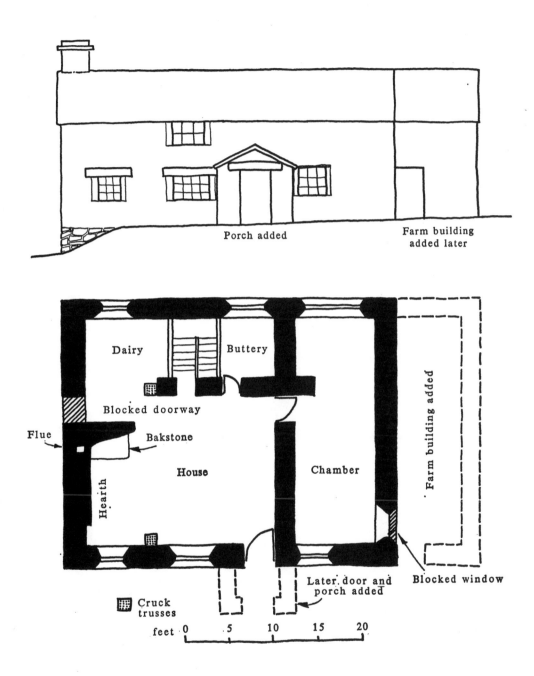

Porch added

Farm building
added later

Dairy

Buttery

Blocked doorway

Flue

Bakstone

House

Chamber

Hearth

Farm building added

Blocked window

Later door and
porch added

Cruck
trusses

feet 0   5   10   15   20

Fig. 2. FAR ORREST, WINDERMERE

ducking one's head and picking one's feet up! Even in the eighteenth century the threshwood still had some mystical significance, and charms such as crossed straws and horseshoes were laid there to prevent the entrance of unwelcome spirits. Having successfully negotiated the threshwood, the visitor found himself in the hallan, which was about four feet wide. The hallan formed a convenient storage place for sacks of corn on the eve of market day and here, too, pigs were hung up after slaughter. Above the door a shelf held various carpentry tools, nails, sickles and the like. The wall on the left of the threshwood, that is, the dividing wall between the hallan and the fire-house, was built of stone, whereas the opposite wall of the passage was merely a 'clam-staff and daub', or wicker partition.[6] At the end of the hallan opposite to the threshwood, two doors opened, one into the down-house, the other into a short passage, the 'mell', leading to the 'house'.

The down-house was often unceiled and open to the rafters; this was the service area of the farm where washing, baking, brewing and pickling were carried on, and here the 'elding', peat or wood fuel, was kept.

The mell passage leading off the hallan into the living quarters was about six feet long and was formed by a stone or wooden partition which shielded the fireplace from draughts (see fig. 3).* The 'house' was the main living-room within the farm; often it was floored with pebbles,[7] sometimes merely with earth, though later most farms were flagged with slate slabs. The hearth occupied most of the stone wall which partitioned the 'house' from the hallan; the hearth-stone being slightly raised above floor level, and over it rose the great funnel-like chimney. This took the form of a huge canopy or hood which extended out into the room about six feet above the floor and gradually narrowed to a flue in the loft. The chimney hood was constructed of lath and plaster or, in earlier times, of wickerwork daubed with clay or cow dung.[8] Clearly this was the warmest and best-lit place in the 'house' and so formed the social focal point of the farm. Under the canopy the family gathered and here, too, the various joints of beef, mutton and pork were hung to dry in the smoke. However, this apparently cosy fireside seat had its disadvantages, for in wet weather a black, sooty liquid called 'hallan-drop' fell down the chimney onto the heads of those seated below. John Gough, writing in the nineteenth century, argued that this was the reason why many countrymen were in the habit of wearing their hats when sitting by the fire![9]

Across the chimney breast, from wall to hood, two beams projected, and on these was placed a long beam known as the rannel-balk or randle-tree. This beam was not fixed, so it could be moved back and forward and the cooking utensils which hung from it by chains could be adjusted on the fire. Adjustable iron pot-hangers known as ratten-crooks or racken-crooks were often used in place of chains (page 32), and as Professor E. Estyn Evans has pointed out, they are common to the Atlantic fringes of Europe.[10] Along the heck side of the fireplace was the sconce, a fixed wooden bench under which the elding or kindling for the morning's fire was usually stored, and on the opposite side of the fire was the long settle, its back often elaborately carved and the seat often serving as a clothes chest. On one side of the fire was a small spice cupboard let into the depth of the wall in which, as the name suggests, the household spices and salt were kept dry. The door of this cupboard usually bore the date of the house (plates 21, 22) and the initials of the owner.

Generally the 'house' was lighted by two small oak-mullioned windows in the front,

*There is some confusion about terminology here; some authorities refer to the short passage as the 'heck', others claim that this term referred only to the partition itself, the passage being the 'mell'.

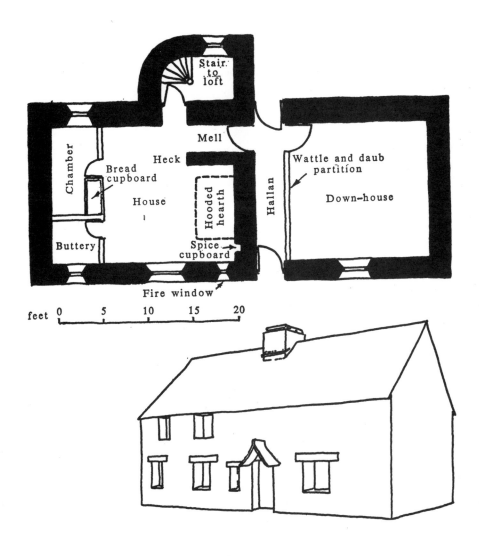

Fig. 3. THE STATESMAN PLAN—A THREE-BAY FARM HOUSE

together with a small fire window which illuminated the hearth; above this window a recess shelf or sometimes a carved cupboard known as the 'catmallison' contained the family Bible. Under the mullioned windows stood the long heavy oak table which, because of its size, invariably had to be built within the 'house', there being no door or other opening which would have admitted it. But the largest and most impressive piece of furniture—indeed, a status symbol—was the carved oak bread cupboard which stood opposite the hearth (plates 24–6). This was a fixture rather than a piece of furniture and often formed part of the partition which divided the chamber and the buttery from the 'house'. Often elaborately carved, these cupboards also bore the date of building and the owner's initials, and in them the oat clap bread (*see* page 34) was stored.

On either side of the bread cupboard doors led through the clam-staff and daub partition, one into the chamber or best bedroom, the other into the buttery which seems to have been located, where possible, on the northern side of the building for coolness.[11] Access to the loft was by a flight of slate stairs leading from the 'house'; here the children and servants slept. The loft was open to the rafters and in spite of the 'mossing' of cracks in the slates, during the winter sleepers might find themselves covered in snow the following morning.[12] The loft was sparsely furnished; one nineteenth-century writer disapprovingly recorded that '. . . a rope was stretched across this nocturnal receptacle of the family, upon which coats, gowns and other articles of apparel, both male and female, hung promiscuously'.[13] In the late nineteenth century most of these lofts were ceiled and partitioned into rooms by clam-staff and daub walls.

This, then, was the basic 'statesman' plan which evolved during the later part of the seventeenth and early part of the eighteenth centuries. It was, in a sense, a response to the upland environment of the fells, for the thick walls and heavy, slated roofs defied the strong wind and driving rain, and the hallan and mell passages ensured a relatively draught-free snugness around the hearth. James Clarke, commenting on recent changes in building styles in 1787, recorded '. . . though I am willing to believe that modern fashions may have given more elegance to buildings, yet I am far from thinking that they have proved better in general for excluding either the wintry winds or the heats of Summer'.[14] Indeed, large windows commanding extensive views of fell and lake are a twentieth-century innovation. But change was inevitable; in the eighteenth century, perhaps under the influence of new urban styles, utility was sacrificed to fashion and many farms were modified so that a door entered directly into the 'house', perhaps protected by a newly erected porch. At Townend,* the Troutbeck house of the Browne family, the abandoned hallan was converted into a pantry when the new entrance was made, and the down-house made into a kitchen. Similarly in many instances the chamber was converted into a parlour and the main bedroom moved to the loft, which was then ceiled. Progressively the great hooded hearth canopies were removed and cast-iron ranges installed, so that now very few remain, although a good example of a lath-and-plaster hood survives at High Birk House, Little Langdale (plate 20). Many of the carved bread cupboards which once graced the statesmen's farms found their way into provincial salerooms and now stand, rather incongruously, in the twentieth-century living-rooms of 'off-comers', assuming a new value as antiques.

Yet in spite of alterations and modernizations, there are many farms which, by their appearance and plan, indicate their origin. Glencoyne Farm, on the shores of Ullswater, provides a good example of a seventeenth-century statesman's home which has subsequently been modified (*see* fig. 4 and plate 1).** Built by the Howard family, it bears a plaster panel in one of the bedrooms inscribed 'TH.DH.1629'. Originally there were only two ground-floor rooms with a hallan crossing the house. In 1700, perhaps because of an enlarged family, a two-bay extension was added at the rear of the house and the original down-house was converted into a parlour. Externally, the stepped gables are a rather unusual feature but the

---

*Townend is a National Trust property and is open to the public every day except Saturday and Monday from April to October, 2 p.m. to 6 p.m. or dusk. In March the house is open on Wednesdays from 2 p.m. to 6 p.m.

**Figs. 1, 2, 3 and 4 are adapted from plans in the late Dr J. E. Partington's Ph.D. thesis, *Rural House Types prior to the Early 19th Century in the English Lake District*. I am indebted to the School of Architecture, Manchester University, and to Dr Partington's brother, for allowing me to study this work.

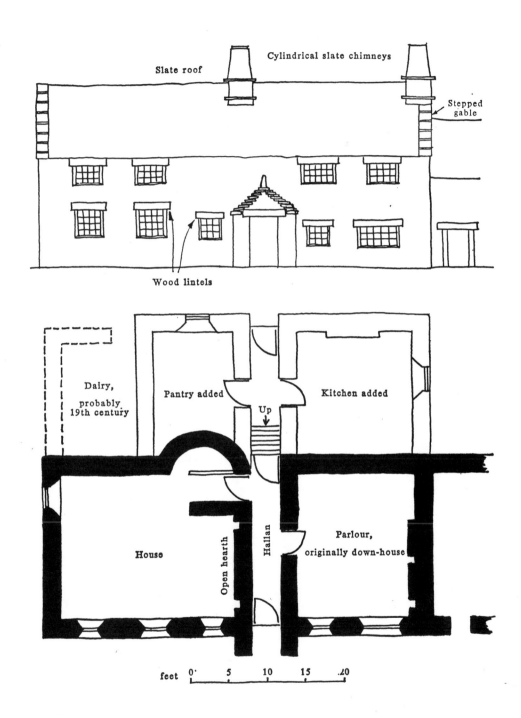

Slate roof

Cylindrical slate chimneys

Stepped gable

Wood lintels

Dairy, probably 19th century

Pantry added

Up

Kitchen added

House

Open hearth

Hallan

Parlour, originally down-house

feet 0 5 10 15 20

Fig. 4. GLENCOYNE FARM AS MODIFIED IN 1700

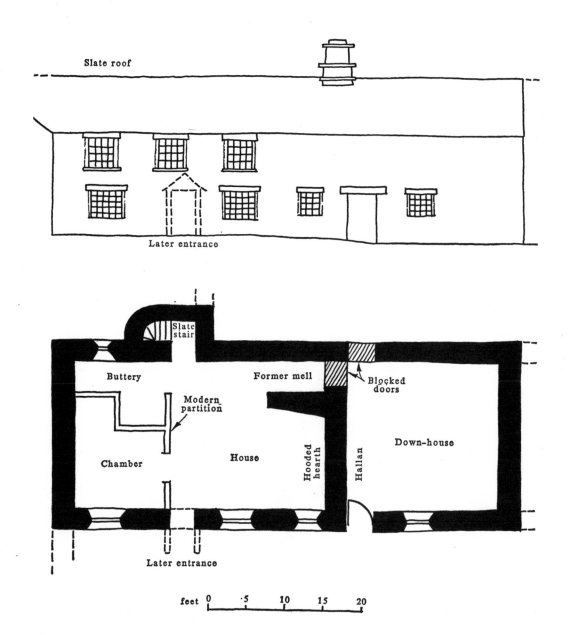

Slate roof

Later entrance

Slate
stair

Buttery

Former mell

Blocked
doors

Modern
partition

Chamber

House

Hooded
hearth

Hallan

Down-house

Later entrance

feet 0   ·5   10   15   20

Fig. 5.   DERWENT FARM, GRANGE-IN-BORROWDALE

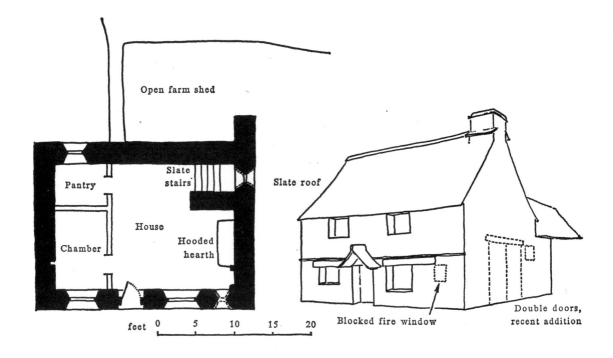

Open farm shed

Pantry

Slate stairs

Slate roof

House

Chamber

Hooded hearth

feet 0   5   10   15   20

Blocked fire window

Double doors, recent addition

Fig. 6.   OLD FARM, HIGH YEWDALE, CONISTON

two cylindrical chimneys are common to many Cumbrian farms, the most widely accepted explanation being that in the absence of suitable freestone, the local rocks lent themselves to this form rather than to the square corners of more conventional chimneys. Like many Lakeland farms, Glencoyne has a white, roughcast exterior; the reason is practical rather than aesthetic, for roughcasting is an efficient method of weatherproofing the rough external walls. Barns and outbuildings are not treated in this way and therefore stand in contrast to the farms themselves. Surprisingly, Wordsworth[15] condemned the Cumbrian practice of whitewashing farms, arguing that they were obtrusive features on the landscape; few would agree with him today, and perhaps it is just as well he did not see the blushing pinks and apple greens which adorn the walls of many Lakeland farms at present.

Derwent Farm, Grange-in-Borrowdale (fig. 5), is a three-bay house, but with the original entrance opening into the down-house. The farm itself is undated, but the adjoining barn was built in 1677 and it seems reasonable to assume that the farm pre-dated this building. It is believed that Sir Hugh Walpole, who lived close by, based his description of a typical yeoman's house in *Rogue Herries* on Derwent Farm:

'In Peel's house the hallan opened straight into the "down-house". This was in his case the great common room of the family, the place of tonight's Christmas feast. . . . The floor tonight was cleared for the dancing, but at the opposite end trestle tables were ranged for the feasting. . . . In other parts of the room were big standard holders for rush lights. All these tonight were brilliantly lit and blew in great gusts in the wind. . . .

'Many were already dancing. It was a scene of brilliant colour with the blazing fire, the red berries of the holly glowing in every corner, old Johnny Shoestring in bright blue breeches and with silver buckles to his shoes perched on a high stool fiddling for his life, the brass gleaming, faces shining, the stamp of the shoon, the screaming of the fiddle, the clap-clap of the hands as the turns were made in the dance—and beyond the heat and the light the dark form of the valley lying in breathless stillness, its face stroked by the fall of lingering reluctant snow.'*

Unlike Glencoyne and Derwent farms, many houses were abandoned to other uses. At High Yewdale Farm on the main road from Coniston to Ambleside the old farmhouse, which probably dates from the late seventeenth or early eighteenth century, has been converted into a store for farm machinery and the gable end now boasts double doors (fig. 6; plate 2). The original farm was probably a two-bay central entry building and later, when both fortunes and family increased, the present farm was built a few yards away. The older building continued in use as a dwelling until the early decades of this century when it was sadly relegated to a sheep pen and storage accommodation.

Although many Lakeland farms were completely rebuilt during the period 1650–1750, others were only partly rebuilt. In particular there are a number of farms which have been grafted on to pele towers, the massively built refuges against Scottish raiders during the border troubles. In many instances the peles are now used as extra storage space, as at Kentmere Hall, Wraysholme Tower, Cartmel, and the remote Ubarrow (or Yewbarrow) Hall in Longsleddale, but elsewhere, as at Cowmire Hall in the Winster valley, the sixteenth-century tower is incorporated in the domestic building.

Such, then, were the houses of the yeomen. There were, of course, other larger houses and mansions, built during the eighteenth and nineteenth centuries, and these we can still see on the landscape of Lakeland today, but it is the snugly built farmhouses which are, as Dr J. D. Marshall has rightly explained, 'the outward expressions of the developing character and experience of entire dales communities'.[16]

FARM BUILDINGS

Although much has been written about the farmhouses of the Lake District, comparatively little attention has been paid to other farm buildings. This is surprising, for barns, cow-houses and stables are as much part of the farm as the house itself. It is hoped that this situation will be remedied for, as Dr R. W. Brunskill has pointed out,[17] because of the technological revolution in farming many farm buildings have become obsolete in the last twenty years; the stable and cart shed have been obsolete since the introduction of the tractor, pig-fattening plants have replaced the pigsty, the silage tower has become a new feature on the landscape, and concrete and asbestos farming factories threaten many farmyards. Yet in the Lake District there are still traditional farm buildings which have retained their original functions. The time-honoured method of cruck-building for farmhouses probably ceased about

*Dr J. D. Marshall (1971, p. 60), however, argues that the description is misleading, for few members of the yeoman class had rooms large enough to accommodate friends and neighbours in this way.

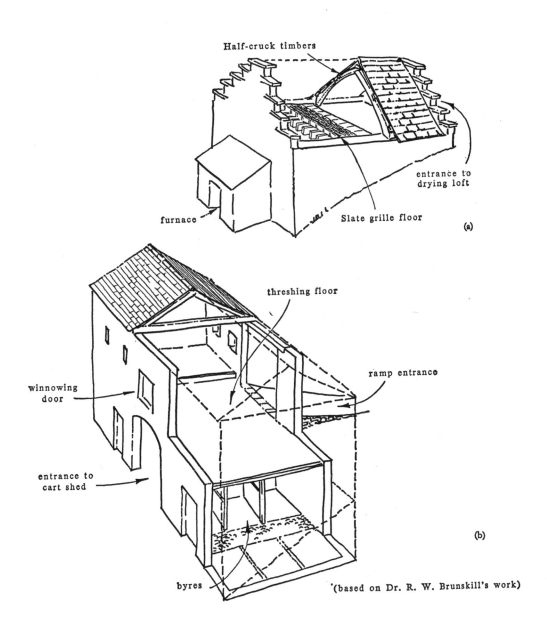

Half-cruck timbers

entrance to
drying loft

furnace

Slate grille floor

(a)

threshing floor

ramp entrance

winnowing
door

entrance to
cart shed

byres

(based on Dr. R. W. Brunskill's work)

(b)

Fig. 7. (a) CORN DRYING KILN, LOW HARTSOP (b) A LAKELAND BANK BARN

the seventeenth century and, as we have seen, there are few remaining examples of houses built in this way. However, cruck-built barns have survived, and from these it is possible to gain some impression of the pre-seventeenth-century farmhouses. Plate 6 shows a fine example of a sixteenth-century barn at Wall End, Great Langdale, and plate 5 a similar example at Field Head Farm, Hawkshead, while plate 4 illustrates a smaller but equally fine cruck barn nestling on the slopes of Great Stickle between the Duddon and Lickle valleys.

Cruck-built barns are, of course, found outside the Lake Counties, but the so-called 'bank barns', or ramp-entrance barns, in Britain are almost entirely confined to this area and the Yorkshire Dales. Basically, as the name implies, this is a barn built on a natural or artificial slope. On the downward side of the barn there is an entrance to the cow-house and stable, while on the upward and opposite side of the building a ramp gives access to the upper storey, where hay is kept (plate 7). Trapdoors enable fodder to be dropped to the animals below with the minimum of effort.[18] One of the finest examples in Lakeland is the barn opposite Townend, Troutbeck. It bears a carved wooden panel with the date 1666 and the initials G. + E.B. The origins of this type of barn are obscure, but examples are numerous in western Norway and also in Switzerland and Pennsylvania.[19] Many such barns had a threshing area on the upper floor where corn was threshed and 'deeted' in an ingenious way prior to the invention of the winnowing machine: opposite the massive ramp-entrance doors was a winnowing door which, when opened, allowed a strong through-draught (fig. 7(b)). After flailing (plate 78) the grain was tossed from a 'weyt' or shallow dish made of sheepskin in this through-draught and the chaff was carried away. On more affluent farms separate barns for corn, known as 'haverlaith', existed,[20] but the grain was 'deeted' in the same way.

Because of the various climatological hazards to farming in the Lake District, cereal crops often had to be harvested damp or not at all. Consequently corn-drying kilns were once common buildings in a farming community, and were probably used jointly by the inhabitants. Few now remain in the Lake District, but Low Hartsop, near Patterdale, has an excellent example which is believed to date from the sixteenth or early seventeenth century[21] (fig. 7(a)). This square-shaped building is built on a steep slope, the entrance to the lower floor, the heating chamber, being from the south and the upper, the drying chamber or loft, from the higher ground on the north. The floor of the drying chamber is formed of slate slabs set edgeways with spaces between each slab to allow the warm air to circulate. The damp grain was probably spread on a horse-hair blanket stretched over the slate grille.

One further characteristic feature of Lakeland farm architecture must be mentioned—the much-photographed 'spinning galleries'. These wooden galleries were often formed when the roof was carried beyond the wall, the space under the extended eaves providing useful storage accommodation. In this sense the name 'spinning' gallery is a little misleading; undoubtedly on fine summer evenings the thrifty Lakeland housewives made maximum use of daylight and yarn was spun by distaff and wheel, and later the cloth was hung after finishing, but in addition the gallery gave access to the upper floor and here, too, peat fuel was stored, as well as various articles of farm equipment. In some cases the galleries are part of the farmhouse as at Hodge Hill Hall, and Pool Bank Farm in the Cartmel Fells, and at Mireside and Thorn House, Low Hartsop (plate 8), while elsewhere the galleries form part of the outbuildings as at Yew Tree Farm, Coniston, perhaps the most photogenic of all Lakeland 'spinning galleries' (plate 9). Although there are exceptions, most spinning galleries are located on the north or east side of the building.[22]

DATE STONES

During 'the Great Rebuilding' it became common practice to build into the fabric of the house a date stone. On the limestones and sandstones which form a broken ring around the Cumbrian dome, the availability of good freestone was assured, but within the fells the slates, shales and volcanic rocks were not satisfactory for this purpose and stone had to be imported or else, as often happened, the date of the house was carved into bread and spice cupboards and other furniture.

Stones dating from the sixteenth century are not common, which makes the inscription on the small Elizabethan Manor House, Hewthwaite Hall, near Cockermouth, all the more interesting (plate 10); it bears the legend:

> John Swynbun esquire and Elisabeth his wyfe
> Did mak coste of this work in the dais of ther lyf
> Ano Dom 1581   Ano Reg 23

Similarly at Crakeplace Hall in the west Cumberland parish of Dean, a sandstone block carries the date 1612 and announces that 'Christopher Crakeplace built the same when he was servant to Baron Altham'. And at Hutton Moor End near Threlkeld a now sadly defaced stone (plate 14) curiously records the date in rhyme:

> THIS BUILDING'S AGE
> THESE LETTERS SHOW
> MDCCXIX
> THOUGH MANY GAZE
> YET FEW WILL KNOW

By the later part of the seventeenth century date stones were more common; the carving was generally in relief and the most frequent arrangement was the initial letters of the Christian names of the husband and wife, with the initial of the surname above and between them, together with the date (plate 11). Those with a right to bear arms—and, indeed, those who had no such right—set up their shields and often added a Latin inscription.

One or two examples still remain of date stones which indicate the occupation of the building; at Randle How, Eskdale Green, once an important centre on the pack-horse route from Broughton to Cockermouth, the lintel of a cottage indicates that the original owner was a blacksmith (plate 16). The date, 1679, and the insignia of the smith's trade, the hammer, horseshoe and pincers, are carved into the sandstone block and the initials 'I. N.' are those of John Nicholson, the seventeenth-century blacksmith who carried on his trade here.[23] The same symbols and the date 1697 appear on a similar sandstone block let into the wall of a barn at Oxen Park in the Furness Fells (plate 15).

By the eighteenth century the practice of carving date stones had declined somewhat, and the technique of producing monograms and dates in relief gave way to a new method of incising the letters and numerals into the stone. Although this art of rustic lettering continued into the nineteenth century, it never again achieved the popularity of the seventeenth century.*

*At Kirkby-in-Furness, on the Duddon estuary, there are some fine examples of nineteenth-century carved inscriptions and symbols on the walls of a stable, while at Wreaks Causeway Bridge on the A595 between Grizebeck and Broughton, there are similar, though earlier, examples.

2 HEARTH AND HOME—SOME FARMHOUSE EQUIPMENT

THE 'HOUSE'

The focal point of Lakeland farmhouses in the past was the fireplace; indeed the words 'hearth' and 'home' were virtually synonymous. Along the Atlantic seaboard of Europe, in areas of damp and often cold climates, the hearth was not only necessary for the warmth and comfort of the family but also essential for the preparation of food. It is not surprising, then, to find the development of hearth-cults in these regions, and there is some evidence in Cumbria of continuous hearth-fires kept burning in lonely farmsteads perhaps for centuries. Dr A. C. Gibson, writing in 1864, recorded that the hearth-fires in two remote farms in the Furness Fells, Parkamoor and Lawson Park, had not been extinguished for several centuries.[1] It may be argued, of course, that it was easier to maintain the slow-burning peat fires than to re-light a fire with a flint and 'flourice', or striker, but alternatively it must be recognized that in such countries as Ireland, Scotland, Wales, the Isle of Man, Iceland and parts of Scandinavia the primitive custom of religiously tending the fire is an ancient one. In Ireland, for example, it has been said that when the fire goes out, the soul goes out of the people of the house.[2]

In the older type of 'statesman' house the hearth, under the great chimney hood, was paved and generally raised a few inches above the floor level. This arrangement seems to have been suitable for the burning of peat and wood such as tree roots and ash tops which will burn with the minimum of draught. In the nineteenth century when coal became a more common fuel, hob grates and kitchen ranges replaced many open hearths. The rannel-balk and the hanging chains were subsequently superseded by iron fire cranes which swung across the fire, and from these the ratten-crooks, adjustable pot-hangers, holding the various cooking implements, were suspended (fig. 8 (1, 2); plate 18). Professor E. Estyn Evans suggests that in Ireland the fire crane was invariably pivoted on the left side of the hearth, for it was believed that actions involving the food supply—such as ploughing, casting a net or removing a cooking vessel from the fire—should follow the direction of the sun's movements in the sky.[3] However, within the Lake District, if such a superstition ever existed, it had been forgotten by the eighteenth century, for examples of fire cranes pivoting on the right-hand side of the fire are common (see plates 19, 27).

Most of the hearth-side equipment was necessarily made of iron. A schedule of the goods

Fig. 8. THE KITCHEN HEARTH

1, 2. Fire crane and ratten-crooks, or adjustable pot-hangers. From Townend, Troutbeck.   3. Massive cooking spit from Troutbeck; length of horizontal rod, 6 feet.   4. Iron girdle plate, 26 inches in diameter.   5. Dutch oven. 6. Bottle jack.   7. Girdle with bow handle.   8. Fire-dog or andiron; height 26 inches.   9. Brandreth; height 8 inches.   10. Piggin from Dunnerdale; height of longest stave 6½ inches.

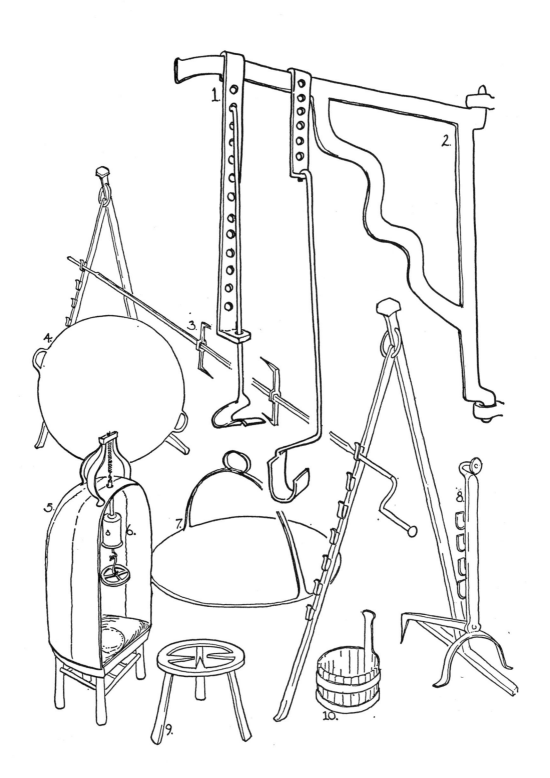

of the late Mrs Elizabeth Sharp of Troutbeck in 1802 contained a special section devoted to 'iron furniture' which included:

'Two pairs of Tongs, one Fireshovel, one Fire poaker, one Box smoothing Iron, two heaters and Iron stand, one Fire Crane and crooks, one copper kettle and cover, one pr. of snuffers and one corkscrew.'[4]

In the days before the introduction of the hob grate, one of the most common pieces of equipment was the iron fire-dog or andiron which stood on either side of the fire to prevent the logs rolling out and also to support the poker and tongs (fig. 8(8) and plate 18).* In addition, many statesmen's hearths boasted cooking spits on which large joints of meat could be roasted on the open fire. At Townend, Troutbeck, an excellent example complete with dripping pan and an adjustable fender may still be seen (fig. 8(3)). Later, such cumbersome instruments were replaced by Dutch ovens which incorporated a bottle jack to turn the meat automatically and cook it uniformly (fig. 8(5)). In small, less affluent farmsteads such refinements were absent since meat was boiled in huge iron pots rather than roasted. Toast-dogs, however, were common in all Lake District farms; their variety is surprising, but essentially they consisted of an iron tripod to which was attached a bar, sometimes adjustable in height, fitted with spikes or prongs on which bread was fixed for toasting. Amongst the other curious fireside cooking implements was, generally, a frying-pan which could, with slight modification, be used for baking wheat bread. When used for this purpose an iron ring two or three inches deep was placed inside the pan in order to increase the depth, and the lid was placed on top of this and the whole covered with burning peat. A variation on this piece of equipment was the kail pot, a cast-iron pan and lid which sat in the fire on three short legs to allow the fire to burn under it. Burning peats were similarly heaped on top of the lid of this versatile domestic appliance which served as a pan for boiling meat as well as an oven for baking pies, cakes and wheat bread. Alternatively, it could be suspended over the fire from the ratten-crook. Similar 'pot-ovens' were used in Wales for the baking of loaves, cakes and tarts.[5]

Although wheaten bread was occasionally baked this was certainly not the traditional bread, for in these damp fells the meal of the black oat was the staple flour and the basis of the diet. Bread made from this meal was often termed 'haver' bread from the Old Norse word *hafrar*, meaning oats, or more often 'clap bread' from the method of manufacture, for the meal and water paste was clapped or beaten with the hand to form a broad, thin cake. This traditional way of making oat bread is not confined to Cumbria, or even to the British Isles, for Professor Evans asserts that this thin, unleavened bread has been common from very early times along the Atlantic seaboard from northern Scandinavia to the Basque country, including Highland Britain and Ireland.[6] Indeed, present-day visitors to Norway from northern England marvel at Norwegian *flatbröd* without appreciating that this is their traditional bread also! The equipment used in the baking of clap bread was very simple—usually a circular iron girdle or 'bakstone' about twenty-six inches in diameter, sometimes possessing a bow handle for suspension from the ratten-crooks, or occasionally merely two iron handles on the rim (fig. 8 (4 and 7)). If not suspended over the open hearth, the bakstone was set on a brandiron or brandreth, an iron tripod about eight inches high (fig. 8(9)). These two pieces of equipment were clearly of

* For an analysis of Welsh fire-dogs *see* Peate, 1972, p. 40.

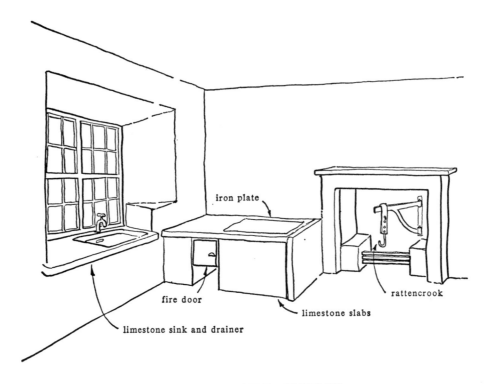

iron plate

rattencrook

fire door

limestone slabs

limestone sink and drainer

Fig. 9. A BAKSTONE IN A FARM AT AYSIDE, CARTMEL

some importance to the household, for they receive specific mention in several ancient wills and inventories; for example, a list of the possessions of John Rowlandson, a sixteenth-century Troutbeck farmer, mentions:

'A girdle, a brandrett, a bottle and a pare of tongs   IIs. Vd.'

And the Rydal blacksmith in the seventeenth century recorded in his accounts book the manufacture of 'a new brandiron' for the princely sum of 2*s.* 6*d.*[7]

Celia Fiennes, a keen observer of such matters, witnessed the baking of clap bread in the Kendal area during one of her remarkable journeys in 1698.

'. . . they mix their flour with water so soft as to rowle it in their hands into a ball, and then they have a board made round and something hollow in the middle riseing by degrees all round to the edge a little higher, but so little as one would take it to be only a board warp'd, this is to cast out the cake thinn and so they clap it round and drive it to the edge in a due proportion till drove as thinn as a paper, and still they clap it and drive it round, and then they have a plaite of iron same size with their clap board and so shove off the cake on it and so set it on coales and bake it . . . if their iron plaite is smooth and they take care their coales or embers are not too hot but just to make it look yellow it will bake and be as crisp and pleasant to eate as any thing you can imagine.'[8]

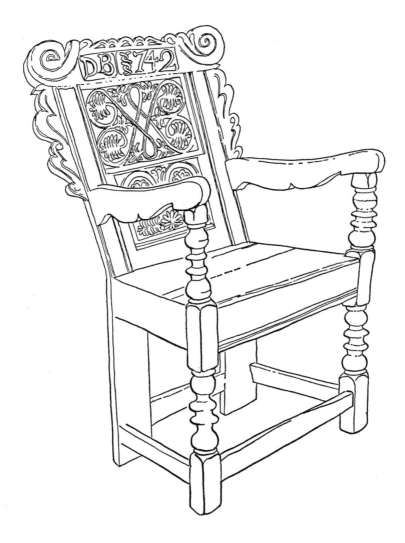

Fig. 10. Carved chair dated 1742, from Townend, Troutbeck.

In the nineteenth century it became customary to have built-in bakstones, usually in the down-house or kitchen. It seems highly probable that originally the bakstone was just that— a slab of slate or stone heated by fire, but by the nineteenth century the built-in bakstones, square iron plates, seem to have superseded the original material. Few now remain *in situ*; plate 30 shows an example formerly at Spring Gardens, Spark Bridge. Here the iron plate measured four feet by two and was fired from below by beechwood shavings purchased at $1\frac{1}{2}d.$ per bag from the nearby bobbin mill. The bakstone was in use in the early part of this century but was removed from the house in 1958.[9] Until recently, a very fine bakstone existed *in situ* in a farmstead at Ayside, Cartmel, but this has now been removed to the Museum of

Lakeland Life and Industry in Kendal. Fig. 9, based on a drawing by Mr Arthur Frearson, A.R.I.B.A., shows its position in the farm.

The baking of haver bread usually occupied a full day and sufficient was baked to satisfy family needs for a month or more.* The bread was usually stored in the carved oak cupboards which often occupied the wall opposite the hearth in the fire-house (see plates 25, 26).

Although mass-produced oat cake is still to be found on many Scottish breakfast tables, its popularity has declined sadly. The reason is not difficult to see—the drastic fall in the price of wheat in the 1880s following the import of grain from the New World meant that long-established eating habits were changed by economic circumstances, so that the once traditional clap bread is now no more than a gastronomic curiosity.

In many old farmhouses an oven was built into the wall next to the fireplace. Constructed of hand-made bricks, they were usually circular in plan with a domed slate roof formed by corbelling out the slate; the opening or door was approximately a foot square. To bake in such an oven required first of all a fire inside the oven to heat it; after a sufficient time, the fire was removed and replaced by the food, the oven was then closed until the baking was done. With the introduction of cast-iron ranges in the late eighteenth and early nineteenth centuries, the brick ovens became obsolete and many were filled in; however, there are one or two still to be seen. Mr Arthur Frearson has drawn my attention to a fine example at Townson Hill, Woodbroughton, near Cartmel, and another at Barnside, Oxenpark, in High Furness.

The fire-house generally was furnished in the simplest possible manner; as well as the built-in wall cupboards, the sconce and the huge oak table already described, there were usually one or two wooden chairs. In poorer farmsteads these were merely fashioned from the trunks of hollow trees,[10] but in the homes of more affluent statesmen solid oak chairs with elaborately carved backs and sides were common. By the eighteenth century 'thrown' chairs, in which the balusters and perhaps part of the back were thrown or turned on a lathe, were introduced (fig. 10). These were clearly much prized and were obviously something of a status-symbol. Bedsteads, too, were often elaborately carved; some of the finest Lakeland examples may be seen at Townend, Troutbeck (plate 31), where the Browne family maintained a family tradition of making their own furniture from the seventeenth century until the end of the nineteenth.

Until the use of earthenware became common, most tableware was either turned in wood or fashioned from pewter, and the inventories and wills of the seventeenth and eighteenth centuries often mention pewter doublers and wooden trenchers.[11] Not surprisingly, the sort of tableware used was an indication of status, for as one nineteenth-century writer tells us '. . . the richer sort of people had a service of pewter; but amongst the middling and poorer classes the dinner was eaten off wooden trenchers.'[12] Such tableware was common throughout Britain at that time and is not peculiar to the Lake District; however, the use of small wooden stave-built vessels for porridge and liquids is worth noting. These 'piggins' were generally made in the manner of miniature half-barrels with one stave longer than the rest serving as a handle (fig. 8(10)). The craft of making these is very old and probably it has roots in the prehistoric past; indeed, Professor Estyn Evans has suggested that it may well be part of an ancient circumpolar culture, for similar 'piggins' are found in Scandinavia and the Asiatic

*J. H. Martindale's claim (Transactions of the Cumberland and Westmorland Antiquarian and Archaeological Society, vol. 13, 1895) that sufficient bread to last for a year was baked during one day seems ambitious.

Arctic.[13]

The Cumbrian farmstead was generally lit by rushlights and candles, at least until the second half of the nineteenth century when paraffin lamps became widespread in the more wealthy homes. Rushlights had the great advantage of cheapness and almost every farm made its own. The basic materials were rushes (*Juncus conglomeratus*) and bacon or mutton fat. The rushes, known within the Lake District as 'sieves', were generally cut in late summer or autumn, care being taken to select only rushes in their second year of growth, which could be distinguished by their flowers. After harvesting, the sieves were trimmed to about 12–15 inches long and then peeled, though a thin strip of rind was left to support the fragile pith. The peelings were usually made into besoms and crude mats or 'bears'—even in 1822 it was possible to make a living by the manufacture of these items.[14] After drying, the sieves were passed through hot fat; often bacon fat was used, but a combination of equal parts of sheep and bullock fat was considered to be superior and not liable to smoking or guttering.[15] The resulting rushlights were clearly very fragile and therefore were generally stored in a cylindrical tin 'rush bark' or 'candle bark' which could be hung on the wall (plate 32).

The secret of burning rushlights lay in fixing them in a holder at an angle; if too vertical the light burned dimly, if too horizontal it burned too quickly and dripped. The simplest form of rushlight holder was merely a short iron rod divided to form a V slot, the rushlight being wedged in at the correct angle. A more sophisticated holder operated on the pincer principle, one arm being counterweighted to hold the pincers together and so grip the rushlight. Other holders combined pincers for rushlights with sockets for tallow candles and the variations on this theme are exhaustive, as are the varieties of free-standing and hanging rushlight and candle holders.[16] (Fig. 11 and plates 33–7.)

Some farms had 'standarts', adjustable candle and rushlight holders which stood on the floor; this was described in the early nineteenth century as '. . . a light, upright pole, fixed in a log of wood, and perforated with a row of holes up one side, in which a piece of iron, bent at right-angles and furnished with a socket for holding tallow candles, and a kind of pincers for rushes, was moved upwards and downwards as convenient'.[17]

In the event of it being necessary to rekindle a fire or light a rushlight, a flint and striker were used to ignite tinder—usually charred linen rags. Certainly until a hundred and twenty years ago the flint and steel strike-a-lights were the most common method of obtaining fire within the Lake District. However, such a method had disadvantages out of doors, and in some areas an alternative was used; basically this consisted of a brass tube and plunger, not dissimilar to the modern bicycle pump. Touch-paper was attached to the plunger which was then rammed home in the barrel, the heat generated by compression being sufficient to ignite the paper. It is believed that such instruments were in common use in Lakeland and the Yorkshire Dales, particularly by shepherds.[18]

This, then, constituted the basic furniture of the 'house', but the more wealthy statesmen's houses might boast additional furniture such as a grandfather clock made by the most famous of local clockmakers, Jonas Barber, of Winster, in the late seventeenth century, or

Fig. 11. HOUSEHOLD ILLUMINATION

1. Combined candle and rushlight holder from Townend, Troutbeck. The holder moves up and down the central metal rod. 2. A simple Lakeland rushlight holder. 3. Candle moulds. 4. A combined tinder box and candle holder from Hawkshead, together with the snuffer and the iron striker and flint.

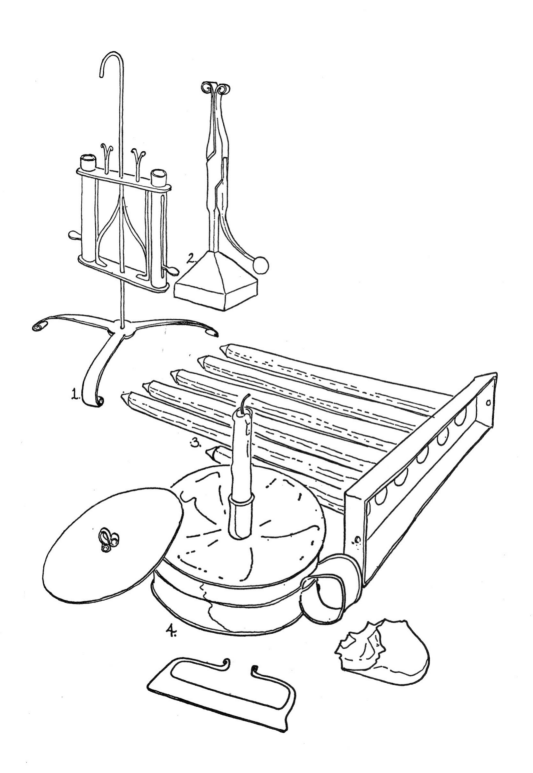

1.

2.

3.

4.

by John Braithwaite or Samuel Burton of Hawkshead. Many farms, too, had a small loom on which the womenfolk wove the cloth for family wear, and by the late eighteenth century the spinning-wheel had become common, though it was relatively late arriving in some Lakeland dales: the ancient method of spinning, using spindle and whorl, persisted in some places until the nineteenth century. Most of the carding, teasing and spinning processes were carried out during the long winter evenings, and in this connection the Brownes at Troutbeck had a simple but effective way of increasing their candle-power—merely a large glass globe which was filled with water and placed in front of a candle, the result being a general magnification of the light intensity.

It is, of course, too easy to over-romanticize the life of a Cumbrian dalesman 150 years ago; we should not forget that 'making ends meet' was often a struggle, that life-expectancy was short, that the standards of living and comfort were far from what we should now consider to be adequate. Yet one thing seems clear, in the dark and often draughty farmhouse the most comfortable, warm refuge was the hearth which, in spite of its smoke and the hallandrop, remained the focus of family life. Around the glow of the peat fire the traditions and folk tales of the Lakeland dales were transmitted orally from one generation to the next, and once again we see a characteristic which is common to the weather-beaten Atlantic seaboard of Europe.

THE DOWN-HOUSE AND THE BUTTERY

Not all Lakeland farms possessed a separate down-house, but in those which did the heavy household chores such as baking, washing, pickling and brewing, were undertaken here. The main piece of equipment was often the bakstone, previously described, used as an alternative to the girdle for the baking of clap bread. Here, too, were kept the great oak 'kists', or arks (fig. 12), holding the oatmeal and barley, as well as the malt mill. Usually these were not unlike the ancient quern mills, having an upper and lower millstone operated by hand. The cumbersome example at Townend, Troutbeck, was made in 1718 and cost £1,[19] but later in the same century a lighter version, mechanically similar to an old-fashioned coffee-grinder, became popular.

In addition, of course, there was a wide variety of utensils used in the preparation of food, bewildering now to the modern cook—the mash vat for brewing, the souse-tub which held brine or sour whey for pickling, the scummer, a long-handled spoon for skimming the salt meat boiling in the cauldron, and the cocklepan, so often mentioned in the Rydal Hall accounts—all are now museum items.

Fig. 12. Dated and intialled panel on a kist at Townend, Troutbeck. The initials are those of George Browne and his wife Ellinor.

Most farmhouses had a buttery, and although the dairy industry was not as important here as in the Yorkshire Dales, nevertheless every household possessed the basic equipment for butter and cheese making. On the whole the production of cheese was mainly for household consumption, but occasionally one or two farms produced cheese for sale in the market; for example at Borwick Ground in Hawkshead parish in 1818 a sale book lists thirteen items of cheese, ranging from 10 lb. to 12 lb. each, which were sold at between 5½d. and 6¾d. per pound.[20] Blue milk cheese was commonly found on most Lakeland tables; this was generally known as 'wangy cheese' because it was reported to be tough enough to make 'wangs' or thongs! The Whillimoor area of West Cumberland was particularly famous for 'Whillimoor wang', a cheese which, when sold in Carlisle market, was described as being 'lank and lean but cheap and clean', a slogan hardly designed to promote sales!

Cheeses were pressed wherever the cheese-press could be conveniently located. In many cases this meant under some nearby tree from which hung the great stone weight. In the nineteenth century more sophisticated presses operated by screw threads were introduced, but the principle remained the same. Cheese-rims were used in this process; the cheese-rims seem to have been 'circular wooden frames of coopered staves, without top or bottom in which the milk [sic] was confined and pressed from above by a heavy weight or wood with a stone on the top of it'.[21] Similar utensils were used in the Yorkshire Dales, where they were known as 'chesfords'.

Milk was brought to the farm from the fields in wooden pails supported by a wooden yoke, or alternatively in a 'backcan' specially shaped to fit on the back of the carrier and worn rather like a rucksack (fig. 13(1)). The usual butter churn was either a simple 'up and down' churn or a box churn, though later the coopered oval churn superseded both (fig. 13(2)). In a remarkable, though regrettably incomplete, paper[22] written early in the nineteenth century, William Close, the Furness apothecary, recorded a description of the churns then in use in the southern part of the Lakes:

'. . . an oblong [or] square box closed by a cover and furnished in the inside with a winged agitator which is turned round on a horizontal axle by a winch or handle on the outside, and performs the operation of churning by dashing through the cream. The square churns are put together with nails and commonly made by joiners; but there is an oval kind made by coopers and hooped with iron, which begins now to obtain the preference over the others as tighter in the joints and likely to be much more durable. The cost of one of the box churns, either oval or square, is about 40 shillings.'

After the milk had been allowed to settle, the cream was skimmed and left to 'ripen' in a large crock until churning day; it was usually reckoned that a quart of cream made one pound of butter. The ripened cream was placed in the churn with some water and churning continued until the contents thickened; an experienced butter maker could tell by the swishing noise within the churn the exact stage the process had reached. When the butter had 'come', the buttermilk was allowed to drain away, clean, cold water was used to wash the butter, and later salt was added to make brine. Finally, the butter was 'worked' in order to squeeze out any remaining water, then salted and rolled before being divided into pats with 'Scotch hands' (fig. 13(4)). However, the churning of butter was a notoriously fickle occupation, dependent, as often as not, on prevailing weather conditions. Consequently the whole operation was surrounded by superstition and folk lore; it was firmly believed—even in the nineteenth

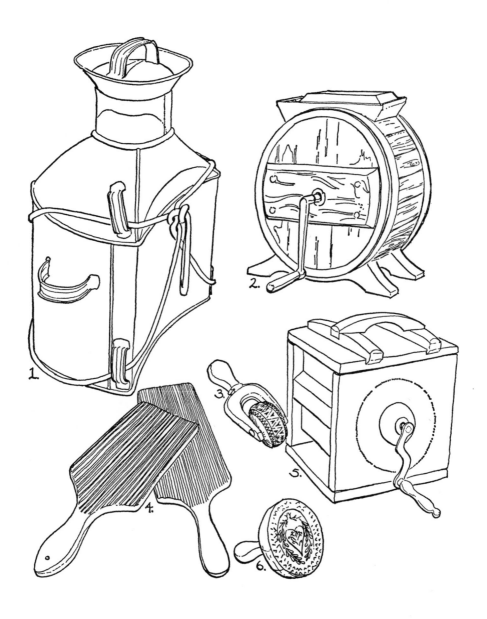

Fig. 13. DAIRY EQUIPMENT
1. A backcan used for bringing milk to the farmhouse from remote areas. 2. A late nineteenth-century oval churn. 3, 6. Butter patterns. 4. 'Scotch hands' for working butter. 5. An early nineteenth-century box churn.

century—that cream which would not churn was bewitched and, as an antidote to this, several remedies could be employed: a holed 'dobbie' stone hung in the byre would protect the cows and their milk from any sorcery (*see* page 83); alternatively, a twig of rowan placed in the churn or even used to stir the milk would prove effective, or so it was believed. If all else failed, a garland of rowan leaves around the churn was a sure guard against witchcraft. All these superstitious charms applied equally in Ireland, and there, as in Lakeland, it is interesting to note the use of the rowan, the sacred tree of the Scandinavians (*see* page 70). It is all the less romantic, then, to learn that the difficulties experienced in the churning of butter probably had a scientific basis—when the number of cattle on a farm rarely exceeded three or four, and when these beasts were poorly fed for most of the year, the butter-fat content of the milk was necessarily low and so the butter was often slow in forming.

Today little butter and cheese are made in Lakeland farmhouses and those who are able to buy local cheeses in the markets of Ulverston, Kendal and Keswick are lucky indeed. For the most part the surplus milk and cream from the farms near to the main holiday towns such as Windermere, Keswick and Ambleside find their way into the great processing plants at Kendal and Milnthorpe where—one hopes—the risk of witchcraft is at a minimum!

3 CUMBRIAN FARE AND FOLK DRESS

'The refinement and general condition of a people are in nothing more apparent than in the kinds and qualities of their food, and their methods of preparing it.'

Rev. J. Hodgson,
Westmorland As It Was, 1822

Within the Lake District, environmental limitations such as the high rainfall, shortened growing season, steep slopes and thin, acid soils have always exerted considerable influence on the types of crops which could be grown. Whereas wheat could be harvested in Low Furness and on the Cumbrian coastal plain, here in the fells oats and bigg, a form of barley, were the traditional grains. Clap bread, an essential part of the diet of all Lakelanders until the mid nineteenth century, was made from oatmeal (*see* page 34), but, in addition, oatmeal was used in other ways: 'hasty pudding' or 'poddish' was a kind of porridge made with oatmeal and water and generally eaten with butter, milk and treacle. This formed the basis of both morning and evening meals; writing of Westmorland, William Dickinson[1] in 1852 pointed out that '. . . a great quantity of oats is ground into meal and made into porridge; and this with milk, bread and sometimes cheese constitutes the breakfast and supper of the chief part of the farm households in the county'. Alternatively, oatmeal was made into 'crowdy', a form of soup in which the stock from the boiling of beef was poured over the meal.

Occasionally, when there was a disastrous harvest or when the price of oats rose, a substitute had to be found; in 1799 and 1800 the price of oatmeal increased to eight shillings a stone, a reflection of its scarcity. Consequently, in order to stretch the available grain supply, many households turned instead to turnip bread made in the following manner:

'Take off the skin from your Turnips and boil them till soft; bruise them well and press out the Juice; add an equal weight of Wheat Flour and Knead them up with a sufficient Quantity of Salt and bake them.'[2]

Until the Agricultural Revolution and the introduction of fodder crops, the autumn slaughter of animals was an important ritual, taking its place in the farming year along with seedtime and harvest. Consequently Martinmas was the time when beef and mutton were cured for family use during the coming winter; much of this was pickled in brine in the large vats which every farm possessed and the rest was dried in the smoke of the huge chimneys. Indeed it was said of the Cumbrian yeoman that he considered a well-stocked chimney to be the most elegant furniture with which he could adorn his house! Certainly James Clarke's claim that in 1787 he saw seven sheep hanging by their hind legs in one Borrowdale chimney was no exaggeration.[3] The habit of eating dried meat was one which died hard; as late as 1822 smoked beef was preferred to fresh meat in spite of the fact that it cost twice as much.[4] Usually a 'collop' or cut of meat was boiled on a Sunday morning and eaten hot for dinner, but thereafter it was served cold at subsequent meals.

Dried beef, mutton and oatmeal can hardly have provided a nourishing and balanced diet, and it is believed that many of the prevalent internal disorders and 'agues' were a direct result; anyone leafing through eighteenth- and nineteenth- century diaries and commonplace books will be well aware of the frequency of such ailments. Perhaps as a means of counteracting this, or merely as a variation, herb puddings were made in spring, consisting of the leaves of Alpine Bistort, called here 'Easter-ledges', groats, young nettles, the leaves of the great bell flower, one or two blackcurrant leaves and a few blades of chives boiled in a linen bag together with the meat. Eaten with veal, it was regarded as a great delicacy. The following recipe for herb pudding is a traditional one from Caldbeck and includes 1½ lb. of bistort, 1 lb. of nettles, ½ cup of barley, a bunch of chopped chives and a leaf of blackcurrant boiled in a bag for 2½ hours; before serving, it was usual to add a lump of butter and a beaten egg. Apart from onions and red cabbage, which was often pickled, garden vegetables were unknown until the early nineteenth century—even potatoes were not in common use until after 1730.[5] However, Sir Frederick Eden, writing in 1797, claimed that potatoes when 'chopped and boiled together with a small quantity of meat cut into very small pieces . . . then formed into a hash with pepper, salt, onions etc. . . . by sailors called lobscouse'.[6] No doubt they were Mersey seamen! Pies made of minced mutton mixed with fruit and sugar occasionally afforded some variety for the jaded palate; generally these were made for the Christmas festivities, and it is believed that around the 1830s, on every 24th December, some 700 to 1,000 sheep were slaughtered in the town and neighbourhood of Kendal for this purpose.[7]

On the whole, fish did not feature prominently in the diet of Lakelanders in spite of the oft-quoted example of the Kendal apprentices who, in their indentures, covenanted that they should not dine on salmon or other fish more often than three times per week. Alpine trout, or more commonly 'char', became popular in the seventeenth and eighteenth centuries, and the Rydal Hall documents and accounts are full of references to char pies and potted char; indeed, Sir Daniel Fleming made the char 'an instrument of social diplomacy, whereby he sweetened (or savoured) his intercourse with politicians and friends at court'.[8] In the nineteenth century, although there is considerable evidence that the numbers of char declined because of over-fishing, potted char and char pie remained popular and special earthenware char dishes were produced, many having a picture of the fish incorporated into the design round the side. Such dishes are now rare and consequently valuable (plate 28).

Almost all Cumbrian farms brewed their own ale and this was drunk with every meal, but on festive occasions ale-possets were made, particularly on what was known as Powsowdy night. This particular beverage, usually served in basins, was brewed by boiling ale and rum with bread, and seasoning it with sugar and nutmeg. Sometimes 'penny-fairs', dedicated to the delights of drinking, were held; James Clarke described one such fair in 1787 in St John's Vale:

'On the Sunday before Easter all the inhabitants of the parish, old and young, men and women, repair to [the] alehouse after evening prayer: they then collect a penny from each person, male or female, but not promiscuously, as the women pay separately: this money is spent in liquor, and at one of these meetings . . . amounted to three pounds, so that there must have been 720 persons present.'[9]

The more affluent, of course, indulged in stronger drink—though not always with happy consequences; William Fleming of Pennington in May 1810 recorded this *cri de cœur* in his diary:

'Last Night I drank two or 3 Glasses of Spirit and Water with Mr. Shaw at his House when I let him the Fields and today find myself much disordered, the Spirit Dealers certainly adulterate their liquor with something unwholesome and of deleterious Quality. . . . Home-brewed Ale is the most Wholesome Liquor.'[10]

However, William Fleming's hangover was nothing compared with the dire result of a Hawkshead wager in 1689, which is recorded in the Parish Registers. It seems that two young men, William Braithwaite and William Stamper, bet a third, Bernard Swainson, that if he 'coulde drinke of nyne noggins of brandy', then they would pay, but if Bernard failed, then he must pay for what he had drunk; 'now this Bernard drunke of those nyne noggins of brandy quickly; and shortly after that fell downe upon the floore: and was straightway carried to his bed where hee layde two and twenty hours: dureinge which tyme hee coulde never speke, noe nor never did know any body though many Came to See him and Soe he dyed.'[11]

By the end of the eighteenth century tea began to challenge the supremacy of the traditional home-brewed ale. Yet not everyone was conversant with the new-fangled methods of brewing 'the cup that cheers . . .'; the story is told of the old lady who, on receiving a pound of tea as a present from her son in the metropolis, promptly filled her clay pipe and smoked it, proclaiming it to be better than the best Virginian! A similar—and equally unverified—tale is related of another dales-woman who, on first receiving a gift of tea, made a somewhat unusual herb pudding![12] The introduction of this harmless brew was not always greeted with enthusiasm; the *Cumberland Pacquet* of 23rd October 1792 saw it as nothing less than a blow to moral fibre:

'A correspondent says that in the neighbourhood of Greystoke, during the late harvest, added to an increase of wages, the female reapers had regularly their tea every afternoon, and the men toast and ale. How different is this from the beef-steak breakfasts of old! How degenerate is the present age, and how debilitated may the next be!'

Traditionally in the Lake District certain foods have been associated with certain events or occasions. Regrettably, few of these now remain. Many of them were connected in some way with Lent; for example Collop Monday was the Monday preceding Lent when the remaining 'collops' of salted and dried meat were eaten; and according to one writer[13] hashes and stews were associated with Ash Wednesday. The fifth Sunday in Lent was 'Carling Sunday', when 'carlings', brown peas softened by soaking and fried in butter, were the accepted delicacy, while it was considered almost profane not to dine on 'Fig Sue' on Good Friday. William Fleming records how this was made in Furness in the early nineteenth century:

'It has been an immemorial Custom in this Corner of England, on Good Friday, to eat a kind of Porridge, called here, Fig Sewe, made of Figs cut in Quarters, with Wheaten Bread cut into small Square Pieces and boiled in Ale or Beer seasoned with Sugar or Treacle and nutmeg;

this is much relished by most People and eaten to Dinner before salt or Fresh Fish.'[14]

And of course Easter Day was associated with pace eggs,* hard-boiled and coloured with redwood, alum or onion skins. Traditionally children met at some appointed place and bowled the eggs against one another until the shells cracked, like some great 'conker' game. Associated with this pace-egging was the pace-egg mummers' play which, although not confined to the Lake District, was linked with the North Lancashire area of Cumbria and in particular with the village of Satterthwaite. In common with many similar plays the characters include Lord Nelson, King George, the Doctor, Tosspot and Bessy Brown Bags, and undoubtedly the seemingly nonsensical plot[15] has its origins in history, although it is difficult to ascribe a date to this Furness version. Recently the Furness Morris Men have resurrected the play and it has been performed with considerable success in the streets of many Furness villages (plate 42).

Even in the most primitive societies and religions, food and drink have been associated with the rituals of birth and death and it is certain that such traditions have their roots in the dawn of prehistory. In Cumbria the custom of serving mourners with 'arvel' bread after the burial is a very ancient one. Opinions differ as to the origin of the word 'arvel', some authorities insisting it means 'inheritance', others that it is an ancient Scandinavian word for funeral, but about the bread itself there is little dispute. Generally, small wheaten buns or cakes were given to each of the mourners in the open air, to be taken home with them, symbolizing, no doubt, a last parting gift. Occasionally, too, arvel cheese was served. The tradition remained in the fells until the nineteenth century; at Troutbeck, for example, the arvel bread was given at the funeral of Elizabeth Longmire in 1834.[16] Many of these funeral gatherings seem to have been designed to cheer the survivors rather than to show their grief for the departed! In the Dalton area of Furness the mourners retired to a public house where they sat down in fours, each group then being served with two quarts of ale and the arvel bread to be eaten at home.[17] And at the funeral of Benjamin Browne of Troutbeck in 1748 two hundred and fifty-eight people attended: the following account shows the sort of meal which was provided for them:

14 dozen Wiggs [Wiggs are tea-cakes or buns with caraway seeds] and
16 dozen of bread.

Cakes, 6 dozen at 2d.	00. 12. 00.
Beef a Quart[r].	00. 15. 06.
Veal a side.	00. 04. 06.
Two sheep . . . at 6s. apiece.	00. 12. 00.
Malt a load (for brewing).	01. 07. 00.
Wine, white and red, 2 gallon.	00. 17. 06.

The birth of children provided happier occasions for feasting, and once again certain traditional foods were deemed appropriate. Often the midwives, called locally 'houdy-wives',[18] cooked the celebration dinner; William Fleming, the Furness diarist, records such an event in 1818:[19]

'The Wife of a Farmer of mine was brought to Bed a few days ago and Preparations had

* 'Pace' or 'pasche' is derived from the word 'Paschal'.

been made previous to the expected Event. As soon as the good Woman was delivered, some Ale was put on the Fire with Spices to warm and a Cheese (better than Common) and a large loaf of fine Bread. The accoucheur [a male midwife] cut a slice or two of the Cheese, then cross cut them into Pieces about the size of a Finger and Shook them in his Shirt lap; these were distributed among the unmarried Women to lay under their Pillows at Night to dream of. This cheese is called the Groaning Cheese of which all present ate heartily and drank the warm Ale mixed with Rum or Brandy after which the married Women leapt over a Besom or Birch Broom and she who did not clear the Broom was pronounced the next for the Straw.'

One wonders what the Church thought of this obviously pagan ritual! As well as 'groaning cheese', rum butter was usually provided at a christening feast, for it was believed that the mother would recover from her confinement more rapidly if fed on this sweetmeat. Made from butter, brown sugar, rum and nutmeg, this traditional Cumbrian delicacy still appears at christenings, though it is now made commercially and sold in great quantities to tourists. Another traditional christening dish, buttered sops, is no longer made, but Joseph Budworth recorded the recipe in 1792:

'Upon the day of celebrating the ceremony, all the matrons in the neighbourhood assemble at the joyful house, and each brings as a present to the good woman in the straw either one pound of sugar, one pound of butter, or sixpennyworth of wheaten bread. The bread is cut in thin slices and placed in rows one above the other in a large kettle of 20 or 30 gallons. The butter and sugar are dissolved in a separate one, and then poured upon the bread, where it continues until it has boiled for some space and the bread is perfectly saturated with the mixture. It is then taken out and served up by way of dessert.'[20]

As for the new-born child, its head was immediately washed with rum and from this arose the custom of 'weshin't barn's heead', an excuse for the proud father and his friends to make merry.

Until the isolation of the Lake District was breached by the turnpike roads of the eighteenth and early nineteenth centuries the fell farmer was self-sufficient; as we have seen, few items of his diet were imported, and similarly most of his clothes were made from the wool of his own sheep. In order to avoid the expense of dyeing cloth, black and white wool was mixed to produce 'self-grey' or 'hodden grey', a common colour for coats and waistcoats; this, of course, is the origin of John Peel's 'coat so gray'. Clarke gives the example of John Bristow, an old dalesman from the Greystoke area who wore clothes made from the wool of his sheep either dyed by a neighbour 'or what is called here Skiddaw-grey, viz. black and white wool mixed'.[21] However, the fact that Clarke felt it necessary to mention this at all suggests that by this time (1787) the practice had already become the exception rather than the rule.

In the guttering light of rushlights and tallow candles, both men and women knitted hosiery and any spare minutes were occupied in this activity; indeed, Joseph Budworth in 1795, writing of the Kendal area, claimed that 'both men and women were knitting stockings as they drove their peat carts into the town.'[22] This cottage industry often supplemented the meagre income of the dales folk; in 1801 2,400 pairs of stockings was the average weekly supply sent to Kendal market, most of these coming from east Westmorland, particularly Ravenstonedale and Orton. Even as late as 1868, six elderly knitters in Orton supplied seventy-two pairs of

1. *Glencoyne Farm, Ullswater.*
This fine example of seventeenth-
century vernacular architecture
was built by the Howard family
in 1629 but extended and altered
in 1700. Note the cylindrical
chimneys so characteristic of Lake-
land farms.

2. *The old farmhouse at High*
Yewdale, near Coniston. Probably
built in the late seventeenth or
early eighteenth century, the house
was finally abandoned in the early
part of this century and converted
into a vehicle store for the adjacent
farm.

3. *Low House, Troutbeck, built*
in the late seventeenth century.
The house is no longer used as a
dwelling.

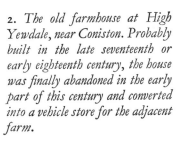

4. *Stickle Barn near Broughton Mills.*

5. *Barn at Field Head Farm, Hawkshead.*

6. *Barn at Wall End, Great Langdale.*

7. *A bank barn at Holme Ground,*
   near Tilberthwaite.

8. *A 'spinning gallery' at Thorn House, Low Hartsop (see also Plate 61.)*

9. *Yew Tree Farm, near Coniston, showing the famous 'spinning gallery'.*

10. *The inscribed date stone at Hewthwaite Hall near Cockermouth is one of the finest in Cumbria. The inscription reads:* John Swinbun esquire and Elisabeth his wyfe did mak coste of this work in the dais of ther lyf Ano Dom 1581 Ano Reg 23.

11. *Date stone, 1683, at Askham.*

12. *A dated lintel stone, 1592, at Millbeck, near Keswick.*

13. *Dated wooden lintel in the barn at Townend, Troutbeck.*

14. *A curious date stone at Hutton Moor End, near Threlkeld:*

THIS BUILDING'S AGE
THESE LETTERS SHOW
MDCCXIX
THOUGH MANY GAZE
YET FEW WILL KNOW

15. *Blacksmith's sign built into a wall at Oxen Park, High Furness.*

16. *Lintel stone at Randle How, Eskdale Green, Cumberland. In 1679 John Nicholson was the village blacksmith.*

17. *Date stone, 1738, on a barn in Far Easedale, near Grasmere.*

18. *The fireplace at Glencoyne Farm near Patterdale, c. 1903. This remarkable photograph shows the open fire with the fire crane and an assortment of ratten-crooks. Note the fire-dog in position to prevent the fuel rolling away from the fire, the two spice cupboards, one on either side of the fireplace, and the trophies proudly displayed.*

19. *An Eskdale interior, Brotherilkeld Farm, c. 1890. Note the cast-iron range, the fire crane, and the spice cupboard.*

20. *An unusual view of the fireplace hood at High Birk House, Little Langdale, Westmorland. The photograph, taken from the loft, shows the way in which the hoods were constructed.*

21. *The interior of a Tilberthwaite farmhouse, 1972. The large fireplace has been replaced by a modern one, but its original position can clearly be seen. The spice cupboard dates from the early eighteenth century and the ham hanging from the beams is evidence that the art of ham curing is not yet dead.*

22. *An eighteenth-century spice cupboard at Rydal Mount, William Wordsworth's final home.*

23. *A Longsleddale spice cupboard, 1662, now in the vestry of Longsleddale church.*

24. *Carving on a bread cupboard, 1646, from Ashlack Hall, High Furness, now at Hare Hall, near Broughton-in-Furness.*

25. *A carved oak bread cupboard typical of seventeenth-century Cumbrian farmhouses. This example is now on display in the Museum of Lakeland Life and Industry, Kendal.*

26. *An outstanding example of a carved oak bread cupboard dated 1660 at Lanehead, Patterdale.*

27. *An eighteenth-century cast-iron range with fire crane and ratten-crooks, in the down-house at Townend, Troutbeck.*

28. *A seventeenth-century char dish. Many of these earthenware dishes were made in Liverpool.*

29. *Below, left: An iron frying pan with bow handle, and a circular girdle on which clap-bread was often baked.*

30. *Below, right: A bakstone formerly at Spring Gardens, Spark Bridge, High Furness. A fire inside this crude oven heated the stone slab (later, cast-iron) and on this large quantities of clap-bread were baked. Used in the early part of this century, this bakstone was fired with shavings from the nearby bobbin mill. It was broken up in 1958.*

31. *A seventeenth-century carved oak bedhead at Townend, Troutbeck. The initials are those of George and Ellinor Browne.*

32. *A 'candle bark' at Hare Hall, near Broughton-in-Furness. Most eighteenth- and nine-teenth-century housewives kept the rushlights and tallow candles in these cylindrical metal boxes which were often hung on the wall.*

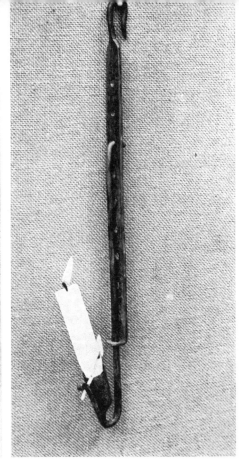

33. *Far left: An adjustable spiral candlestick from Cumberland.*

34. *Left: A hanging adjustable candle and rushlight holder.*

35, 36. *Below, left and centre: Combined candle and rushlight holders.*

37. *Below: A simple rushlight holder from Cumberland.*

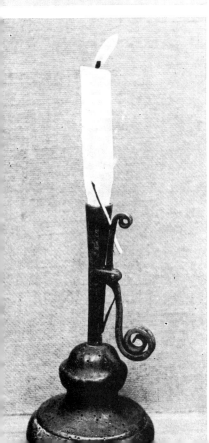

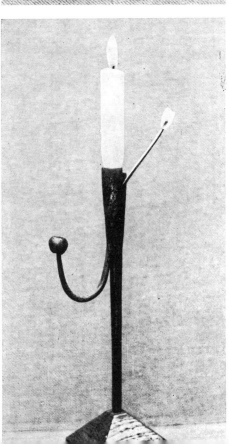

38. *A Wasdale classroom, c. 1894. Within the last twenty-five years, selective rural migration has resulted in many young families moving away from the remoter valleys, and several of these small schools have been closed.*

39. *A rush-bearing procession at Warcop.*

40. *Carrying a 'burden' at the rush-bearing.*

41. *Part of the annual rush-bearing celebrations at Ambleside.*

42. *Members of t*
Furness Morris Me
perform the ancie
Pace Egging Play ou
side the castle
Dalton - in - Furnes
Easter 1972.

43. *A grisly talisma*
at Askham, Wes
morland—a deer's foo
and a horse-shoe naile
to the door of a byre.

stockings a month to a firm in Kendal.[23] In order to make the new stockings last as long as possible, many frugal housewives adopted a simple but effective technique; the heels of the stockings were smeared with pitch and then immediately dipped into the ashes of the turf fire, forming a hard and flexible layer which resisted the formation of holes.[24]

In the eighteenth century, shirts were made of 'harden' cloth, a very coarse material made from hemp or flax. Wearing them must have quickened one's admiration for the medieval penitents in their hair shirts! In order to make them more tolerable to wear they were soaked in water and beaten with a battling wood.[25] By the beginning of the nineteenth century harden cloth had been superseded, and John Gough remarked that few women in Kendal knew the art of spinning flax.[26]

Wooden-soled clogs were universally worn by both men and women, the distinction being that the women's clogs had brass clasps rather than iron. This somewhat cumbersome footwear was expedient rather than elegant for, it was argued, '. . . it would be impossible to wade through the wet and dirt of a farmyard in winter without these guards'.[27] The making of the alder soles and leather uppers was a skilled task and cloggers in towns like Kendal, Keswick and Ulverston were kept busy. The wooden soles were usually shod with iron 'corkers' or 'caulkers'. Clogs are still manufactured and even today are preferred by some farmers for their warmth and comfort, though the number of cloggers has sadly declined.

Many isolated valleys and farmsteads were visited in the eighteenth and nineteenth centuries by pedlars, known locally as 'Scotchmen' irrespective of their actual nationality, but no doubt a reflection of the number of Scottish pedlars in the north of England. These itinerant tradesmen generally carried with them lengths of printed cotton cloths, calicoes and the like which found a ready market in these remote communities. Similarly, itinerant tailors visited remote areas once or twice a year to make up the duffel or hodden grey into clothes. These craftsmen were usually paid 10d. to 1s. per day with board and lodging, often remaining a week or more until the new wardrobe for the family had been completed.

Such, then, was the dress of the eighteenth-century dalesman, but the more affluent statesman could afford to dress his family in a manner which befitted his status. The following extracts are from an early eighteenth-century account book of a Troutbeck yeoman:[28]

1722 Feb. 9.	A pair of stockings for my wife.	1s. 5d.
Nov. 23.	To Cooper for making my sheepskin breeches.	2s. 6d.
Sept. 10.	To Mr. Ferrys for making 14 yards of plush of my own wool 21 lbs. at 2s. 2d. a yard.	£1. 10. 0.
,, 24.	For dying the said plush.	2s. 0d.
May 30.	Irish Linen of Mr. Elliott 4 yards at 16d. for myself a shirt.	5s. 4d.
July 7.	Kirkby Harden 6 yards for aprons.	4s. 0d.
1728 Nov. 15.	To Geo. Shoomaker for shooes for myself.	6s. 6d.
	My wife shooes a pair.	2s. 6d.

By the nineteenth century 'the rust of poverty and ignorance', as one writer termed the apparent backwardness of Cumbria,[29] had begun to wear off; improved communications and the transmission of new ideas and fashions meant the erosion of long-standing traditions both in food and dress. When Kendal and Ulverston mirrored London fashions, and mantua-makers, tailors and milliners had premises there, it was no longer necessary to be self-sufficient or to rely on the visits of the pedlar and the itinerant tailor. In 1774 Thomas West, writing of Furness, recorded that 'within the memory of man every family manufactured their own wearing apparel; at present, few wear anything that is not imported'.[30] Similarly, John Gough in 1812 also witnessed the changing traditions in dress: '. . . the yarn hose and coarse druggets of former times have been supplanted by the manufactures of the West of England, Yorkshire, Manchester and Nottingham; so great indeed is the aversion to a home-spun dress at present, that the poor buy a new kind of second-hand finery from dealers in old clothes.'[31] The age of mass-produced fashion had dawned—and with its arrival died an honourable tradition of folk costume.

4 SOME CUSTOMS AND TRADITIONS

All areas of Highland Britain are rich in folk traditions and the Lake District is no exception; many of these customs are shared in common with parts of the 'Celtic fringe', but others appear to be peculiar to Cumbria. One thing is certain, that almost all have their origins far back in history, though most are no longer respected.

BIDDEN WEDDINGS

In closely knit societies such as existed in the fells, 'bidden weddings' afforded an opportunity for social contact, for generally the entire dale was 'lated' or invited to a wedding. The couple were often preceded to church by a fiddler—a custom which still prevails in the fjord country of western Norway—and after the ceremony a race on foot or on horseback to the bridal house followed, the victor receiving a riband from the bride.[1] Wrestling and leaping contests as well as foot races—in which the women guests also participated—were the accepted part of a Lakeland wedding celebration, as was the strange custom of breaking a wedding cake over the bride's head. This was not as fearsome as it might first appear, for the bridecake was a thin currant cake rather than the substantial iced centrepiece of today's receptions! The bride's head was covered with a white cloth and the bridegroom, standing behind her, broke the cake which was then distributed. The same custom also existed in Ireland.[2] The bride later sat in state while the assembled guests placed money and other gifts in a plate on her knee. The festivities often ended with another time-honoured tradition—that of throwing the stocking: '. . . a custom which refinement has proscribed as indelicate, though it offered no offence to the decorum of the rude simplicity of the people amongst whom it prevailed. It was, however, accessible only to a chosen party. While the new married couple sat upright in bed, with the curtains open only at the foot, the young men attempted to hit the bridegroom and the young women the bride, by throwing the bride's stockings over their shoulders. Those who were successful in the attempt went away assured that their marriage was near.'[3]

In High Furness the happy couple's peace, and that of the surrounding countryside, was further shattered by 'friends' who fired shots over the roof of the bridegroom's house in the early hours of the morning.[4] 'Public' weddings were often widely advertised in the manner of a fair or a theatrical performance. The marriage in 1807 of Joseph Rawlings and Mary Dixon of High Lorton was one such 'festival' which was publicized by printed handbills.[5] The invitation was extended to 'Friends, Acquaintances and others', who were assured that '. . . every effort . . . will be used to accommodate the company, and render the day agreeable'. Amongst the prizes were 'one saddle to be run for, and two bridles to be trotted for, by horses; two belts to be wrestled for, two hats to be run for, gloves to be leaped for, and a tankard to be shot for, by men'. The festivities ended with a 'Pantomime Exhibition . . . to be performed by Actors of the first Distinction', after which the 'guests' were expected to make a monetary contribution to the happy couple.

On a more discordant note, although divorce and separation were almost unheard of, occasionally such scandals were revealed. William Fleming gives one example of a situation which Thomas Hardy has described in Wessex, and Hugh Walpole in Cumbria;[6] it seems that an unfaithful wife and her lover were pursued from Furness to Whitehaven by the aggrieved husband. The erring and unrepentant lady, being unwilling to return home, was led to the market place with a halter round her neck and auctioned, whereupon she was sold to her lover 'for something less than one shilling'.[7] Whether or not it was a bargain, Fleming does not record! The outcome of this affair was perhaps fortunate, for in other circumstances the lady would have been obliged to 'ride the stang'. This curious custom, generally performed by proxy, was usually reserved for adultery by men or women, although it was also a punishment for wife-beating and, if some authorities are to be believed, for husband-beating![8] The character nominated by the community to impersonate the guilty party was carried through the village at night on a plank or pole, known locally as a 'stang', by a noisy, shouting mob. Stops were made at each door, when the rider explained his appearance in doggerel rhyme, the final halt being made at the house of the culprit before the company adjourned to the alehouse, no doubt to reminisce of other 'stang ridings'.

WAKES AND FUNERALS

Superstition and death are an inseparable part of folk lore and all primitive peoples have customs and traditions associated with death. In Cumberland, even in the nineteenth century, it was believed that a dying person could not, in fact, expire on a bed which happened to contain pigeon feathers. Consequently, if it appeared that the person was sinking slowly, it was customary to remove him from the bed to the floor in order that he could pass away in peace.[9] Undoubtedly this rough treatment often precipitated the fatal result, thereby adding credibility to the superstition! In Ireland the removal of a dying person from the bed to the floor was believed to ease the escape of the departing spirit.[10] As soon as the person had died, it was believed necessary to 'tell the bees', and a special messenger was sent to the hive for this purpose and often the hive was decorated with black ribbon. The meaning of this curious custom is obscure; it was practised in Cumbria, East Anglia, Ireland and Scandinavia at least until the late nineteenth century.*

Just as guests were 'bidden' to a wedding feast, so too it was customary to invite representatives of the homesteads in the dale to attend the funeral. In the more remote and thinly populated valleys it was customary to 'bid' two people from each farm, but in areas where the population was greater, only one was 'bidden' at each house. If the representative failed to attend, it was regarded as a gross insult to the departed and his family. Although Cumbria has no tradition of wakes such as existed in Ireland, nevertheless the corpse was watched constantly until the day of the funeral[11] and visitors arriving to express condolences were expected to undergo the ordeal of touching the body. This arose from an ancient superstition which held that if the murderer touched the corpse of the person he had killed, it would bleed,

*George Ewart Evans has traced the origins of the tradition to Classical mythology. See 'Folk Life Studies in East Anglia' in G. Jenkins, *Studies in Folk Life*, London, 1969.

consequently all mourners had to pass this test to indicate that they were not responsible for the deceased's death.[12]

The corpse was carried from the house to the church by jealously guarded 'corpse-ways', and any departure from these recognized routes would have been regarded as an ill omen. In Troutbeck there are records of fences which had to be removed so that a funeral procession could pass along a traditional route, established by ancient custom.[13] During the procession the church bell tolled, indicating by the number of tolls whether the corpse was a man, woman or child. The Troutbeck 'passing bell' tolled nine times and then a pause for a man, six times for a woman, and three times for a child, but the number of tolls varied from place to place. After the interment, the party then proceeded to the funeral feast, where the 'arvel' bread was distributed (*see* page 47).

In the more remote Lakeland dales the corpse had to be carried to the distant church either on a crude form of bier or sledge, or, alternatively, strapped to the back of a pack-horse. Corpse roads along which these doleful processions passed were once common in Cumbria. Often the bearers had to rest at intervals along the road, and 'resting stones' were erected on which the coffin was placed. In such cases it was usual to distribute the arvel bread before the procession started; each bearer received one and a quarter arvel cakes, the quarter being eaten as refreshment at the first halt. Several folk legends are associated with these corpse roads; one of the best known concerns the Coniston area. Before there was a burial ground at Coniston, corpses had to be carried to Ulverston for burial; following his death, a gentleman named Jenkins was being conveyed on a sledge to that town when, crossing a small beck some quarter of a mile from Coniston Church, the body slipped into the stream. It was some time before the loss of the principal personage was discovered, but after a search he was found and duly interred safely in Ulverston. The beck is still known as Jenkins Syke. An even more macabre legend is told of the corpse road which ran from Wasdale Head to Eskdale over the bleak and windswept Burnmoor. During the funeral of a young man, the horse carrying the coffin took fright and galloped off into the swirling mist and was lost. The man's mother died shortly after and at her funeral in the snow the same thing occurred. Ultimately the mourners found a horse—but one which bore the young man's coffin; the woman's corpse was never found.[14]

BARRING-OUT

Although not essentially a Cumbrian tradition, the annual schoolboy riot of 'barring-out' the master from his school remained until the nineteenth century and perhaps even later. The object seems to have been to persuade the master to grant longer holidays by what today might be called a 'sit-in'. Most 'barring-outs' were good-natured, though they could be protracted affairs: at St Bees the school charter restricted the rebellion to 'a day and a night, and the next day till one-o-clock in ye afternoon', but elsewhere the ceremony usually lasted for one day only. Doting parents invariably gave sums of money to their rioting sons; Sir Daniel Fleming of Rydal regularly gave money to his children 'at their barring-out' which generally took place between December 7th and 15th each year and was clearly in anticipation of the Christmas holiday.[15] John Bolton, writing in the nineteenth century of his schooldays in Urswick-in-Furness, remembered with affection the barring-outs and the schoolmaster who 'quietly submitted to have a little dirty water thrown over him when he attempted to storm our barricade, and as he never could succeed, being always forced to retreat, it was not with frowns and threatenings for another time, but with a good-natured smile at his defeat'.[16] Student-teacher confrontations today have regrettably lost this degree of amicability!

TREE WORSHIP AND CULT OBJECTS

Customs associated with trees, plants and stones are as old as Man himself; they have their origins in the prehistoric, pre-agricultural phase of human history. Until recently, several traditions associated with trees were respected within the Lake District. One of the most widely observed was the carrying of rowan branches to the Beltane fires which were generally lighted on the eve of May Day. These bone-fires, so-called because bones were originally burned, were clearly a relic of fire-worship and the branches of rowan were carried as a protection against evil influences. Thomas Pennant, passing through Cumberland during one of his tours to Scotland in the eighteenth century, noted that '. . . till of late years the superstition of the Beltain was kept up in these parts, and in this rude sacrifice it was customary for the performers to bring with them boughs of the mountain ash'.[17] Even in the middle of the nineteenth century, rowan twigs and leaves were inserted into keyholes and hung over doors of houses to prevent witchcraft,[18] and it was widely believed that a twig of rowan placed in the milk during churning would soon make the butter come (page 43).

Clearly, then, the mountain ash or rowan was regarded as no ordinary tree, and indeed it was venerated by Scandinavian peoples and figures prominently in their folk lore as the sacred tree of Thor. It is possible that the Irish-Norse settlers arriving in Cumbria in the ninth and tenth centuries brought with them these traditions, but it may be suggested that the origins of such superstitions could be considerably earlier. Professor E. Estyn Evans argues that in Ireland the rowan, holly, elder and whitethorn were endowed with special magical properties because these plants became common in Neolithic times as weeds of cultivation associated with the primitive agriculture of the first cultivators. In this way they became symbols of the farming year, the blossoms heralding spring and the red berries being a token of the promise of rebirth after the harvest.[19]

In Ireland and the Isle of Man it was customary, even in this century, to decorate with rags certain trees near to springs or wells, and in Derbyshire, well-dressing continues to the present. Certainly the same custom was observed in the Lake District at the end of the nineteenth century, for W. G. Collingwood recorded that an oak tree overhanging a fountain at Satterthwaite and another at Hawkshead Hill were both decorated with crockery and coloured rags on Maundy Thursday, 1894.[20] At Brough near Kirkby Stephen, the holly tree was used in an unusual ceremony on Twelfth Night when the tree, suitably illuminated with rushlights or candles, was carried through the town and later thrown amongst the crowd, where the younger and more daring members attempted to seize it and carry it off to rival inns where drinking and dancing continued far into the night.

Although cult objects other than trees do not feature as prominently in the folk lore of Cumbria as they do in Ireland, nevertheless there is some evidence for the continuation of such practices until the last century. Mention has already been made of the 'dobbie' stones which were believed to be possessed of magical powers (page 43; *see also* page 83), but in some areas large stones were visited and decorated at certain times of the year. In Low Furness the inhabitants of Urswick near Ulverston regularly celebrated Midsummer Day by dressing a large limestone boulder with coloured rags and flowers, and at the same time covering the surface with sheep salve, tar or butter.[21] The origin of this obviously pagan votive offering can only be guessed at, but it was certainly carried out in the nineteenth century.

RUSHBEARING

The strewing of rushes on church floors is by no means solely a Lake District ritual, for it was a festival of the early Christian Church, probably organized to supersede some ancient pagan celebration, and as such it was widely respected throughout England. By the eighteenth century, however, the custom had lapsed in all but a few places in the north of England, and within Cumbria it is now held only at Warcop, Musgrave, Ambleside, Grasmere and Urswick. There was more to the tradition than mere ceremony, for in pre-Reformation times, and, indeed, in many cases until the eighteenth century, the floors of the churches were of soil. Moreover, burials were undertaken in the naves of the churches; for example, interments continued within Grasmere Church until 1823 and, because of the resultant sinking of the ground, the benches had to be constantly relocated. The renewal of sweet-smelling rushes, then, was as much a necessity as a ritual. In some churches near to the coast, for example Walney Chapel and at Dalton-in-Furness, marram grass from the sand dunes was substituted for rushes. Kneeling on this spiky grass must have been a penance in itself!

The great annual strewing was naturally undertaken in high summer, when the rushes or sieves on the fellsides were fully grown, and the labour was regarded as a boon service by the parishioners. This was a good time for festivities within Lakeland, for by then the two main harvests, wool and hay, were both gathered in, and the rushbearing was seen as an excuse for merry-making and drinking.

James Clarke witnessed a Grasmere rushbearing at the end of the eighteenth century and described it as follows:[22]

'This is an ancient annual custom, formerly pretty universal here, but now generally disused . . . About the latter end of September,* a number of young women and girls (generally the whole of the parish) go together to the tops of the hills to gather rushes; these they carry to the church, headed by one of the smartest girls in the company. She who leads the procession is stiled the Queen and carries in her hand a large garland, and the rest usually have nosegays. The Queen then goes and places her garland upon the pulpit, where it remains till after the next Sunday; the rest then strew their rushes upon the bottom of the pews and at the church door they are met by a fiddler who plays before them to the public house, where the evening is spent in all kinds of rustic merriment.'

Being a boon service, the rushbearers who undertook the actual strewing of the church floor expected no reward, but as early as 1680 the Grasmere Churchwardens' accounts show:

For Ale bestowed on those who brought rushes and repaired the Church   00. 01. 00.

---

*Writing in 1787, Clarke here records a rushbearing which had taken place several years earlier, and it seems that he is confused about the month in which the ceremony occurred. Before 1845 the Grasmere rushbearing was held on the Saturday nearest to St Oswald's Day, 5th August.

Four years later the amount spent on ale was increased to two shillings, and in 1685 it reached 5s. 6d. but thereafter, perhaps under pressure from more temperate parishioners, the charge 'to Rushbearers' remained fixed at 2s. 6d. until 1774.[23] From 1819 the Grasmere rushbearers, by this time almost solely children, were given gifts of 'rushbearers' cake', the famous Grasmere gingerbread, still sold from a small shop in the corner of the churchyard. Apart from a lapse of thirteen years in the mid nineteenth century, the gingerbread tradition has been maintained to the present day.

The Grasmere church floor was eventually paved in 1840 and it was no longer necessary to strew rushes; the ceremony, however, continues, although its character has changed and it has now become essentially a children's flower festival. The same is true of the Ambleside celebration; certainly a hundred and fifty years ago the rushbearing here bore the stamp of a rustic medieval fair. The following extracts are taken from an interview in 1898 between Canon H. D. Rawnsley, Vicar of Crosthwaite near Keswick, and Miss H. Nicholson, then aged eighty-five:

'In my young days we met at the Village Cross on the Saturday nearest St. Anne's Day, at 6 o'clock in the evening. Old Tommy Houghton, the clogger, came; he was a very clever jigger, best dancer hereabout ... he was a kind of clerk and village constable ... who marshalled us. Everyone who chose came—young and old; and all who carried "burdens" [garlands on poles] received a good big cake of gingerbread, made by Old Mickey the baker. ... Folk came for miles to see the procession, and Wordsworth never missed; he and the Rydal party would sit in our little room to see the procession start ... we all met— a hundred and more—and then an old man played on his fiddle or his pipe and off we all went round the village, up street and down street, to the same old tune. We only knew one tune in those days—"The Hunt is Up". ... We became refined in later days, and then we had a band—the Steamer Band [from the Windermere steamers]—and my mother, who collected for the gingerbread, had to collect an additional sovereign for the band.'[24]

Rushbearings are still celebrated in Lakeland (see plates 39–41) but other aspects of folk customs have been forgotten, albeit only in the recent past. Few people today know of the once popular 'bidden weddings' or the riotous 'barring-outs' or, indeed, of the magical properties of the rowan, yet a hundred years ago such traditions would have been widely remembered in Cumbria, if not widely respected. The Age of the Mass Media, some would say an 'enlightened' age, has meant the almost complete decline of folk traditions and our culture is the poorer for it.

5 FOLK MEDICINE

Until comparatively recently the Lake District was remote and isolated and this, in turn, meant that the dalesmen were necessarily both self-sufficient and self-reliant. Although by the early nineteenth century most Lakeland communities had the services of a resident doctor, many countrymen preferred to rely on the age-old herbal remedies and cures passed on to them by their fathers and grandfathers. To be fair, many of these well-tried cures were in some measure medically effective, but others were superstitious nonsense rather than rational remedies. Superstition and folk medicine die hard in rural communities and it is therefore not surprising to find that some of these ancient and primitive cures have survived until the twentieth century.

In these days of anaesthetics and antibiotics it is difficult to imagine the dangers to health which the nineteenth-century dalesman had to accept as his lot; the ever-present fear of disease, a difficult childbirth, an infected cut turning to septicaemia — all could be fatal, and against such adversities medical knowledge was almost as ineffective as some of the folk remedies. Even a broken limb, if badly set, could result in maiming and lameness for life. Little wonder, then, that anyone acquiring even the slightest degree of skill in setting bones was a much sought-after person—and not only for the setting of human limbs, but those of animals as well! Not that these amateur osteopaths were always successful; the seventeenth-century account books of Sir Daniel Fleming of Rydal give us an insight into the problems of broken limbs, in this case the leg of Sir Daniel's son, William:

1658	Aug. 10.	Given unto George Browne of Troutbeck, a bone setter, when Will was hurt	£00. 02. 06.
	Aug. 11.	Given unto William Story of Seadgwicke near Sighser [Sizergh]— bone-setter—for looking at Will's thigh	£00. 07. 06.
	Nov. 12.	Given unto John Rawlings, a bone-setter, for Will	£00. 10. 00.

One of the most fascinating pieces of folk medicine in Cumbria concerns the so-called skin disease 'King's Evil', or scrofula. During the seventeenth and eighteenth centuries it was widely believed that the most effective remedy was the monarch's touch, hence the name.* This belief remained until the early eighteenth century when, with the death of Queen Anne, the tradition was broken.[1] The belief in this cure was common throughout England, and there are several references to Cumbrians travelling to London to be 'touched'; one of the earliest appears in the Crosthwaite (Westmorland) church registers:

---

*The origin of the custom of 'touching' may be traced to Edward the Confessor, but after the Restoration it became extremely popular; between 1660 and 1682 Charles II 'touched' 92,107 people. R. J. Mitchell & M. D. R. Leys, *A History of the English People*, 1950, p. 356.

73

1629   14th Feby. Given to John Rig of Staveley who hath the King's Evil to go
              up to be cured thereof.   1/-

In the Fleming account books the following entry appears:[2]

1669   Oct. 2.   Given unto my brother Roger towards his charges in going
                    unto London to get the King's Touch for the Evil.   £10. 0. 0.

And the Grasmere Parish Registers contain the following entry:

'Wee the Rector and Churchwardens of the Parish of Grasmere in the County of Westmorland
do hereby certify that David Harrison of the sd Parish aged about ffourteen years, is afflicted
as wee are credibly informed with the disease commonly [called] the King's Evill; and (to
the best of o[r] knowledge) hath not heretofore been touched by His Majesty for ye s[d] Decease.
   'In testimony whereof wee have hereunto set o[r] hands + seals the ffourth day of ffeb:
Ano Do: 1684

            Henry ffleming, Rector.

            John Benson   ⎫
            Jo[n] Mallinson ⎬ Churchwardens
                           ⎭

'Registered by John Braithwaite, Curate.'

   Unfortunately there are few indications of the success or failure of these 'touchings'; on the
face of it, the success rate cannot have been high, but on the other hand the effectiveness of
psychosomatic cures cannot be discounted. Indeed, charms and other semi-religious magic
played no small part in many of these ancient folk remedies, and undoubtedly the psychosomatic
element must have played an important role in any 'cure'. It was widely held in Lakeland
dales that various scriptural texts written on scraps of paper by a 'wise man or woman'
could readily check haemorrhage, cure ague and jaundice, and relieve toothache. At Skelwith
Bridge in the middle of the eighteenth century the following formula was used:

'To stop bleeding in Man or Beast at any Distance, first you must have some Drops of ye
Blood upon a Linen Ragg and wrap a Little Roman Vitrioll upon this Ragg put it under
your oxter [armpit] and say these words thrice into yrself "There was a Man Born in
Bethlehem of Judea Whose name was Called Christ—Baptised in the River Jordan in the
Watter of the flood and the Child also was meak and good and as the watter stood So I
desire thee the Blood of Such a person or Beast to stand in their Bodie, in the name of the
father son and Holy Ghost Amen." Then Look into the Ragg and at that moment the
Blood stopeth the Blew powder is Turned into Blood by sympathy.'[3]

Similarly, the eighteenth-century commonplace book of Christopher Birkett of Troutbeck
(Westmorland) contains the following remedy 'for a Fevour or an Ague':

'When Jesus did see the Crosse whereon his body should be crucified, his body did shake.

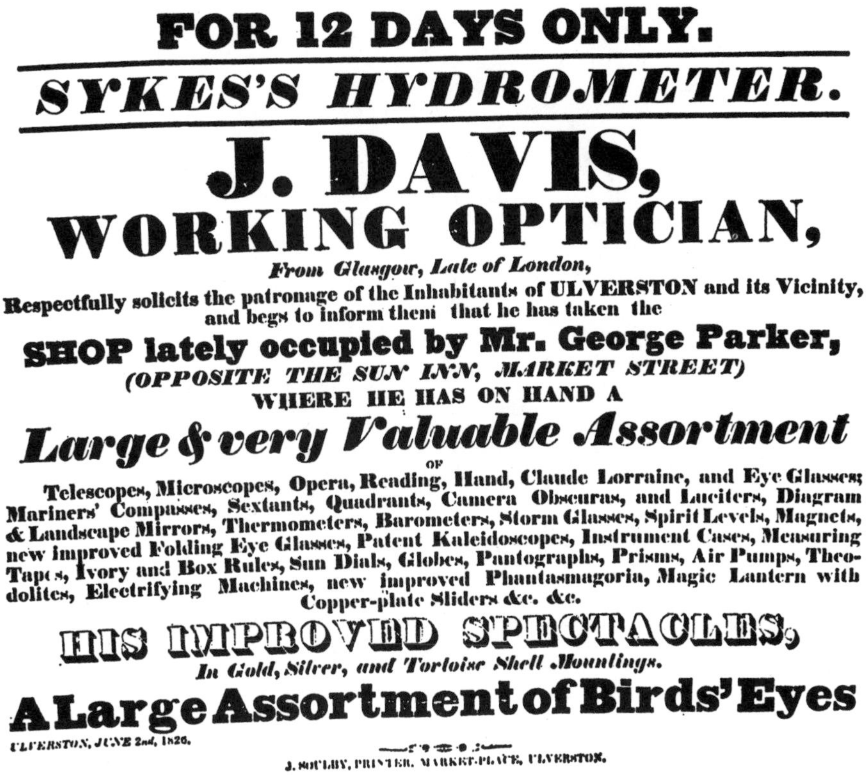

FOR 12 DAYS ONLY.

SYKES'S HYDROMETER.

J. DAVIS,

WORKING OPTICIAN,

From Glasgow, Late of London,

Respectfully solicits the patronage of the Inhabitants of ULVERSTON and its Vicinity, and begs to inform them that he has taken the

SHOP lately occupied by Mr. George Parker,

(OPPOSITE THE SUN INN, MARKET STREET)

WHERE HE HAS ON HAND A

Large & very Valuable Assortment

OF

Telescopes, Microscopes, Opera, Reading, Hand, Claude Lorraine, and Eye Glasses; Mariners' Compasses, Sextants, Quadrants, Camera Obscuras, and Luciters, Diagram & Landscape Mirrors, Thermometers, Barometers, Storm Glasses, Spirit Levels, Magnets, new improved Folding Eye Glasses, Patent Kaleidoscopes, Instrument Cases, Measuring Tapes, Ivory and Box Rules, Sun Dials, Globes, Pantographs, Prisms, Air Pumps, Theodolites, Electrifying Machines, new improved Phantasmagoria, Magic Lantern with Copper-plate Sliders &c. &c.

HIS IMPROVED SPECTACLES,

In Gold, Silver, and Tortoise Shell Mountings.

A Large Assortment of Birds' Eyes

ULVERSTON, JUNE 2nd, 1826.

J. SOULBY, PRINTER, MARKET-PLACE, ULVERSTON.

Fig. 14. Handbill of Mr Davis, optician.

The Jews did ask him if he had an Ague. He answered and said whosoever keepeth this in mind or in writing shall never be troubled with an Ague nor a feavour soe Lord help thy servants, they that put their trust in thee.'[4]

Elizabeth Birkett, also of Troutbeck, used a different remedy for the ague in 1699:

'Take a spider and lye it quick in a cloth and hang it about the party's neck, they not knowing of it, and take it away when the fitt is over.'[5]

Even more bizarre cures were sometimes attempted; as late as the nineteenth century, sufferers from toothache in Hawkshead sought out the remains of the ancient gibbet or gallows, made a stopping from the wood and were soon cured—or so the story says.[6] In some areas it was believed that to improve the teeth of a child it was necessary to rub them 'with the brains of an Hen, or let a Horse breathe into the Child's Mouth twice a day, which may prevent convulsive fits'.[7] It is safe to assume that such a remedy would today induce a convulsive fit rather than prevent one! Whooping cough was treated in a variety of ways—either by passing the patient under the belly of a donkey, taking him into

```
┌─────────────────────────────────────────────────┐
│  JOHN SUMMERS,                                    │
│       DENTIST,                                    │
│  TAKES the Liberty of acquainting his Friends and the Public, that │
│     he is just arrived from Newcastle, and will commence pursuing his │
│  Profession here with the utmost Attention and Care, and may be found │
│  at the House of Mr. JOHN BURNETT, Innkeeper, in Ulverstone; or, upon │
│  Application, will wait on any Lady or Gentleman at their own House. │
│                                                   │
│     He begs leave to observe, that he is the only Person in the Kingdom │
│  who can extract a Tooth even in the most decayed State, without Pain │
│          to the Patient ; He also professes       │
│                                                   │
│     CLEANING, SCALING and PLANTING TEETH,         │
│           From one to a Complete Set.             │
│                                                   │
│     N. B.——He makes POWDERS and TINCTURES, for Hardening │
│        the Gums, Cleaning the Teeth, and Sweetening the Breath. │
│           BOX 1s. 6d.--BOTTLE 2s. 6d.--Duty included. │
│        *₊* His Stay in this Place will be for a few Days only. │
│  November 15th, 1803.          G. ASHBURNER, PRINTER. │
└─────────────────────────────────────────────────┘
```

Fig. 15. Handbill of Mr Summers, dentist.

'an underground excavation'[8] or, at Skelwith Bridge, riding the afflicted person across the bridge with his face to the animal's tail![9] This latter cure was known to have been practised about 1817.

The commonplace book kept by Elizabeth Birkett of Troutbeck[10] contains a wealth of seventeenth-century hedgerow cures; 'ffor falling sickness' the sufferer was subjected to a brew comprising the dried and powdered intestines of three goslings in a 'draught of ale without Hops', and 'stone and gravel' was cured by a dose of warm white wine to which had been added the powdered roots of nettles. For a headache the brow of the afflicted person was soothed with an infusion of marigold flowers and distilled water, after which it was recommended that the patient be allowed to sleep 'if he can'.

Fortunately, folk medicine did not depend entirely on blind superstition. At the end of the eighteenth century—indeed, at the same time as the primitive 'kill or cure' remedies were still being practised—scientific medicine had its origin. As early as 1799, surprisingly only a year after Jenner's original experiments, vaccination against smallpox was introduced into the Furness area of Lakeland by a Dalton apothecary well ahead of his times, Dr William Close. His experiments were successful and by the early nineteenth century the practice of vaccination had spread to other parts. William Fleming, a nineteenth-century Furness diarist, commented:

'Friday, March 15, 1816: In spite of the Vaccine Inocculation the Small Pox rages in Ulverston with deadly Violence and spreads fast among the Children there, but I do not hear of any

WILLIAM ROSS,

BEGS leave to acquaint the Inhabitants of *Ambleside* and its *Vicinity*, that he practises Midwifery.

W. R. should have thought it unnecessary to have troubled the Public with the present notice, but that he wished to correct a report which has been propagated with great industry, for the purpose of injuring him in the public opinion, that he did not practise Midwifery.—During the four Years he studied at the University of *Edinburgh*, he attended the Midwifery, in common with the other Medical Professors in that University, and hopes by a diligent attention, in this, as in every other part of his Professional Duty, to Merit and Share the Public Favour.

J. Soulby, Printer, Ulverstone.

Fig. 16. Handbill of Mr Ross, midwife.

being infected who have been cut for the Cow Pox; however, its Efficacy in preventing the Small Pox will most likely now be put to the Test and many Doubts removed.'[11]

Cholera, however, was a different matter. Medical knowledge in the early part of the nineteenth century was virtually powerless, and often drastic measures had to be taken in order to try to contain the disease. William Fisher, a yeoman farmer in the small argricultural hamlet of Barrow, recorded the alarm occasioned by a cholera outbreak in 1834:

'Oct. Elizabeth the wife of Nickles Fisher of Little Mill Stile begun in the Cholera on the night of the 7 and died on the 8 her Grand Daughter residing with her begun on the 12 and died on the 13 Nicholas Fisher husband of the above Elizabeth Fisher begun on the 14 and died on the 15 a daughter took it a few days after but recovered again it threw the country in to such an alarm it was thought nessary [*sic*] to prevent its further spreading to burn every article in the House the Clock alone was saved and it had the desired effect. I write this Dec. 22 and there has not been another case the loss will be mad up by the Parish.'[12]

Blood letting was an old and much-trusted remedy for all manner of ills; in his account book for 1663 Sir Daniel Fleming records the expenditure of one pound 'to Mr. Kemp for blooding me and other phisick', and it may be added that the same cure was used for sick animals (*see* page 81). In the nineteenth century, however, it became common to apply leeches to human patients. In October 1810 William Fleming complained that he had paid 'Half a Crown for the Bites of four Leeches' but conceded that he gained some relief after

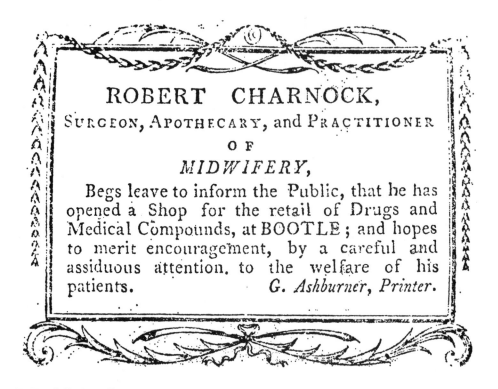

Fig. 17. Handbill of Mr Charnock, surgeon.

the leeches had been 'set to bite on the back Part of the Neck and these Places allowed to bleed freely for 7 Hours'.

Many eighteenth- and nineteenth-century cures relied for their potency on wines and spirits: in 1784 the Hawkshead Parish Accounts record the expenditure of one shilling and sixpence 'for one gill of Brandy and one quart of ale for Sarah Usher to stop the ague'. One wonders if, in alleviating the ague, this remedy did not also produce certain side effects! Spirits were not only used medicinally but also as the basis for various rubs and embrocations: William Fisher endorsed the following nineteenth-century prescription as being 'perfect remedy' for whooping cough:

'Infuse 2 Cloves of Garlick in a quarter of a pint (ale measure) of Rum for twenty four hours; rub the back and soles of the feet of the person afflicted for three or four successive nights at Bed time; at the same time abstaining from all animal food.'

In spite of the somewhat strange method of application, this remedy was no doubt preferable to being passed under the belly of a donkey—and may even have been more effective!

The eighteenth-century commonplace book[13] kept by John Hall of Leasgill, near Heversham, is largely made up of various animal cures, but here and there a 'human' remedy may be found. One such unusual 'cure' describes a 'plaster for Worms for a young Child; take 1 head of Garlic, 1 Sprig [of] rue, 1 thimble full of Gunpowder, 1 halfpenny worth of bitter alice [aloes]; heat the above well in a mortar, mix it with honey and spread it on leather or coarse cloth, lay it on the breast for 24 hours or according to the strength of the patient let it not get lower than the breast'. Hall also recommends as a cure for typhus fever a tablespoon of yeast in a gill of warm porter repeated every six hours until the fever subsides. Amateur practitioners such as John Hall did not always confine their attentions purely to medicine; in the mid nineteenth century in Patterdale, John Walton exercised his skills as a waller, a joiner and a tinsmith—but he also enjoyed a reputation in the area as an excellent tooth-puller! Similarly, Samuel Relph, a vicar of Sebergham, seems to have been the parish doctor as well as the local clergyman, for in one volume of the parish registers he recorded his remedy for lameness: 'Take the yoke of a new-laid egg let it be beaten with a spoon . . . add three ounces of pure water, agitating the mixture continually that the egg and water may be well incorporated apply this to the part, cold or milk-warm by a Gentle Friction for a few minutes 3 or 4 times a day.'

For sufferers from toothache who could not seek relief from the splinters of the Hawkshead gibbet, there were other palliatives: 'a sovereign remedy for toothache' was known to be camphor, ether and laudanum in equal quantities applied to the troublesome molar,[14] a prescription which undoubtedly afforded some relief. The commercial mining of graphite or black lead at Seathwaite in Borrowdale introduced another strange cure; the patient took as much as would lie on a sixpenny piece in white wine or ale as a cure for '. . . the cholick, [and] it easeth the pain of stone and strangury . . .'[15] Eighteenth-century Borrowdale had further attractions for the infirm—the salt spring at Manesty.[16] Even in 1740 it was visited by hopeful invalids for it was believed that '. . . in Dropsical, Cachochymic, cachectic disorders; foulness of the Stomach, slipperyness of the Bowels from Relaxations, or much Mucus, some icteritious [jaundiced] disorders, it is of service to several'.[17] James Clarke, the eighteenth-century surveyor and author, claimed that the same spring was 'a never-failing cure for cutaneous eruptions in man or beast by washing only. I attended it several years (but not of late) on account of rheumatic pains in my left shoulder about mid-summer, five or six years successively. It so cured me that I have not had the slightest touch of it these twelve years past.'[18] One wonders if Mr Clarke had tried other cures for his affliction, for there were many; an eel's skin wrapped around an arm or leg was a powerful charm against rheumatism, so, too, was a living toad carried somewhere on the person, although a lump of brimstone, a potato, or a nutmeg in the pocket was believed by some to be equally effective. Alternatively, bee stings were supposed to have some remedial effect, and there are those who would today endorse such a cure, as indeed there are those who support the theory that nettle stings will cure lumbago. In view of the somewhat strange nature of some of these remedies, perhaps James Clarke was wise to stick to his medicinal waters from Manesty.

Cures for warts seem to have been almost as common as the warts themselves; 'buying' them, rubbing them with apples, raw meat, and even black slugs are remedies which are used today, although these cures seem to be psychosomatic rather than medicinal. On the other hand, several of these curious folk remedies have some validity; the use of honey for wounds and various skin disorders is still common, as is the use of spiders' webs to help stem bleeding from a cut and, anticipating antibiotics by several generations, many Lakeland families used mouldy apples to cure sore throats and mouldy cheese and bread to treat boils and sores.

During the eighteenth and nineteenth centuries several of the large towns in the Lake

District, such as Kendal, Keswick and Ulverston, began to receive regular visits from itinerant physicians, dentists and opticians. Their stock-in-trade, as well as the way in which they solicited custom, strike the modern reader as curious; Mr J. Davis of Glasgow, a travelling optician, carried a wide variety of telescopes, compasses, landscape-glasses, barometers, 'improved spectacles' and 'A Large Assortment of Birds' Eyes' (*see* fig. 14). Mr Telzifair, a surgeon dentist, offered the public his 'new mode of constructing artificial teeth [which] effectually supersedes the usual injurious and insecure fastening by ligatures, wire, hoop or spiral springs'. Similarly, a number of male 'midwives' offered their services (fig. 16). However, as well as these undoubtedly reputable gentlemen, there were other less qualified individuals who can only be described as mountebanks. The Lake District certainly had its share of these colouful characters; Sam Fitton, who styled himself 'The Herb Planet Doctor', and supposedly practised in the Keswick area in the seventeenth century,[19] was a firm believer in the combined powers of herbs and the Heavenly Bodies. In the eighteenth century James Mossop, or Pill Jim, an Ambleside man, had a 'practice' which extended from Buttermere and Eskdale to Braithwaite and Grasmere. His cure-all was a somewhat potent herb beer which bore the sinister name 'Black Drop', but which was nevertheless much prized. The Wasdale area, too, had its own itinerant physician in the late nineteenth century; 'Jackio', believed to be of Romany origin, was skilled in minor surgical operations which were carried out in his herb-strewn caravan. The Kendal and Gosforth regions were visited by a woman charlatan who was known as the 'Mother Superior'. Among her collection of remedies were toothache drops, baby tantrum powder, Virgin Water, guaranteed to preserve that state in the imbiber, and a nostrum called 'Green Fire' which warded off colds and chills.

The fact that such quack doctors plied their arts as late as the nineteenth century indicates significantly the conservative nature of Lakeland dalesmen and a reliance on herbal cures and hedgerow medicine which even today is not entirely dead.

6 EARLY VETERINARY PRACTICE

Until the Agricultural Revolution, which in Cumbria was somewhat later than in many other parts of England, veterinary science was unsophisticated. Such animal medicine as existed was mainly a curious mixture of ancient well-tried remedies and blind superstition, similar in many ways to the kill-or-cure folk remedies which were practised on human patients (*see* chapter 5). Yet, out of necessity, the farmers in the more remote districts had to acquire some knowledge of veterinary techniques. Bleeding, that universal panacea for both man and beast, was commonly adopted, and the services of farmers and others who were skilled in this operation were much in demand. In the seventeenth century Sir Daniel Fleming of Rydal Hall regularly resorted to such treatment for his horses and cattle; typical entries in his Account Books[1] include:

1657　February 23 Given for the blooding of Hobson—horse at Ambleside.　£00. 00. 04.
1679　Oct. 1 Given to ye Miller of Ambleside for blooding and giving a Drink to my Cowes for ye murrain.　　£00. 01. 00.

Such methods persisted even until the twentieth century. Figure 18(4, 5) shows the instruments used in this bleeding process; after a string or thong had been bound around the animal's neck in order to make the veins stand out, a vein was opened with a fleam or bleeding knife which was driven in with a mell, or bloodstick, a light wooden mallet. As much as two pints of blood might be drawn off an animal, or even more if a high-spirited horse was being bled to pacify it. For a horse with inflamed lungs, John Hall, an eighteenth-century Westmorland farmer, recommended 'speedy, large and repeated bleedings; First take 3 quarts, next day 2 quarts, and if no better 1 quart daily'[2] After such massive bleedings one wonders if the poor animal survived!

As well as such implements as the fleam and mell, the nineteenth-century Lakeland farmer possessed other standard equipment. In the days when cow remedies consisted of various powders mixed with water and treacle, it was necessary to use a drenching-horn, generally a large cow-horn (fig. 18(10)) from which the dose was poured into the animal's mouth. It is fairly certain that the Miller of Ambleside who gave 'A Drink' to Daniel Fleming's cows used such an implement. Even today many farmers refer to the administering of medicine to animals by mouth as 'horning'. Horses were less passive than either cows or sheep and it was often necessary to employ a gag (fig. 18(3)) when giving them liquids, in order to keep the mouth open. By far the most primitive treatment, however, was the rowelling of cattle and horses; basically the remedy consisted of the insertion of an irritant between the skin and flesh of the animal just above the forelegs. Sometimes this consisted of a leather disc, small wads of setter-grass (*Helleborus foetidus*), a piece of onion or a ball of cotton-wool which was allowed to remain for twenty-four hours. After removal, the wound was kept open for a week or more with a ball of lard and salt, and in this manner it was believed that 'evil humours' were drained from the animal. Another equally grim 'cure' was applied until comparatively recently to sheep which had contracted an ailment which the dalesmen call 'sturdy', 'the turn' or 'gid'. This is essentially a disease transmitted by dogs or foxes which have tapeworms; the parasite sometimes finds its way to the sheep's brain where the worm eggs develop into cysts. The afflicted animal often becomes blind in one eye and wanders round and round ('sturdy' from the Norman French *étourdi*, meaning giddy). In the early decades of this century certain shepherds developed a skill in trepanning; with a sharp knife an incision was made in the skull, exposing the brain and the small bladder or cyst which was the cause of the trouble. This was then extracted by means of a probe or, more often, a goose quill. At the end of the nineteenth century an even more drastic method was used—the skull was burned through with a hot mazling iron in order to expose the brain. A curious superstition existed that 'sturdied' sheep were not to be operated on until the full moon, for it was believed that the skull was soft at that time. Following the operation the incision was usually treated with green salve or a mixture of egg-white and lint-tow and covered with a tar plaster, although some shepherds insisted on placing a silver threepenny or sixpenny piece over the incision before applying the tar plaster![3]

One of the strangest remedies was 'double scalp', 'scaup' or 'scappie', applied to hoggs, yearlings and shearling ewes. Generally the symptoms of the ailment were a poor fleece and a decline in condition of the animal; technically a calcium/phosphorus deficiency produced a soft rarefaction of the frontal bone of the skull. The cure was simple—the skull of the unfortunate animal was merely thumped hard with the knuckles in order to fracture the outer wall of the frontal sinus. However, it should be mentioned that the condition is often associated with worm infection, and since 'double scalping' was applied at the same time as the spring 'worming' it seems more than likely that any apparent benefit was due more to this than to knocking the skull.[4]

By the early nineteenth century several of the remedies in use on Cumbrian farms were probably quite effective. William Fisher, the Low Furness yeoman, recorded several of these in his commonplace book:

A Receipt for a Wound or Bruse in Hors or Cow

Blue vitterol and Verdigrass	each ¼ ounce
Coppras and Broach Allum	each ½ ounce
Salt Peetre	2 ounces

To be Boild in one Quart of Vinegar

A Good Gripe drench for a horce and will Cure a Cow that is hove or blown by eating Clover which will relive in a ¼ of an hour

1 oz. sweet spirits of Nitre.
1 oz. salt of Tartar.
1 pint of mild warm Ale

to be repeted about 6 or 8 hours afterwards to prevent a relaps.

Wherever possible, of course, the farmer used ingredients which were readily available on his farm or which could be easily and cheaply procured. For example, John Hall in 1787 advocated the use of an ointment 'for strangles', the basic ingredient of which was foxglove flowers and butter: 'take in by stamping in a mortar then put them in a pot and stand for a fortnight or longer to rott, then boil them and strain them for use'.[5] Similarly, honey, beeswax, liquorice, linseed oil, rain water, black pepper, mustard, saffron and a wide variety of plants all played a part in these primitive but well-tried remedies, and undoubtedly some of them had a beneficial effect—though not all. In 1819 William Fleming tried out a potent brew of 'chamberley and brimstone' on an ailing pig with little effect, so he administered 'some milk which had been poured upon Iron Ore and it died immediately'.[6]

But all was not sweetness and light, for the forces of superstition were still powerful. It was a strongly held belief in many parts of Lakeland that diseased and sick animals were a direct result of bewitchings, and even as late as 1857 it was argued that several holed stones hung in a stable would prevent evil spirits disturbing the horses.[7] Similar charms and 'dobbie-stones' were credited with the power of hindering evil spirits from disturbing the household or preventing cream from churning, and 'flaying' or bewitching cattle.* But one of the strangest superstitions concerning the bewitching of cattle comes from Troutbeck in Westmorland. The commonplace book of an eighteenth-century farmer, Christopher Birkett, states that '. . . If they be chattell that are bewitched, Take some of the hair of every one of them and mix the haire in faire watter, or wet it well . . . lay it under a Tile, set a Trivet over the Tile, make a lusty fire, turn your Tile oft upon the haire, and stirr upp the haire ever and anon, after you have done this by the space of a quarter-of-an-hour let the fire alone, and when the ashes are cold, bury them in the ground toward that quarter of heaven where the suspected witch lives.' Regrettably the commonplace book does not record the outcome of such measures!

The barbarous practice of calf immolation was widespread in the Lake District—indeed it did not cease until the second half of the nineteenth century. It was believed to be a remedy against contagious abortion or brucellosis. As late as 1866 a bull calf was roasted alive in the village of Troutbeck because all the cows were calving males.[8] Similarly if a cow slipped its calf which then showed signs of life, it was buried alive under the threshold of the byre. *The West Cumberland Times* in April 1876 carried the following report:

'A farmer living within one hundred miles of Lake Bassenthwaite has been rather unfortunate with respect to some of his cows being addicted to slipping their calves. Somebody advised him that, in order to prevent a continuance of similar misfortunes, he should bury a calf in sight of its dam. The cruel suggestion, we are credibly informed, was actually carried into effect.'

Undoubtedly such practices have their origins in the mists of antiquity, but it is surprising to find that they lingered almost to within living memory.

Animal diseases, and in particular that known as murrain (foot and mouth disease), were much feared; against them primitive veterinary science was almost powerless. Murrain, of course, could spread very rapidly through an area, carried not only by animals but by human agents and even birds. *The Complete Cow Doctor*,[9] a volume which was found in many nineteenth-century farmsteads, contained a murrain-preventive remedy consisting of a draught of myrrh, Epsom salts, sulphur, antimony and diapente powder mixed with a quart of rue tea, but the efficacy of such a potion can have been minimal. In view of the virulent nature

*The 'dobbie-stone' at Bleaze Hall, Old Hutton, near Kendal, is a well-worn axe-hammer, probably of prehistoric origin. The Lake District was not alone in its belief in the powers of these talismens; witchstones were also common in the Yorkshire Dales. See M. Hartley and J. Ingilby, *Life and Tradition in the Yorkshire Dales*, London, 1968, p. 60.

of the disease it is not surprising to find that superstition played an important role in the supposed cures, and in particular the belief in the powers of 'needfire'.* This was undoubtedly a relic of ancient fire-worship, and traces of the same practice may be found in Norway, Sweden and parts of Scotland. Essentially the needfire was kindled by friction after all other fires had been extinguished; in order to create 'plenty of reek', straw, potato tops, green leaves and other damp fuels were heaped on and the cattle—and indeed other animals—were driven through the smoke. Harriet Martineau, in her *Guide to the Lakes,* tells the delightful story of one dalesman who, when all his cattle had been fumigated by the needfire smoke, subjected his ailing wife to the same potent charm! The results are not recorded. There is considerable evidence of the use of needfire within the Lake District in the nineteenth century—at Finsthwaite about 1837, Sawrey 1845–7, Monk Coniston 1847, the Keswick area in 1841, when the fire was brought over Dunmail Raise from farm to farm,[10] and at Troutbeck in 1851, the last recorded occurrence.

In the days before the introduction of sheep dipping, the flock had to be 'salved' by hand in order to protect the animals and waterproof the wool. Exactly when this practice originated is unknown, but certainly Sir Daniel Fleming spent considerable sums on the protection of his sheep. In 1645 Richard Harrison, the steward at Rydal Hall, paid £4 5s. for 'greasing ninescore and fifteen days', which works out to about 5d. per day 'without meat or drinke',[11] and in April 1661 Sir Daniel's account book[12] records:

Item (paid John Banckes) which hee had paid to Great John for two dayes
salveing of hoggs ** with tobacco.   £00. 01. 00

The salve was usually a mixture of tar and rancid salt butter, though sometimes tobacco was used. In 1698 the salve for the Rydal flock was made up of butter from Hawkshead costing £3 14s. 11d, and tar brought from Ambleside, £2. 13s. while the bill for labour amounted to £4 16s. 4d. The steward noted that year that the hoggs required 6 gallons of tar and 5 stones and 3 featlets (a featlet=4 lb.) of butter, while the old sheep required 25 gallons of tar, 16½ stones of butter and 3 stones of tallow.

Salving continued well into the nineteenth century, indeed for Fell and Herdwick flocks it was practised in some parts of the Lake District until 1905, when the Board of Agriculture issued a compulsory dipping order to eradicate sheep scab. The composition of the salve continued to be butter and tar, the usual proportions being 16 lb. of butter to 4 quarts of tar. During the nineteenth century this was sufficient to salve 35 to 40 sheep at a cost of approximately 6d. per head. Salving was generally undertaken at 'the back end', between mid October and mid November, just before the onset of winter. The operation itself was a slow one: the 'smearer' divided the fleece along the back of the animal and applied the salve to the skin with his forefinger from head to tail, repeating the process until the sheep was salved. A good smearer

* Possibly from *neat* fire or oxen fire.
** Before their first shearing lambs are known as hoggs or hoggets (*see* pp. 89)

Fig. 18. SOME VETERINARY IMPLEMENTS

Top: A mid nineteenth-century advertisement for Bigg's sheep-dipping apparatus. 1. Gelding irons. 2. Implement for extracting cows' teeth. 3. Horse gag. 4. Fleam, or bleeding knife, with three blades. 5. Mell, or light wooden mallet, used with the fleam. 6. Breaking bit with five keys, from Hawkshead. 7. Mazling iron. 8. Probe. 9. Horn trainer for cows. The cups were usually made of lead. 10. Drenching horn.

A, The Dipping Tub.   B, The Drainer.   C, The Inclined Plane.

THE ABOVE SKETCH IS AN ACCURATE DESCRIPTION OF

BIGG'S SHEEP-DIPPING APPARATUS,

(Which obtained prizes at the Meeting of the Highland and Agricultural Society of Scotland, at Berwick-upon-Tweed; at the Yorkshire Agricultural Society's Meetings held at Hull, 1841, and at Richmond, 1844; and also a Silver Medal from the Royal Agricultural Improvement Society of Ireland, at their Meeting, held at Dublin, August, 1844.)

LAMB DIPPING COMPOSITION," which requires NO BOILING, *and may be used with Warm or Cold Water*, for effectually destroying the Tick, Lice, and all other insects injurious to the Flock, preventing the alarming attacks of Fly and Shab, and cleansing and purifying the skin, thereby greatly improving the wool both in quantity and quality, and highly contributing to the general health of the animal.

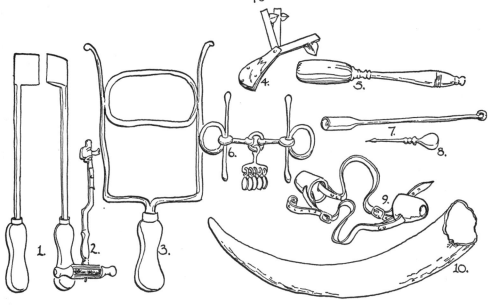

could salve between ten and twelve sheep in a day, for which he was paid 2*d.* per animal.[13] By the second half of the nineteenth century, the salve was made into a liquid and poured onto the skin from a long-spouted can, but although this innovation meant that more sheep could be treated in a day, two men were required for the operation. By 1850 sheep dipping, using Bigg's dipping composition and troughs (fig. 18), was replacing salving, and economics hastened the process, for by 1868 sheep could be dipped for 1½*d.* per head compared to salving at 8*d.*, and at the same time the dipped wool brought 1½*d.* to 2*d.* per pound more on the market than salved wool.[14] In the twentieth century scientific veterinary methods, with insecticides and chemical dipping compounds, have abolished the ancient practice of salving, and with it has gone—perhaps mercifully—the odour of sheep smelling pungently of rancid butter!

Horse and cow 'doctors' remained in practice until the middle of the nineteenth century and later; at Crosthwaite, Westmorland, Thomas Harrison kept an account book[15] between 1769 and 1803 which illuminates the activities of one of these early veterinary practitioners. Much of his income was derived from the sale of 'drinks', salves, pills and potions to his neighbours, but in addition he made visits to sick animals when requested. The following extract gives an indication of his transactions:

1776 To Jos. Taylor.		s. d.
Jan.ʸ 8	to a Cow Drink	8
Feby. 11	Do. 2 Cow Drinks.	1. 4
March 24	Do. a mustard Drink.	6
Aprell 7	Do. Cow Drink.	8
June 17	Do. plaster.	4

Harrison occasionally bought supplies such as butter and herrings for his customers on a commission basis and supplemented his income by curious 'bargains' such as that made in 1774 between John Atkinson and himself whereby Atkinson agreed 'to shoe the old mare for two years to come after the first time of her wanting shoeing' in exchange for an old Galloway 'which I got in a swap at Kendall'.

But for those dalesmen who could not afford to call in a cow 'doctor' or who were too remote for him to be summoned there were the printed manuals which not only described in vivid detail the symptoms of the ailment but also set out a variety of cures. Two of the most widely distributed publications, printed in Penrith by A. Soulby, were *The Farmer's Jewel*, written by 'a Person of Thirty Years' Experience', and *The New Cow Doctor*, by J. Cundall, both indispensable to the eighteenth-century do-it-yourself vet! With these and similar volumes on his shelves and with a basic knowledge of the medicinal properties of plants, the Lakeland farmer was able to fend for himself and his animals.

7 MOUNTAIN SHEEP

'Sing, my bonny harmless sheep
That feed upon the mountain steep;
Bleating sweetly as ye go
Through the winter's frost and snow.
Hart and hind and fallow deer
Not be half so useful are:
Frae kings to him that hods the plow
Are all obliged to tarry woo'.'

From an old Cumbrian spinning song.

The breed of mountain sheep which has long been associated with the Lake District is the Herdwick (plate 53); strictly speaking, this term refers to the pasture where the sheep are kept, but it is now widely accepted as the name of the breed.[1] The stories concerning the origin of the Herdwick breed are many; they might even justifiably be considered as part of Cumbrian folk lore. Some authorities suggest that the breed originated from forty or so animals washed ashore on the Cumberland coast from the wreck of a Spanish Armada vessel, others, adopting the same basic story, claim that the ship wrecked was Scandinavian. Certainly the Cistercian monks of Furness Abbey had 'Herdwyck' farms centuries before the year of the Armada, which seems to discount the first hypothesis. There is, however, a similarity between sheep marks used in Norway and those used in the Lake District, but this in itself does not necessarily signify that the sheep themselves originated in Scandinavia, but merely that the shepherds or their forebears originated there.[2] Finally, it might be argued that the Herdwicks are derived from the indigenous species which first became domesticated in Bronze Age or even Neolithic times.

The earliest description of Herdwicks is that given by James Clarke in 1787, which is worth quoting in full:

'There is a kind of sheep in these mountains called Herdwicks which, when properly fed to the highest growth seldom exceed 9 or 10 lbs. a quarter. They, contrary to all other sheep I have met with, are seen before a storm, especially of snow, to ascend against the coming blast and to take the stormy side of the mountain, which saves them from being overblown. This valuable instinct was first discovered by the people of Wasdalehead. They, to keep this breed as much as possible in their own village, bound themselves in a bond that no one should sell above 5 ewe or female lambs in one year. But means were found to smuggle more, so that all the shepherds now have either the whole or half breed of them, especially where the mountains are very high, as in Borrowdale, Newlands and Skiddaw, where they have not hay for them in winter. These sheep lie upon the very tops of the mountains in winter as well as summer.

'If a calm snow fall, the shepherds take a harrow and drag it over the tallest heath or ling; the snow then falls to the bottom and the sheep feed upon the tops of it and upon the moss which grows upon the stones.

'Whence this breed first came I cannot learn. The inhabitants of Nether Wasdale say that they were taken from on board a stranded ship. Till within the last few years their number was very small. They grow very little wool, 8 or 9 of them not producing more than a stone, but their wool is pretty good.'[3]

This oft-quoted description has, with the passage of time, gained a degree of authenticity which it perhaps does not fully deserve; for example, the suggestion that in stormy weather the Herdwick will seek the exposed mountain side rather than the lee side seems more legendary than real. Peter Crosthwaite, the famous eighteenth-century Keswick museum keeper and himself of farming stock, makes this comment in the margin of his copy of Clarke's 'Survey':

'O, for shame, Mr Author! Neither the present Generation nor their forefathers before them ever knew Cumbrian Sheep keep the weather side of a mountain in a storm when they could get to the leeward.'[4]

Similarly, to suggest as Clarke does, that Herdwick wool was 'pretty good' savours of exaggeration, for it was well known that the wool was coarse and contained 'kemps', or hairs, intermixed with the fleece. Yet, in spite of these criticisms Clarke was correct in his assertions that the Herdwick could withstand exposure better than other breeds. Indeed Herdwicks have been described, not inaptly, as 'the breed best standing starvation',[5] for they are able to nibble a living from the coarsest bent grass and the toughest heather shoots and survive on the most bizarre diet.

In the period before the Agricultural Revolution it was necessary to use any available fodder to keep as many sheep as possible alive throughout the winter. Often sheep were fed with hay but auxiliaries such as ash leaves, pease straw and even corn straw were fed to animals. It was an offence under the orders of the Court Baron of the Manor of Windermere in the seventeenth century to 'cutt down or breake any other Men's Ash leaves', indicating that ash leaves were carefully harvested for winter food.[6] In the eighteenth century it was customary in High Furness for the shepherd to browse his sheep with sprigs of holly and ash. Thomas West, in 1774, records that 'at the shepherd's call the flock surround the holly-bush, and receive the croppings at his hand, which they greedily nibble up and bleat for more. The mutton thus fed has a remarkably fine flavour. A stranger unacquainted with this practice would imagine the holly-bush to have been sacred amongst the fellanders of Furness'.[7] There is evidence to suppose that the browsing of sheep in this manner continued until the mid nineteenth century and perhaps even later.

As well as an ability to thrive on poor pasture, the Herdwick can withstand burial in a snow drift for up to two weeks, living off its own fat; sheep cocooned in this way have even been known to suck their own wool for sustenance—and survive to produce offspring at lambing time.

One final characteristic which recommends itself to the fell farmer is the remarkable propensity of the Herdwick to stick to its own 'heaf', or the pasture where it was weaned.

On the open, windswept fells this incredible homing instinct is clearly an advantage for it results in fewer strays, and there are many tales of farmers who have sold sheep to farms miles away across the fells—only to find that weeks later the same sheep are once again contentedly grazing their own 'heaf'. It must be rather like selling homing pigeons! In order to retain the 'heaf' instinct it was common, in the days of tenant farming, for the flock and sheep marks to remain as an integral part of the farm, rather than for the farmer to take the sheep with him when he moved. Although Herdwicks are the characteristic sheep of the Lakeland fells, they are certainly not the only breed; 'Swaddles' (Swaledales), 'Teeswatters' (Teeswaters), Rough Fell (plate 54) and Silverdale or Warton Crag are all common. In many areas cross-bred sheep outnumber the Herdwick, for they provide both saleable mutton and wool: however, if the resistance of the flock seems to be waning the introduction of the Herdwick 'tup' amongst the ewes soon reintroduces a hardy strain.

Undoubtedly one of the most fascinating aspects of Cumbrian sheep farming concerns the distinctive dialect names given to animals and the methods used to mark them, for in many of these customs we can trace a direct link with the Norse-Irish settlers who colonized the Lake District in the ninth and tenth centuries.[8] A lamb, either male or female, before shearing is known as a 'hogg' or 'hogget', a term commonly used by the medieval monks of Furness Abbey when recording their sheep. After the first clipping the animal becomes a 'twinter' or 'twowinter', and in the following year a 'thrinter', age-names which are still in common use in Iceland. Similarly dialect words such as 'gimmer', a yearling ewe, and 'rake', meaning to gather, are further links with Scandinavia. But the most powerful evidence for a common cultural inheritance concerns the marking of sheep and in particular the lug marks. Generations of Cumbrian children have been reprimanded by the threat of a 'clip round t'lug' and the word has today become synonymous with the ear, but it is derived from the old Norwegian word *lög*, a law, so in other words the farmer put his lawful ownership mark on his animals, usually on the ear. As well as this the farmer usually has a 'smit' mark which is daubed on the sheep's fleece.[9] Under Norse law any sheep farmer who cut off the ears of his sheep entirely was liable to punishment, for clearly if this was carried out there was no reliable means of proving identity, for any 'smit' mark could be removed at clipping time. Any sheep which had had their ears removed were therefore suspect. In the Lakeland fells a similar ruling prevailed; no sheep farmer was allowed to crop a sheep on both ears unless he lived on a hall farm belonging to the Lord of the Manor and the lord alone had the right to use a mark which took off most of the ears, a privilege which, it was believed, could be entrusted to him alone.

FOLD BITTED	KEY BITTED	FORKED
RITTED	HALVED	PUNCHED
CROPPED	SNECK BITTED	SLIT
SHEAR HALVED	TWICE RITTED	STOVE FORKED

Fig. 19. LAKELAND LUG MARKS

Sheep Stealing.

Five Guineas

REWARD.

Whereas for about twenty years past Sheep and Lambs have been annually stolen from the Mountain Sheep Pastures belonging to the *Black Hall* and *Gaitscale* Estates, at the head of the division of Ulpha, in the Parish of Millom, Cumberland, and the Farmer there has not been able to detect the Thief or Thieves.

Notice is hereby given,

That if any Sheep or Lambs shall in future be stolen from the Flocks belonging to either Estate, any person giving such information to Mr. GEORGE TYSON of Black Hall, as shall lead the Offender or Offenders to conviction, shall receive a reward of Five Guineas.

THE MARKS ARE;

BLACK HALL STOCK.—A red smit stroke down the near side; and both Ears cropped and upper Key bitted.

GAITSCALE STOCK.—A red smit mark over the Shoulder; and some of them also a red pop on the near Hook Bone, as a gathering mark for a particular part of the pasture; and both Ears cropped and under Key bitted.

Last year a Lamb of the Black Hall Stock which had been stolen, returned with one Ear cut off leaving the appearance of a Short Fork.

N. B.—Any communication made to Mr. WILLIAM BLENDALL, Solicitor, Broughton in Furness, will be forwarded to Mr. TYSON.

Black Hall; 19th August, 1849.

MARY TYSON, PRINTER, KING STREET, ULVERSTON.

Fig. 20. Sheep stealing was clearly something of a problem in certain Lakeland dales as this early nineteenth-century handbill emphasizes.

Just as the lug marks varied from farm to farm so, too, the smit marks also differed. Some used the owner's initial together with a 'pop' mark in black or red; others an individual insignia or device. In the days before chemical dyes, rudballs made from red haematite iron ore were used for marking purposes; for example, the 'setting book' of Rydal Hall records in June 1693 the expenditure of two shillings 'for 3 hundred Rudballs for the clipping'. In the nineteenth century iron ruddle dug from the Langdale fells by that infamous illicit whisky distiller Lanty Slee was sold for sheep 'rudding', and in Borrowdale pure graphite from the Seathwaite black lead mines continued to be used for 'smitting' until the eighteen-thirties. Even in the twentieth century many farms made their own 'ruddle' by boiling grease, Stockholm tar and Venetian Red, but the cheapness and availability of commercial dyes have ousted this eye-stinging, acrid-smelling preparation, though not always with complete success, for one imported Australian dye was completely washed out of the fleeces after a week's exposure to Lakeland rain!

The many variations of lug marks (fig. 19), together with an equally varied collection of smit marks—and sometimes horn brands as well—gave a wide permutation of individual ownership marks, and in the nineteenth century it became necessary to have a register of sheep lug and smit marks. The first of these 'Shepherd's Guides' was compiled in 1817 by a Martindale yeoman farmer, Joseph Walker. Dealing with the eastern fells of the Lake District, its object was simply 'that everyone might have the power of knowing the owner of a stray sheep and so be able to restore to everyman his own'. Each farm was represented by two fierce-looking sheep, one showing the appropriate lug marks, the other bearing the smit marks (plate 52). The idea was clearly successful, for within a few years other areas of Lakeland produced their own guides or 'smit-books', and even today well-thumbed later editions of these guides may still be found on farmhouse mantelshelves.

Perhaps one of the most fascinating pieces of folk lore concerned with sheep, and one which has lasted since Celtic times when Cumbria was part of the great Celtic kingdom of Strathclyde, is the traditional dialect way of counting sheep. Although there are variations in numerals from valley to valley within Lakeland, there are marked similarities, particularly in the numerals one, five and ten, between the Old Welsh language, Cornish and Breton, for all these areas were once part of 'the Celtic Fringe'. This seems to have been a method of counting sheep in fives, and though there are still shepherds who can recite—or rather sing—these numerals, the tradition is fast dying.

Sheep Scoring Numerals, One to Ten

	Coniston	Borrowdale	Eskdale	Old Welsh	Cornish	Breton
1.	*Yan*	*yan*	*yaena*	*un*	un or Onan	unan
2.	Taen	tyan	taena	dou	deu or dyw	daou
3.	Tedderte	tethera	teddera	tri	try or tyr	tri
4.	Medderte	methera	meddera	petuar	peswar or pedyr	pevar
5.	*Pimp*	*pimp*	*pimp*	*pimp*	*pymp*	*pemp*
6.	Haata	sethera	hofa	chwech	whe	chouech
7.	Slaata	lethera	lofa	seith	seyth	seiz
8.	Lowra	hovera	seckera	wyth	eath	eiz
9.	Dowra	dovera	leckera	nau	nau	nao
10.	*Dick*	*dick*	*dec*	*dec*	*dek*	*dek*

Based on T. Ellwood, 'Sheep Scoring Numerals'. *Transactions of the Cumberland and Westmorland Antiquarian and Archaeological Society* (old series), volume 3.

In spite of the Herdwicks' heaf-keeping characteristics, sheep sometimes strayed over the watershed of the fells into an adjacent valley and so, for centuries, Cumbrian shepherds have gathered at 'meets' in order to sort out the strays. Until 1835 one of the most famous 'meets' was held on the summit of the High Street range, an easily accessible location for the shepherds of Mardale, Hartsop, Troutbeck and Kentmere. In 1787 James Clarke visited the 'meet' and recorded that 'the neighbouring shepherds assembled there and held festival, during which there were horse racing, wrestling and other such-like country diversions; hither likewise everyone brings the stray sheep he has found during the preceding year, that they may be owned; they also, at this time, frequently amuse themselves with foxhunting'.[10] Shepherds' Meets are still held, though now in less exposed locations than the summit of High Street; the Walna Scar Meet, one of the largest, congregates in the more convivial atmosphere of a local pub, one year at the Newfield Inn, Seathwaite, the next at the Blacksmith's Arms, Broughton Mills, and the following year at the Church House Inn, Torver. The horse racing and wrestling have given way to hound trailing, but the festivities usually round off with a traditional 'merry neet' and a 'tatie-pot' supper.

The ageless cycle of gathering, lambing, dipping and clipping continues to govern the pattern of farming activities in the fells as it has for centuries. Every year the farmer takes care not to put the 'tups' or rams to the ewes too soon for this would mean early lambing, perhaps when snow is still lying in the 'intak' fields. Generally late November is considered soon enough to let the tups run with the ewes; if a wandering tup visits the flock before this, the lambing programme may well be ruined. Towards the end of February the sheep are gathered from the fells for dipping (plates 58, 59) to guard against lice and keds, which can sadly weaken a flock, and at the beginning of March the ewes are brought down to the 'inland' pasture where the lambs are dropped from the middle of April until the middle of May. Unlike the clipping, lambing is no time for festivities; the work is long and arduous and the shepherd is required to use all his store of veterinary skills and subtle ploys. For example, it may be necessary to persuade a bereaved ewe to suckle an orphaned or abandoned lamb, but often this is not easy, for unless the birth smell is present the lamb will usually be rejected. In order to encourage acceptance, one farmer is known to have dosed a ewe with whisky and sprinkled some of the same spirit on the lamb's fleece! A less expensive though no less ingenious method commonly employed involves smearing scented soap over the ewe and its intended foster-lamb, a novel and interesting use for some of the proprietary brands currently advertised on television. Sometimes sprinkling the lamb's fleece with the ewe's milk will encourage acceptance, but occasionally the ewe's dead lamb has to be skinned and the skin draped over the orphaned lamb. Certainly lambing is not for the squeamish or the sentimental!

By mid May, when the croziers of bracken are beginning to unfold on the fellsides, the ewes and the lambs are returned to the 'heaf' (plate 49), to remain there until early in July when the clipping begins. It was formerly the practice before shearing to wash the sheep in a dub or deep pool (plate 60), but this is no longer undertaken, although sheep folds near to dubs may still be seen along many a Lakeland beck.

Clipping time has always been one of the most important festivals of the farming year; fifty years ago it was common for farmers and their men to visit each farm in turn. By their combined effort the flocks were soon sheared and sports and dancing went on far into the night, the clippers being fortified by a 'clipping drink' of specially brewed strong ale. Today,

Fig. 21. MOUNTAIN SHEEP

1. Horn branding iron.   2. Sheep dipping poles, approximately 5 feet 7 inches long.   3. Lug marker.   4. A cruder form of lug marker.   5. Sheep shears.   6. Sheep marker and tar costrel.   7. Clipping stool.   The Herdwick sheep has a forked lug mark.

however, this co-operation is largely a thing of the past and each farmer shears his own sheep with whatever help he can hire. At Rydal Hall the Fleming sheep were clipped by the tenants, who were obliged to pay a day's boon service, but Squire Daniel made sure that there were sufficient incentives; ale, bread and cheese were always supplied in abundance and often tobacco was bought 'for the clippers'. In addition the Rydal account books show that Squire Daniel entertained his workers with music:

1684 June 20th. Given to Renny, fidler for playing this day unto my clippers   £00. 00. 06d.
1685 August 25th Given to Geo. Benson, Piper, for 2 dayes being with my shearers
       who did shear all this day   £00. 01. 00d.

Although some of the larger fell farms have invested in electric shears, many farmers still use the hand clippers, implements which have changed little over the centuries (fig. 21(5)). The Cumbrian dalesman is both conservative and an individualist and he will argue that although electric shearing is quick, it is not as efficient as the old methods. Seated astride his wooden clipping stool (fig. 21(7)), a good shearer, assisted by a helper who brings the sheep to him, can clip between seventy and eighty animals a day (plates 61–69).

   Mrs E. Lynn Linton, a keen observer of local activities, has recorded a colourful account of a nineteenth-century clipping:

'. . . the sheep are . . . dragged out by boys as they are wanted, and flung on their backs into the lap of a clipper seated on a long kind of settle—"sheep forms" they are called—who tranquilly tucks the little pointed head under his arm, and clips away at the under part of the wool, taking care to keep the fleece unbroken; the art being to hold the middle way, and neither to graze the skin by going too close, nor to loosen the fleece by cutting above the welted fibres. All four feet are now tied together, and the beast is hauled round as a solid kind of rug, when its back is sheared in the same way, the fleece hanging down like a bit of carpet or small crib blanket. When the whole is off, the legs are untied, and it is lugged— that is the only word to express it—panting and terrified to the place where the man stands with the ruddle pot and branding iron, where it receives its distinctive smear and letter of assignment, and is then dismissed to its huddled group of companions clustering together at the remotest spot in the yard available. . . . The little figures of the boys learning of the men; . . . the pretty young house girls, looking so quiet and gentle, dressed in their Sunday best and carrying great jugs of beer—the strongest that can be brewed—laughing and yet shy, as they penetrate into the mass of men and animals in the yard; the cows milking by the byre doors; the purple hills and the calm lake . . . these are the incidents which make sheep-shearing a striking thing to see.'[11]

   After clipping, the naked, newly 'smitted' sheep return to the heaf until August, when once more they are 'laited', or gathered for another dipping against blowfly 'strike'. Until the end of the nineteenth century fell flocks were 'salved' (see pages 84–6) with butter and 'roany' tar to discourage parasites and to waterproof the fleece, but compulsory dipping introduced in 1905 has eradicated not only scab and other diseases, but also the drudgery of salving. But there were other advantages, for it was cheaper to dip sheep than to salve them and, moreover, the wool of dipped sheep brought a higher price on the market than the 'tarry wool' of the salved sheep.[12] Little wonder, then, that the ancient practice of salving declined in the face of scientific farming.

Apart from the shepherds' meets, the tup fairs, when rams are hired out or sold for breeding purposes, are opportunities for farmers to gather and cast experienced eyes over the livestock and, like the meets, they are also social gatherings. The Eskdale Tup Show is one of the most famous in Cumbria; it is graphically recalled by Mrs S. J. Bulman, who describes a show during the early decades of the present century:[13]

'The great event of the year was the Eskdale Tup Show, held over fifty years at the "Woolpack", the last Friday in September, when tups were shown and hired out for the season. The sheep, pure Herdwick, arrived the previous day having walked over the fells from Borrowdale, Wasdale, Coniston, Seathwaite, Bootle and elsewhere. The inn was transformed, furniture stored away, floors were sawdusted, windows were barricaded, bedrooms full to overcrowding, one hardly knew who was sleeping where. This was a time to celebrate and meet your friends, and they did. Beer at three pence per glass, and spirits at four pence, soon had them singing in each room, one above the other. Special staff was engaged each year to help, and each knew his own job. The big, hefty butcher, who supplied nine rounds of beef and six hams to be eaten on the day, was chief barman. Pickles were stored in huge crocks. Large squares of apple pasties by the dozen, loaves by the hundred, and all made on the premises. Little Tommy Pharaoh (he was about five feet tall) strutted about the field in a grey topper and fancy waistcoat, casts-off from Lord Muncaster, just like one of his game birds.

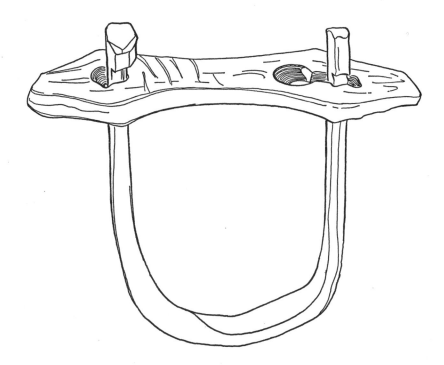

Fig. 22. Sheep band used for tethering.

Mr. Inman from Coniston, always sober and dignified, Ned Nelson from Buttermere, looking like one of the prophets, quoting the Bible and stroking his black beard. Mr. Rothery from Wasdale Head with his high choker collar and frock coat looking more like a parson than a flockmaster . . . one old chap with a red beard aired his views in no uncertain manner about "lasses now wearing low necks", for fashion had moderated the high neck a little. . . .'

In October the fells are raked once again and the gimmer ewes drafted for breeding purposes, some being sent for wintering to Walney Island and the Solway marshes. The wethers or castrated sheep are sent to be fattened for market. By mid November all the sheep have been gathered from the high fells. At the end of the month the tups are allowed to run with the ewes—and the farming cycle recommences once again.

44 *(above left)*. The late Isaac Cookson of Gillhead, Bampton, who attended the Mardale Shepherds' Meet on sixty-four occasions.

45 *(left)*. A nineteenth-century fell farmer.

46 *(above right)*. Mr A. E. Irving of Bridge End Farm, Boot, Eskdale, and his dog, Glen, after 'laiting' his flock from Birker Moor.

47. *Hand feeding in winter.*

48. *Digging out a ewe from a snow-drift near Windermere.*

49. *The spring-time return to the 'heaf'.*

50. *Sheep at Glencoyne Farm, Ullswater.*

51. *Sheep in All Hallows Lane, Kendal, c. 1950.*

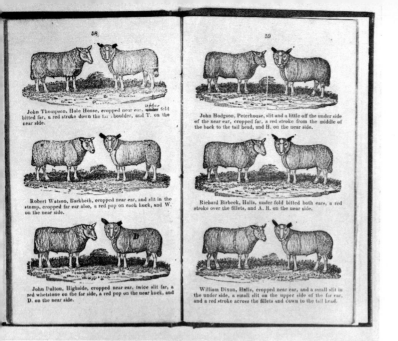

58

John Thompson, Hole House, cropped near ear, under fold bitted far, a red stroke down the far shoulder, and T. on the near side.

Robert Watson, Barkbeth, cropped near ear, and slit in the stump, cropped far ear also, a red pop on each huck, and W. on the near side.

John Dalton, Highside, cropped near ear, twice slit far, a red whetstone on the far side, a red pop on the near huck, and D. on the near side.

59

John Hodgson, Peterhouse, slit and a little off the under side of the near ear, cropped far, a red stroke from the middle of the back to the tail head, and H. on the near side.

Richard Birbeck, Halls, under fold bitted both ears, a red stroke over the fillets, and A. B. on the near side.

William Dixon, Halls, cropped near ear, and a small slit in the under side, a small slit on the upper side of the far ear, and a red stroke across the fillets and down to the tail head.

52. *Pages from* The Shepherd's Guide, *1817.*

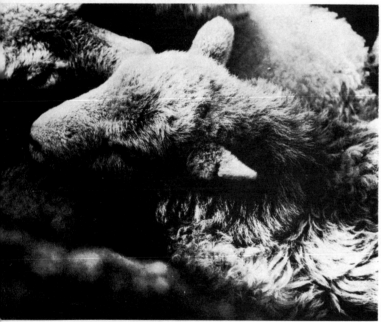

53. *A Herdwick with a key-bitted lug mark.*

54. *Mr J. Hudson, of Black Moss Farm, Windermere, marking a Rough Fell shearling.*

55. *A fine group of rams at Steel End Farm, Wythburn. The ram on the left has had part of its horn removed to prevent it growing into its face.*

56. *Horn branding.*

57. *Dosing a yearling sheep— a far cry from some of the veterinary practices of the eighteenth and nineteenth centuries.*

58. *Sheep-dipping was made compulsory in 1905 and this did much to eradicate scab, but it also meant a decline in the ancient practice of salving sheep with tar and rancid butter. Here an apprehensive-looking flock waits to be dipped.*

59. *Sheep-dipping at Mearness Farm, Cartmel, c. 1920.*

60. *In the nineteenth century it was common to wash sheep before shearing. Here a group of men prepare to wash a ram in a 'dub', a deep pool in a river bed.*

61. *Shearing at Thorn House, Low Hartsop, about 1880. Note the 'spinning gallery' and the tar costrel in a recess in the wall (see also Plate 8).*

62. *Clipping day in Eskdale, c. 1895.*

63. *Shearing at Brockstones Farm, Kentmere.*

64. *Rolling fleeces after the clipping.*

65. *Before and after . . . Rough Fell sheep with and without fleeces.*

66. *After shearing the sheep are 'popped' with 'ruddle'.*

67. *Above left: Mr J. Hudson shears his Rough Fell tups by hand.*

68. *Above: Mr William Birkett shearing Herdwicks at Tilberthwaite, July 1972.*

69. *Mr and Mrs J. Hudson rolling fleeces, Kirkstone Pass, July 1972.*

70. *An eighteenth-century plough team in Eskdale. This remarkable oil painting was rescued from a barn and is now in the Woolpack Inn. Probably painted by an itinerant artist at the request of the farmer, seen here in his Sunday best guiding the plough, it shows the ancient method of harnessing two horses, one behind the other, and two yoked oxen. These heavy wooden ploughs required at least three men to operate them—one to guide the plough, one to drive the team and one to hold the plough beam to prevent the ploughshare from slipping out. If the land was particularly heavy, a fourth man would follow the plough to break up the clods with a spade.*

71. *Centre: Horse-ploughing near Loweswater, Cumberland.*

72. *High-level ploughing. During war time when food is in short supply the level of cultivation moves up the fellside. This photograph was taken in the late 1940s.*

73. *Horse-harrowing at Syke Farm, Buttermere, in the 1950s.*

74. *Broadcasting seed in the Great Lang-dale valley in the early 1950s.*

75. *Sowing with a 'fiddle', Cartmel. The bag of seed feeds a flywheel which is operated by a 'bow' and the seeds are scattered evenly.*

76. *Reapers at Raisthwaite, Woodland, High Furness, c. 1890. In the nineteenth century much of the harvesting was done by bands of itinerant Irishmen who preferred to use the sickle rather than the scythe. In this photograph the sickles can be clearly seen. The man on the right is making 'bands' with which to tie the sheaves.*

77. *Horse-reaping in south-west Cumberland, c. 1920.*

78. *One of the oldest agricultural instruments, a flail, in use in the Lyth valley. Grain was threshed with flails in some parts of Cumbria until the 1930s.*

79. *A steam threshing machine and farm-hands, south-west Cumberland, c. 1920.*

80. *Haymaking in High Furness,* c. *1890. The carts have 'shelvins' fixed in order to increase the capacity.*

81. *Horse-mowing on the shores of Grasmere.*

82. *Haymaking with a horse and sled. On steep slopes a wheeled vehicle might overturn, but a sled remains stable.*

83. *Loading baled hay, Cartmel.*

84. *Leading the hay through the medieval gatehouse in Cartmel, 1950s.*

85. *Mr Joe Youdell using a reaping hook and 'gebbie', or grain stick, to trim roadside verges in the Duddon Valley, 1972.*

86. *Mr Mitchell of Rawfold, Dunnerdale, scythes bracken for winter bedding for his animals.*

87. *Peat-cutting at Witherslack. The man graving the peat is wearing pattens strapped to his clogs to prevent him from sinking. Note the peat barrow and the circular rick or 'mount' in the background.*

88. *Stacking peat in 'winrows' to dry. Note the swill basket in use on the left.*

8 SOME AGRICULTURAL TOOLS AND TECHNIQUES

Until the second half of the eighteenth century farm implements were both few and primitive and their form had changed little since medieval times; the sickle, flail, plough and ox-team depicted in the fourteenth-century Luttrell psalter would have been instantly recognized and appreciated by the eighteenth-century Cumbrian yeoman, for even in the 1750s most agricultural equipment was still made of wood and mechanization was virtually unknown. Within a hundred years, however, the Agricultural Revolution had brought with it great changes, not merely new farming techniques, new crops and new methods of breeding animals, but also some revolutionary developments in farming equipment.

FARM CARTS

Until 1750, according to William Dickinson, the agricultural writer, only yeomen and the larger occupiers owned carts, for most of the farm produce such as hay, corn and peats was transported on sleds. This is eminently sensible, however, for on steep fellsides a sled remains stable under conditions which would cause a wheeled vehicle to overturn, and even today bracken and hay sleds are still to be found in Lakeland dales for precisely this reason (plate 82 and fig. 23). James Clarke made the possibly exaggerated claim that until the 1760s wheeled vehicles or carts were unknown in Borrowdale[1] and comments that

'. . . in carrying home their hay (for they make no stacks) they lay it upon their horses in bundles, one on each side; . . . the traveller may even see hay carried in this manner through the streets of Keswick. Their manure they carried in the same manner, putting it in wicker baskets;* in the same manner they carried the smaller wood for firing, the larger logs they trailed.'

But the fact that in 1787 Clarke felt it necessary to mention this anomaly suggests that by then this method of transport was declining, and by the end of the century, when Bailey and Culley were compiling their agricultural report, the single-horse cart had become common.[2]

These 'tummel cars', however, were crudely constructed; built entirely of wood, they bore little resemblance to the comparatively sophisticated farm carts of the nineteenth century. They had two solid clog-wheels made of three pieces of wood fastened together with wooden pins, and these were fixed to the axle which turned under the cart. Such a vehicle could be made for £5 in 1794,[3] but they certainly had their disadvantages; the body of the cart was easily displaced from the wooden pins which were supposed to secure it to the revolving wooden

*These panniers were known as 'holts' or 'halts'.

113

A BRACKEN SLED AT FELL FOOT FARM, LITTLE LANGDALE

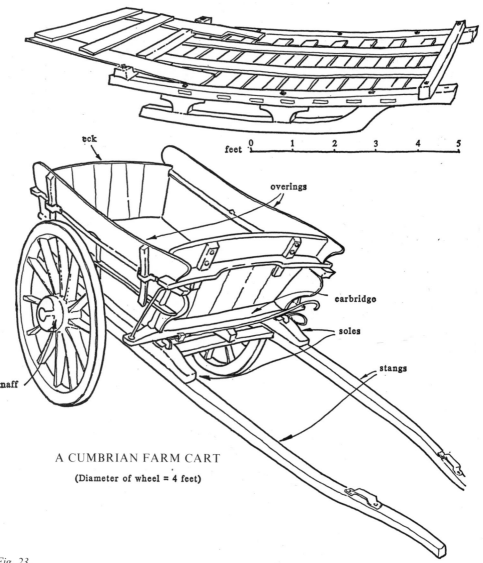

eck

feet 0 1 2 3 4 5

overings

earbridge

soles

stangs

naff

A CUMBRIAN FARM CART
(Diameter of wheel = 4 feet)

Fig. 23.

axle, so that it was somewhat unsafe. Moreover, the crude mechanics produced an unpleasant squeaking, as James Stockdale recalled in Cartmel:

'. . . the revolving axle-trees of the clog-wheeled carts, scantily greased, making each a most unnatural squeak . . . disagreeable music . . . about as pleasant as that produced by "the cleaver and marrow bones"!'[4]

In some cases the noise was so bad that drivers carried a cow's horn filled with animal fat which was periodically applied to the axle-tree. Harness was equally primitive and 'braffins', or horse-collars, were generally home-made by plaiting 'symes' of hay or straw; bridles were made of cord, but halters were more often of hemp and sometimes of plaited sieves or rushes. And only affluent yeomen had leather saddles, for 'sonks' or green sods, girthed on with hay bands, served as substitute saddles, both for farmers and for their wives and daughters!

Slowly at first, but with quickening momentum, new techniques of cart building infiltrated into the Lake District, and wheelwrights began to construct wheels with 'naffs' (hubs), spokes and felloes, rimmed with iron, which turned *on* the axle, not with it. William Close, writing at the beginning of the last century, has recorded his impression of these new carts:

'The wheels are commonly dished or made a little concave by the receding of the spokes, and run loose upon a wooden axle-tree about 12 inches wider at top than at bottom, where the distance of one to the outside of the other is 4 feet. . . . The dimensions of these carts are as follows: the breadth is 3 feet 6 inches; the inside length is 4 feet 2 inches at bottom and 4 feet 8 inches at top; the depth of the fore end is $14\frac{1}{2}$ inches and $13\frac{1}{4}$ inches at the other end. The length of the shafts or poles, before the body of the cart is 6 feet. The wheels are commonly 3 feet 10 inches, and sometimes 4 feet high; $2\frac{1}{4}$ inches broad and generally hooped with 9 or 10 stones of iron. The cost of the whole complete is about £8. 18. 0d.'[5]

These single-horse carts remained the most common agricultural vehicle until the 1930s, when internal combustion engines began to replace the horse, and much skill and effort went into their making. The regional variation of farm carts throughout England and Wales has been the subject of recent research, and although the Cumbrian carts were basically similar in design to those used in the Yorkshire Dales (see *Life and Tradition in the Yorkshire Dales* by M. Hartley and J. Ingilby), the vernacular terms for the various parts of the cart are worth recording before they are entirely forgotten (fig. 23). There are slight variations in these dialect terms, for example in the Cartmel area the word for the movable tailboard of a cart is 'eck', in other areas 'heck' or 'skut' might be used; similarly in certain parts of Cumbria, the shafts of the cart are known as 'stangs', while in other parts of the Lake District, particularly in the east, the term 'limmers' is more common. The following list, dating from 1926, not only gives several dialect words, but also indicates the prices of various parts at that date:

	s.	d.
1 pair of stangs [shafts]	12	0
1 pair of soles	8	0
2 top overings	3	0

1 set of shelving wood
  [shelvings were frames used to extend the length of a cart]
1 earbreed [earbridge—*see* fig. 23]   8
1 endboard top   1 4
1 frontboard top   2 0
1 bottom rail   6

The making of a 'dished' cart wheel was an art which demanded much skill and an experienced hand and eye. The wheel hubs, or 'naffs', were generally of seasoned elm, the felloes, or component parts of the rim, were of ash pinned together with oak dowels, and the spokes were of oak, preferably riven rather than sawn (plates 89, 91). On the completion of the wheel, it was hooped with an iron rim, usually by the blacksmith. This involved heating the rim in the log fire for about an hour until it was red-hot, fitting it over the wheel on a tyring platform, and then slaking it with cold water so that it contracted and tightened on the felloes (plate 90). To complete a cart wheel took four days and cost between £3 10s. to £4 a pair in the 1930s; 'built-in obsolescence' was unheard of and many of the wheels built then are still in service, yet, like so many rural crafts, the wheelwright's art has declined almost to the point of extinction.

PLOUGHS AND PLOUGHING

The transformation from the cumbersome 'tummel car' to the light, single-horse cart of the late nineteenth century was considerable, but so too was the development of the plough. In 1850 William Dickinson was able to recall

'a venerable plough-wright who used to ridicule his younger brethren "with their planes and their paint" working several days over "a bit of a plew", and then it had to be sent to the smith after all! Where he could have cut down the timber, borne it home on his shoulder, and finished his plough the same day without assistance, and no smith required—all being of wood except the coulter and sock, which would be supplied from the old plough'.[6]

No doubt Dickinson had this in mind when, in 1876, he wrote:

Fig. 24. SPADES AND PUSH-PLOUGHS

1. Peat spade from Lowick, High Furness; length 4 feet.   2. Tom spade used for cutting drains in upland areas; length 3 feet.   3. Front and reverse side of a peat spade; length 3 feet 2 inches.   4. Sough, a wooden spade sheathed with iron, used to clean out drains in soft ground; length 3 feet 11 inches.   5. Drainage spade used to cut narrow trenches for tile drains.   6, 7. Push-ploughs. Note the wing, at right angles to the face, which acted as a coulter and was sharpened with a stone; length (6), 6 feet, (7) 7 feet.   8. A peat barrow from the Lyth Valley. Note the horizontal bar connecting the legs and the broad metal wheel which prevents the loaded barrow from sinking into the soft ground.

Below: A push-plough in use.

Now out wid a heam-mead roan-tree plue,
Wid ironin' scanty eneuff,
Lait up strea braffins—reap traces enue,
And see 'at they're o' draft preuff.[7]

James Stockdale also repeats the story of ploughs made in a single day from suitable trees, but adds that in order to season the green wood, it was held over a blazing fire made of gorse and bracken.[8] Such home-made ploughs can hardly have been efficient and they often required two horses and two oxen to work them. The horses were harnessed one behind the other and the oxen yoked in pairs; one man drove the team, another held the plough beam down to prevent the ploughshare from slipping out, while a third man guided the plough. If the land was 'heavy' a fourth man followed the plough, breaking up the clods with a spade. A remarkable painting in the bar of the Woolpack Inn, Eskdale (plate 70), illustrates this ancient ploughing technique; the farmer, clearly wearing his Sunday best for the occasion, drives a crude, wooden plough, assisted by two labourers who control the horses and oxen and hold the plough beam. Painted in oils on wooden boards, the picture is believed to date from about the middle of the eighteenth century. (N.B.: It is now, 1987, privately owned)

By the end of the eighteenth century Colonel John Bolton, of Storrs Hall near Windermere, had introduced an iron plough into the Lake District; made by Wilkie of Glasgow, it soon superseded all other kinds and became a pattern for plough-wrights throughout the area. By 1850 William Dickinson could record that 'they are . . . remarkable for neatness of finish, an absence of nick-nackery, and a simplicity and lightness of construction, with strength adapted for the stony soils of the county, and weighing from 12 to 13 stones each'.[9] Ploughs such as these continued to be made by such firms as Stalkers in Penrith until the 1940s, and many present-day farmers will remember learning to plough behind one of these implements drawn by two Clydesdales. Even as late as the Second World War and the immediate post-war period when food was scarce, horse-drawn ploughs were to be seen working at altitudes which had not grown crops since the Napoleonic Wars, if then (plate 72), emphasizing the fact that the agricultural landscape is a product of both physical and economic factors.

Although not a plough in the accepted sense of the word, the push-plough or breast-plough deserves a mention here, if only as one of the oldest and most primitive tools used in agriculture, yet one which was still in use in Cumbria in the nineteenth century.[10] Basically these implements were similar to pointed spades with a flange or 'wing' at right angles to the face which acted as a coulter and which was kept sharpened with a stone. The shaft or 'pole' of the plough was usually about six feet long and often braces were used to strengthen the handle, or 'crown', which was pushed by the operator's chest or thighs (fig. 24). In very difficult terrain, a second man was sometimes harnessed to the plough to pull from the front; it is not surprising, then, to find that such work has been called 'the most slavish task in husbandry'. The purpose of breast ploughing was to remove the shallow acid turf from the surface of a field, and this was allowed to dry before being burned, after which the ashes and lime fertilizer were ploughed in. During the enclosure of the commons in the eighteenth and nineteenth centuries, this was the way in which thousands of acres of land were brought into production, though the overall cost in terms of soil deterioration was probably excessive. Nevertheless, crops of oats could be coaxed from all but the most rocky and unpromising land.

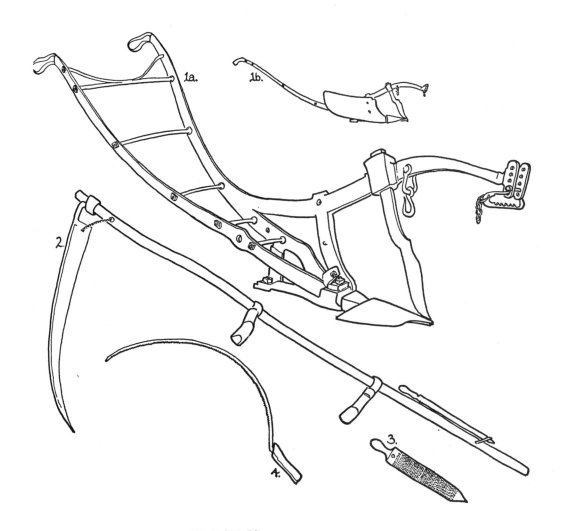

Fig. 25. PLOUGHS, SCYTHES AND SICKLES

1a. An iron 'Stainton' plough, illustrated here without the mould-board but with the coulter and ploughshare.
1b. The 'Stainton' plough showing the position of the mould-board.   2. A 'ley', or scythe, 4 feet 6 inches in length.
The 'strickle' is attached to the pole to give it balance.   3. A 'strickle' used for sharpening the ley. Originally
these were made of wood pitted with holes and smeared with bacon fat, and later dusted with sharp quartz sand
from mountain tarns.   4. The Cumbrian sickle, approximately 2 feet 6 inches long and with fifteen teeth every
inch.

SICKLES, SCYTHES AND HARVESTING

The sickle, one of the most primitive of all harvesting implements, continued to be used in the Lake District until the second half of the nineteenth century. This apparent backwardness was partly a result of cheap labour, for hundreds of migrant Irish workers flocked into Cumbria for the harvest, and also a reflection of the Irishman's preference for the sickle (plate 76).[11] The implement most commonly used had a blade of approximately two feet six inches long, which was edged with fifteen teeth every inch (fig. 25(4)). The work must have been back-breaking; at the beginning of the last century three men could reap, bind and 'stouk' a customary acre of grain in a day for a wage of four shillings each. The working day was a long one, as this early nineteenth-century account testifies:

'The day is commonly considered from 5 o'clock in the morning to 8 in the evening, of which an hour and a half [is] consumed in meals and taking refreshments at other times, the whole being served in the following order: cheese, bread and beer before the reapers enter the field in the morning; breakfast about 8-o-clock, beer sometimes about 10 in the forenoon; dinner at 12; beer about 3 o'clock; cheese, bread and beer about 5 in the afternoon, and supper after leaving the field about half past 8 in the evening; likewise as much beer at other times of the day as the heat of the weather may render necessary.'[12]

Gradually the sickle was replaced by the scythe, a process which was accelerated, according to F. W. Garnett, when, in the late nineteenth century, it was realized that acre for acre crops could be harvested more cheaply with the scythe than with a sickle.[13] The scythe or 'ley' used in the Lake District was usually 4 feet 6 inches long, and attached to the pole, in such a way that it balanced the ley, was an oak wood 'strickle' for sharpening the blade (fig. 25 (2, 3)). Each of the four sides was pitted with small holes and smeared with bacon fat, after which it was dusted with hard quartz sand collected from the edges of mountain tarns in order to give an abrasive surface. Scythes still have their uses on modern fell farms for they are employed in cutting bracken, which provides winter bedding for animals (plate 86).

Although horse-drawn reaping machines were introduced into Cumbria about the middle of the nineteenth century—one of the earliest was at work at Hackthorpe Hall, Lowther, in 1851—on the whole the mechanization of the harvest was slow, but this was not surprising in view of the fact that agricultural activity was centred on animals rather than grain. After cutting, the sheaves were set up in stooks which remained in the field until the sap had dried out, traditionally 'for three Sundays' before it was carted home to stack; the disappearance of this once common feature is a further reminder of the changing agricultural landscape. Also by the middle of the nineteenth century, horse-powered threshing machines became increasingly common; however, the cost of a two-horse machine, £33 in 1860, made it prohibitive for most small dales farms, and there the rhythmic beat of the flails remained a familiar sound even as late as the nineteen-thirties. Plate 78 shows a flail in use in the Lyth Valley about this time. One of the simplest of all agricultural implements, it consisted of an ash handle to which a 'swingel' of holly or thorn was attached by means of an eel-skin thong, and with this the grain was threshed on the threshing floor, usually by two men working in harmony. The traditional method of winnowing or 'deeting' the grain was to throw it into the wind using a 'weyt', or shallow dish made from sheepskin (see page 30); the heavier grain fell near to the deeter while the lighter chaff was dispersed. Like flailing, this method of deeting

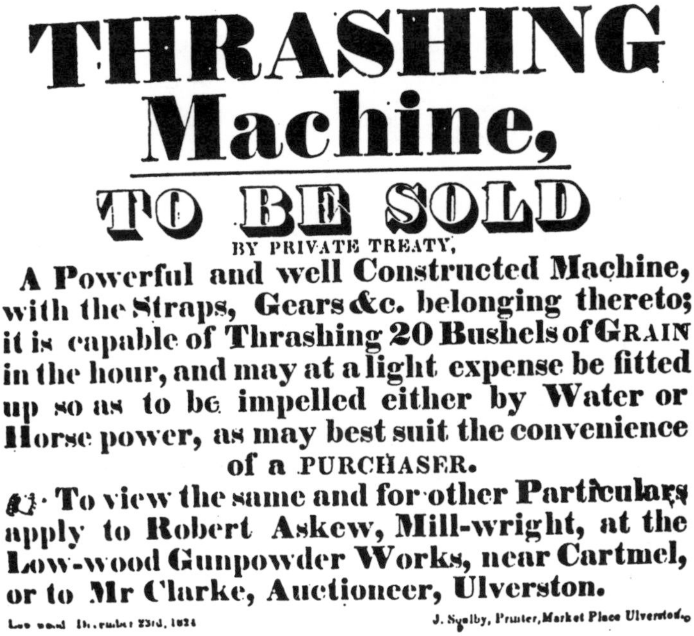

THRASHING Machine,

TO BE SOLD

BY PRIVATE TREATY,

A Powerful and well Constructed Machine, with the Straps, Gears &c. belonging thereto; it is capable of Thrashing 20 Bushels of GRAIN in the hour, and may at a light expense be fitted up so as to be impelled either by Water or Horse power, as may best suit the convenience of a PURCHASER.

☞ To view the same and for other Particulars apply to Robert Askew, Mill-wright, at the Low-wood Gunpowder Works, near Cartmel, or to Mr Clarke, Auctioneer, Ulverston.

Low wood December 23rd, 1824   J. Soulby, Printer, Market Place Ulverston.

Fig. 26. Handbill of 1824.

survived as an archaic farming practice until the present century, but by the second half of the nineteenth century, steam threshing machines had been introduced (fig. 26, plate 79), and these remained in use in Cumbria until the 1940s and 1950s, when they were replaced by combine harvesters. The eclipse of hand-operated implements and the complementary triumph of mechanization, even on Lakeland farms, were the inevitable outcome of a declining labour force, increased wages and a growing demand for agricultural produce; within the last twenty years horse-drawn reapers and steam threshing machines have taken their places in agricultural museums alongside the flails, 'weyts', scythes and sickles of an earlier period.

PEAT

Until the nineteenth century the traditional domestic fuel within the Lake District was peat and, even after the improvements in communications which brought coal to some areas, in the remote dales some farmers continued to 'grave' or 'cast' peats until the 1950s. In the flat-floored valleys of the Winster and the Lyth, as well as on the mosses which fringe the Leven, Kent and Duddon estuaries, peat cutting was a common practice in early summer, and graving was as much part of the agricultural calendar as haytime and harvest. Even amongst the fells, peats were graved wherever conditions were suitable; places such as Skiddaw Forest, Wythop Moss, west of Bassenthwaite Lake, and Flaskow Common at the northern end of the Helvellyn range, all of which had provided the sixteenth-century smelting works at Keswick with peat,[14] continued to supply fuel to local farms until the nineteenth century.

In 1710 the schedule of the agricultural implements of the late William Hawkrigg, a Grasmere farmer, lists a peat spade and three 'fflawing' spades,[15] and this was fairly typical, for until comparatively recently many Lakeland farms possessed these two types of spade which were necessary for peat digging. The 'fflawing' or flaying spade was an instrument rather similar to a push-plough but shorter, which was used for paring off the top layer of peat, while the 'slane' or peat spade was employed in actually graving the peats. Both spades were made by the local blacksmith and therefore patterns varied according to his fancy or the preference of his customers (fig. 24(1, 3)). The peat spade had a small flange or wing which allowed two sides of the peat to be cut at a stroke; unlike the push-plough the shaft was straight and flat for some distance from the cutting edge so that it could be run horizontally under the peat in cutting it. Clearly, the size of the peats depended on the width of the spade and the size of the wing.

A peat 'pot' or working often produced two types of peats. The top layer to a depth of two feet or more gave grey peats containing a high percentage of fibrous material from the ling and heather and, when dried, this was used as kindling; below this lay the black peats which gave more heat and lasted longer in burning. Peats were transported in peat barrows, wooden single-wheeled carts which lacked sides but had a four-inch wide iron wheel which prevented the barrow from sinking in the soft surface (fig. 24(8)). After graving, the peats were allowed to dry by placing them in lines or 'winrows' for three or more weeks, during which time they would be 'ruckl'd', an operation which involved propping up five or six peats against one another to allow the wind to blow through them in order to hasten the drying and shrinkage process. Finally they were stacked in a circular rick or 'mount', again allowing the air to circulate freely, and in this way the peats remained unharmed until they could be led to the farm, usually after the hay had been brought in (plates 87, 88). In a dry summer a farmer might manage to cut enough peats for a year or even two, but as in all other aspects of the rural economy, there was no waste, even the 'flaughts' or 'topping peats' were dried and used as fuel and the 'comb' or 'mull', the fine, dry peat dust, was especially prized on days when clap bread was made, for it produced a hot fire.

HAYMAKING

Next to wool, hay is perhaps the most important harvest in Lakeland, but even haymaking has become mechanized and scythes, rakes and 'tumble-toms' which were used forty and fifty years ago now collect dust and cobwebs in many a Cumbrian barn. Until the mid nineteenth century grass was cut with scythes, but in spite of men like George Brownrigg of Troutbeck who, in 1861, was able to cut 2 acres of grass in 8 hours 55 minutes for a wager,[16] the operation was a slow one. In the same year in which Brownrigg won his justly earned wager, and only a couple of miles away at Low Wood, one of the earliest two-horse mowing machines in Cumbria cut 22 acres in 18 hours. The time-saving advantage of mechanization, so important in the fickle climate of the fells, was immediately apparent and soon one- and two-horse mowing machines were in use throughout the Lake District, and these and similar machines remained in service until comparatively recently (plate 81).

Now the modern baling machine disgorges its standardized packages at regular intervals over the surface of the hay field, and although much of the colour and atmosphere have been lost from haymaking so, too, has much of the sweat and backache! Fifty years ago things were different; one of the first tasks at haytime was 'hacking out' with a scythe the edges and corners of the meadow where the horse-drawn mower could not reach, after which the mowing machine did its work. The mown grass was then strewed and tossed or cocked, according to the weather conditions: eventually the meadow would be swept with a horse-drawn 'gate sweep', or 'tumble tom', which was a wooden beam with spikes projecting from it which slid beneath the hay and collected it. When the sweep was full, the driver slightly lifted the sweep by the handles so that the spikes dug into the ground, the horse continued forward and so the sweep somersaulted, leaving the collected hay behind in a heap. There were several types of sweep in use for, like peat spades, they tended to vary with the whims of makers and farmers. The heaps of hay were then made into tall pikes which would stand safely through all sorts of weather until the hay could be led; the tops of these pikes were often held down by a length of 'Michael' or binder twine, weighted with stones or logs so that it settled with the pike as it dried.[17]

One of the final tasks before leading was 'thin-raking' to gather in the last wisps of hay. This was sometimes done with a horse-drawn rake but often with the wooden hand rakes and the large drag-rakes known as 'nag rakes', 'donkey rakes' or 'T' o'd Meare', and which were merely trailed behind the worker. The hay was led by carts to which 'shelvings' had been added to increase the load, and also, when the terrain demanded it, by sled (plates 80, 82). In ramp-entrance barns (see page 30), the loading of hay into the upper floor was simple, but in other barns it had to be forked up. Very often the youngest or the smallest worker had to 'mew' or tread the mow-stead as it grew in height in order to make room for more hay, finally sliding down to the floor on a rope tied to a beam when the last hay cart had been led and loaded. A far cry indeed from today's balers and elevators.

9 WEATHER LORE

Before the days of radio and television every dalesman knew the signs and portents of good and bad weather as well as he knew his own flock or fellside, for this very necessary art, so important in any farming community, was carefully passed down from one generation to the next. Even today, when sophisticated forecasting techniques can foretell the weather several weeks in advance, many of the traditional maxims still hold good. Farmers living on the coasts of Cumberland and Furness looking westwards at sunset towards the whale-backed silhouette of the Isle of Man knew well enough that rain can be expected some time during the following day—indeed it is said that if the Isle of Man can be seen it will rain soon, and if it can't be seen—it is raining already! Much of this weather lore has been built up by careful observation over many generations, and within a limited area it can be surprisingly accurate. The sound of falling water is regarded by many people as a useful weather indicator; referring to the River Kent in Westmorland, Fuller, in his edition of Camden's *Britannia.* noted that '. . . there be two catadupae or waterfalls; whereof the northern, sounding clear and loud, fortokeneth Fair Weather; the southern, on the same terms, presageth Rain'. James Clarke observed the same phenomena at Swarthbeck falls, Ullswater, and commented that '. . . these sounds are a barometer of the neighbourhood. Traditions handed down from father to son have formed a set of rules by which the farmer is enabled to predict with tolerable certainty the weather of the day from the sound these cascades emit the preceding evening'.[1] And at Keswick the sounds of Barrow and Lodore falls were regarded as weather portents in precisely the same way. Clearly, these sounds are related to the strength and direction of the wind which, in turn, reflect the position of areas of high and low pressure and frontal systems, but such meteorological refinements were unknown until the early twentieth century.

Many of these early weather forecasts were based on the formation of clouds amongst the hills, and one of the oldest of the Lakeland weather maxims is:

> *If Skiddaw wears a cap*
> *Criffel knows full well o' that*

indicating that a cloud layer which affects Skiddaw will almost certainly reach Criffel on the Scottish side of the Solway. Black Combe, that rounded bastion of the fells thrusting south-westwards into the Irish Sea, is another useful meteorological touchstone, for the warm, moist air masses travelling in from the Atlantic are forced to rise over the mountain and condensation produces 'messenger' clouds, often reflecting the shape of the mountain, which foretell rain in the central fells. Clouds can also forecast the arrival of that cold, uncomfortable, rheumatic wind which is the Lakeland equivalent of the 'helm wind' of the Eden valley. In Grasmere folk still keep a wary eye open for that characteristic bar and cap of pale cloud on Fairfield and Seat Sandal, and in Keswick they look for the same signs on Skiddaw and

Blencathra, knowing that the biting, blustery, easterly wind will soon be rattling windows and whirling the dead leaves at Ashness. At the head of Borrowdale the famous 'sop', a cloud which gathers over Sty Head and Sprinkling tarns, has long been used as a significant forecasting sign; if the cloud moves in the direction of Great Langdale, rain can be expected within twelve or twenty-four hours, but if it moves north-eastward and passes east of the Borrowdale Fells, fine weather will continue.

The sunset, that old stand-by of weather forecasting, was a much-looked-for omen; in the Kendal area this contradiction of the well-known 'Red sky at night . . .' rhyme was common:

> *If the sun in red should set,*
> *The next day surely will be wet.*
> *If the sun should set in gray*
> *The next will be a rainy day.*

and undoubtedly this tradition is founded on folk observation, but not all the folk rhymes relating to weather are so based. The curious idea that 'when the owl calls "t'wet", it will rain next day', or 'if the cock crows on going to bed it rises with a watery head' seems rather improbable, as does 'if the sun shines not on Christmas day, the apple crop will surely fail'. On the whole, however, many of these sayings have more than just a grain of truth; 'when the days begin to lengthen, the cold begins to strengthen' surely reflects the very low temperatures in January and February, and similarly, 'a cold May and windy, makes a fat barn and a findy' (i.e. plump, weighty) reflects the farmers' belief that a cold spring often produces a good crop in summer. Conversely, 'a green Christmas makes a fat churchyard' underlines the suspicion associated with a mild December. Candlemas (February 2nd) features prominently in Cumbrian weather lore:

> *If the thrush sings 'fore Candlemas Day,*
> *it does nowt after but repent and pray,*

runs one old rhyme, and 'if Cannelmas Day be sunshining an' warm, ye may mend yer oald mittens an' look for a storm', warns another. Similarly, 'if Candlemass Day be fine and clear, we'll get two winters in one year' suggests that a mild February augurs ill for the rest of the year. Late frosts and sudden storms in April, known as 'hogg-squalls' because they usually coincide with the return of the hoggs to the heaf, often delay the first flush of the new grass and this has probably given rise to an old saying that 'you should allus hev hauf yer hay left at Cannelmas' to safeguard against a late spring.

One of the characteristic features of Lakeland weather is the suddenness with which the local climate can change, and this makes conventional forecasting difficult. Warm, moist Atlantic air moving over the fells from the west can soon turn a bright morning into an afternoon of 'kessened over' skies, and many a sunny haymaking has been rained off after a promising start. 'Too bright too early' is a maxim which is familiar enough to Cumbrian farmers. Similarly, in summer, local convection currents ascending from the fellsides can, under certain conditions, produce ominous cloudbanks while the fields of west Cumberland and the sands of Morecambe Bay shimmer in sunlight. Tourists have for many years noted this trait with understandable exasperation: '. . . at a time when the sky is clear', moaned one 'Laker' in 1792, '. . . a black cloud will start up instantly from behind a Mountain, and if you are not very near a house, ten to one you are wet before you can run a hundred yards'.[2] Some valleys and certain lakes, notably Derwentwater, experience sudden gusty winds known as 'bottom winds' and these, too, can be a factor in the local climate. One late eighteenth-century observer described the effect as follows:

'One part [of Derwentwater] was agitated violently without the least apparent cause, while another was so smooth as to have scarcely moved more than a ripple upon its surface; a boat with two men was tossed up and down in a storm in one part, while a man at no great distance was fishing quietly with a rod and line from another'.[3]

The rainfall figures tell their own story—the central fells have an average 225 'rain days' each year, Grasmere receives 83 inches, Ambleside 72 inches, Seathwaite 129 inches, and Sty Head still holds the record with 250 inches in 1928, but the perversity of Lakeland weather is further emphasized by the number of floods which are experienced. One of the most spectacular occurred in June 1686, when Hawkshead was struck by torrential rain and flooding 'the like of it was never seen in these parts by noe man liveinge, for it did throwe downe some houses and mills and tooke away severall briggs . . . the water wash't upp great trees, stocks, and greate stones a greate way off and lay'd them on men's ground . . .'[4] Again, in August 1749, the Vale of St John was devastated by a water-spout which flooded the valley to a depth of several feet and caused extensive damage. Heavy rains and the bursting of river banks were so common that it is reported[5] that some dalesfolk believed that a summer without a day of flooded streams was abnormal and as such was something to be feared. In Keswick the rain and floods often arrived during late July and early August, and consequently were named 'Morlan' or 'Magdalen' floods, after the saint's feast day on 22nd July.

Floods and torrents such as those which swept down Lingmell Gill on August Bank Holiday Monday, 1936, or washed away bridges and walls in Borrowdale in August 1966, continue to plague Lakeland, and no weather lore or forecast can predict them accurately. As every dalesman knows, mountains make their own weather, and although he will listen to the weather forecast on the radio, nevertheless the farmer—particularly at lambing time and haymaking—keeps a weather eye open for the traditional signs which he knows herald a change in the weather in his particular dale—whatever the Meteorological Office might say to the contrary! Even men of the cloth have been known to put their faith firmly in traditional weather signs, and the story is still told of the Westmorland clergyman who, on being requested to offer a prayer for a fine haymaking, replied, 'It's nae use es lang es t'wind is in this quarter'!

10 DRY-STONE WALLS

Few visitors to the Lake District can have failed to marvel at the dry-stone walls which snake and wind across the mountains, surmounting steep, rocky crags with ease, and apparently growing out of the fells like the rowan and the blaeberry. Even the most car-confined tourist must be conscious of these stone fences so unlike the wooded hedgerows of the midlands and the south of England, and thousands of fell wanderers on Great Gable have been elated by the sight of the western sun casting long shadows amid the stone mosaic of the Wasdale Head fields. Indeed, these stone walls are a tangible expression of man's effect on his environment, and are as much a part of the human landscape as the snugly built, whitewashed farms and the dripping, overgrown copper adits and slate quarries. Yet, in spite of their ancient appearance, they are a relatively recent addition to the Lakeland scene, for most of them were built between 1750 and 1850; within the space of a hundred years the transformation from open, unenclosed moorland into a network of dry-stone walls was accomplished.[1]

There is, however, considerably more to a Lakeland dry-stone wall than meets the eye. It would be wrong to regard them purely as field boundaries for, as any fell shepherd knows, the lee side of a stoutly built wall will provide welcome shelter for sheep in inclement weather, a fact which has not escaped the winter fell-walker. The wire fences of the twentieth century, though quick and cheap to erect, can provide no such shelter. Some walls were built to prevent sheep from straying over precipices or into gullies where they might become crag-fast; in the nineteenth century Ennerdale shepherds collectively kept in good repair a wall which prevented their sheep from roaming onto the front of Pillar Rock,[2] and similar walls may be seen along the summit of Dow Crags in the Coniston fells, though these are now sadly decayed. Elsewhere, dry-stone walls have been built to form 'out-gangs', wide-mouthed funnels narrowing down to parallel walls culminating in sheep pens, so that the flocks may be gathered from the fellsides with ease. On some of the more level valley floors the stone walls not only divide the available inland pasture into small, irregular fields, but they also act as stone dumps, for the pasture has been created by the laborious process of clearing the land of boulders and obviously the most convenient method of disposal was to build them into the boundary walls. In valleys such as Borrowdale, Langdale and Wasdale Head, bastion-like walls many feet thick are evidence of this practice (plates 108, 109). In some cases the stones cleared from the land were more than could be used in the building of the walls and consequently huge heaps of stones, or 'clearance cairns', were occasionally left in the middle of the fields, a dramatic testimony to the industry of the men who created the pasture. Jonathan Otley, the nineteenth-century geologist and guide-book writer, commented on these clearance cairns:

'Wasdale Head comprises a level area of 400 acres of land divided by stone walls into irregular fields, which have been cleared with great industry and labour; as appears from the enormous heaps of stones, piled up from the surplus after completing the enclosure.'[3]

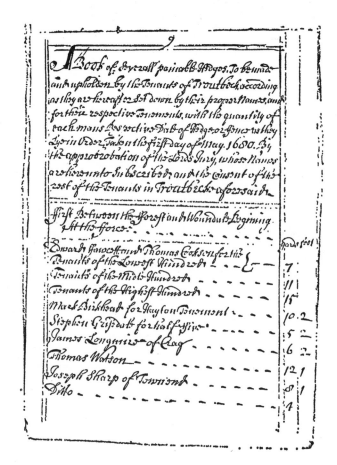

Fig. 27. Part of the Troutbeck Painable Fence Book, as written in 1680. This records the length of stone wall to be maintained by each tenant.

Although most of the Lakeland dry-stone walls were built in the eighteenth and nineteenth centuries, a few are considerably older. The low turf and stone dike which crosses the green, boggy wastes of Lincove in Upper Eskdale was built by the Cistercian monks of Furness Abbey some time between 1284 and 1290, for during that period they successfully petitioned John de Hudleston, Lord of Millom, for the right to enclose certain pastures at 'Botherhulkil' (Brotherilkeld), and 'Lincoue' (Lincove) which adjoined the forest of Egremont. However, this enclosing wall was carefully specified as '. . . . a dyke, wall, or paling as the abbot and monks should think most convenient for them; but such, nevertheless as harts and does and their fawns could leap';[4] in other words, a wall which was designed to prevent sheep from straying but not sufficiently high to hinder the free movement of deer and fawns. Several centuries later, in 1551, the Forest of Troutbeck was divided between Ambleside and Troutbeck by a wall which straggled over the crags of Red Screes and then descended sharply to the summit of Kirkstone Pass.[5] In 1680 the Troutbeck Painable Fence Book[6] was compiled to record those walls for which the township was responsible and to allocate each man's responsibility for a

90. Below: The interior of a wheel-right's workshop, Museum of Lakeland Life and Industry, Kendal. Below the work bench a number of 'naffs', or wheel hubs, of seasoned elm can be seen, while the vice on the bench holds a partly finished felloe, one of the sections of the rim. The rack on the wall carries various planes, saws and measuring devices used in this most skilful craft.

89. Wheel hooping. Mr R. Dewhurst, of Hawkshead, his son and an assistant fitting the iron rim to the wheel. The rim is first heated to expand the metal, then fitted over the wheel on a tyring platform, before being cooled with water in order to encourage the metal to contract and fit tightly over the wheel.

91. A partly finished wheel made by Mr R. Dewhurst of Hawkshead. Considerable skill was required to manufacture a dished wheel and the process could take up to four days to complete. Here, three components may be seen—the elm 'naff', the oak spokes and the ash felloes.

92. This wall at the side of the Garburn Road, Troutbeck, has been built from fissile rock taken from a nearby quarry. The marked tendency to split into thin slabs makes it an unsatisfactory building material and the wall has deteriorated badly.

93. In areas where the Brathay Flags outcrop, fences made of interlocking flags may be found. This example occurs in the Lickle Valley, but there are others at Coniston, Hawkshead and Ambleside.

94. The Borrowdale Volcanic group of rocks make up the central fells of the Lake District and the rugged and angular nature of these mountains is reflected in the dry-stone walls of the area. This wall on Low Pike, near Ambleside, has a fine 'hogg-hole'.

95. In the granite areas of Eskdale the pink crystalline rock has been used for wall building. In this example, on the valley floor, the boulders have been rounded either by ice or by river action.

96. Below left: Around the Cumbrian coast, water-worn sea-shore boulders form the basic material for wall building. This example, near Bootle in West Cumberland, consists of alternate layers of turf and stone.

97. Below: Ingenuity in wall building. An exposure of hexagonal columnar rhyolite at Stephenson Ground in the Lickle Valley has provided the waller with unusual material with which to bridge a small beck. These pillars are similar to, although smaller than, the Giant's Causeway columns in Antrim, Northern Ireland.

98. *A well-constructed wall in Borrowdale Volcanic rock on the Fairfield range. In spite of the steeply sloping ground, the stones are set horizontally.*

99. *Wallers repairing a stone wall on the high fells.*

100. *Repairing a dry-stone wall in limestone country, near Arnside, Westmorland.*

101. *A stone mosaic at Wasdale Head. The small, irregular fields on the valley floor, some containing clearance cairns, contrast with the more regular 'intaks' of a later period encroaching up the fellside.*

102. *One of the Troutbeck 'painable' walls below Red Screes, Kirkstone Pass.*

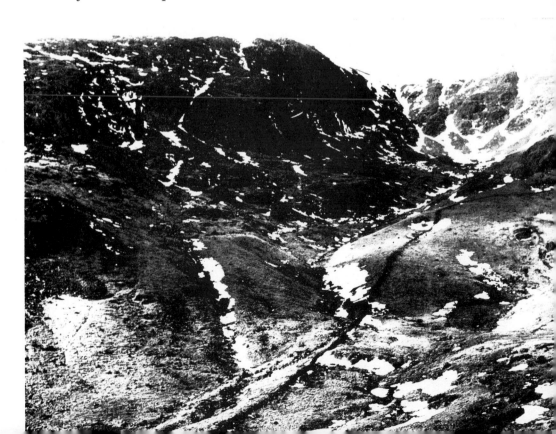

106. *Above: A wall head near Coniston. Clearly marked divisions such as these were built into common walls to indicate ownership and responsibility for upkeep.*

103, 104, 105. *Some Lakeland hogg-holes. Hogg-holes are gaps left in the base of stone walls to allow 'hoggs', or yearling sheep, to pass freely from one part of the heaf to another. Top left: An ornate example in the Lickle Valley. Left: A gable-shaped hole with the blocking stone in position.*
Bottom left: A common form of hogg-hole in Lakeland.

107. *Below: An unusual feature in Lakeland—an initialed and dated gate-post near Rosthwaite in Borrowdale bearing the inscription J.B. and the date 1798.*

108. A 'Cyclopean' wall near Ulpha, Dunnerdale. These enormous boulders are probably a result of field clearances in the late eighteenth or early nineteenth century. The folded Ordnance Survey map in the centre of the picture gives the scale.

109. A Wasdale Head wall many feet in thickness. Walls such as these became stone dumps when the inland pasture was first cleared and reclaimed.

110, 111. *Two Cumbrian blacksmiths. The blacksmith was once one of the most important members of the Lakeland rural community—not only was he a farrier but he could also make and mend items of household equipment as well as spades, ploughs, sickles and a variety of other agricultural tools. With the mechanization of farming in the twentieth century the number of smiths has declined, and those who remain have become 'agricultural engineers'.*

stated section of wall; the 'Lords Jury of Troutbeck' saw to it 'that every tenant, and Tenants shall maintain their painable Fences in good repare or else shall be in pain', that is, fined six shillings and eight pence. Figure 27 illustrates a section of the Painable Fence Book which records the length and location of the walls which each tenant was expected to maintain in good repair, and plate 102 shows one of the 'painable' walls on the fellside below Red Screes.

These are a few of the older dry-stone walls which can be dated by documentary evidence, but without this evidence it is very difficult to assign a meaningful date, though, as a general rule, the older enclosure walls can be distinguished by their rounded corners since, in the days before accurate surveying, it was easier to build a wall without corners than one with.[7]

The arrival of the Agricultural Revolution, which in this remote part of north-west England was later than in many other areas, brought a stimulus to the Enclosure Movement. The new methods of farming, new crops and improved breeds of animals dictated the enclosure of the commons, as did the high price of food during the Napoleonic Wars. These new enclosures were often laid out by trained surveyors, and the regular pattern of large fields stands out in marked contrast to the irregular patchwork of the earlier enclosure of the arable fields. There were two main methods by which land could be enclosed, either by private agreement between the landowners involved, or by Act of Parliament. Most of the Lakeland stone walls were built by Act of Parliament following the General Enclosure Act of 1801; under this legislation the common rights were extinguished and the land reapportioned among the promoters of the legislation and the holders of rights on the old commons. Not everyone benefited from such changes; thousands of small farmers lost rights of pasturage on the common land and many became mere farm labourers, some, paupers. The enclosure awards usually specified a date when all the walls were to be completed, and also named those responsible for maintenance of the walls and the gates. The following extract from the Wasdale Head award, dated 30th January 1808, is typical of many such documents:

'William Ritson his Heirs and Assigns to make and repair two fifth parts of the whole extent of Fence up to Black Cragg beginning nearest the Inclosures and John Benson his Heirs and Assigns to make and repair the remaining three fifth parts thereof and so in the like Proportion to the Extremity of the Boundary.'[8]

Often the walls were built not by the farmers themselves but by bands of itinerant wallers who wandered throughout the area seeking work; it is largely these men who enmeshed the Lake District in a network of stone.

To the layman's eye, dry-stone walls often appear as mere heaps of uncemented stones balanced precariously on top of one another, but nothing could be further from the truth, as anyone who has attempted to build a dry-stone wall in his garden will testify. They are, in fact, structures in equilibrium in which the main load is transmitted down through each skilfully laid stone course onto the foundations below. To build a dry-stone wall which would resist the wily attentions of the lish Herdwicks and the clumsy clamberings of fell-walkers it was necessary to set the wall on a good footing of large, usually square-shaped boulders set in two parallel rows in a shallow trench about three or four feet wide. 'Footing stones' were generally the largest stones to be found in a wall, often being several feet across. The space between the two parallel rows of footing stones was filled with 'hearting', small, irregular fragments which compacted together under pressure. Subsequent 'courses' were then laid on this foundation, care being taken to see that each stone rested on two stones in the course below, and again the space between the two outside faces was filled with 'hearting'. After several courses had been built in

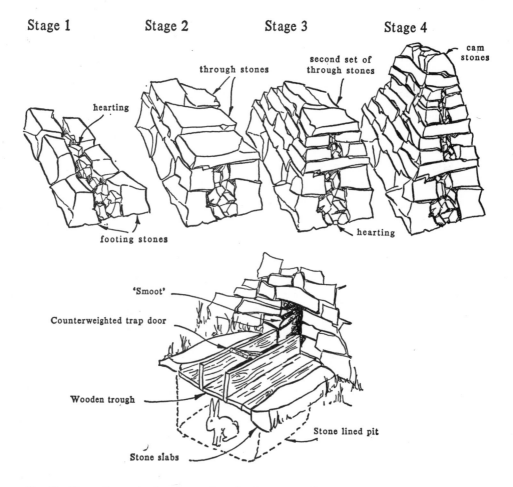

Stage 1   Stage 2   Stage 3   Stage 4

cam stones

second set of through stones

through stones

hearting

footing stones

hearting

'Smoot'

Counterweighted trap door

Wooden trough

Stone lined pit

Stone slabs

Fig. 28. Above: Stages in the construction of a dry-stone wall.
Below: A rabbit 'smoot', Ayside, Cartmel.

this manner, 'through' stones were laid at intervals; as the name suggests, these were stones which ran through the wall and usually projected out from both faces, their function being simply to tie the two faces together and to prevent the wall from 'bellying out'. A well-built wall often had two or more lines of 'throughs' at different heights above the footing (fig. 28). As the wall gained height, the width decreased to perhaps one or two feet; this was achieved by setting the stones into the wall slightly, so producing a wall which was considerably thicker at the base than at the top. Many eighteenth- and nineteenth-century walling contracts specify not only the number of through courses, but also the amount of 'batter' the wall should have, and in order to attain the correct height and batter, a wooden frame corresponding to the dimensions of the required wall was sometimes used. The wall was completed with a row of 'cams', slate-like stones roughly the same size stacked on edge and all lying at the same angle; their main purpose was to discourage sheep from leaping over the wall.

This brief account of dry-stone wall construction merely catalogues the stages in the construction of a wall, without taking into account the secrets of the craft which every waller acquired. Observant fell-walkers will have noticed how, on steeply sloping ground, the stones in the wall remain horizontal irrespective of the angle of slope, so that there is less possibility of stones slipping down hill. A further characteristic which is less known, though of considerable importance, concerns the angle at which the stones are set within the wall; wherever possible they slope outwards so that rainwater drains off the wall, rather than inward where it would soak the hearting. In this way the interior of the wall is kept dry and the risk of damage by frost expansion in winter is reduced. Should the hearting be attacked by frost, whole sections of wall may 'rush', or collapse. Anyone who has been fortunate enough to observe a craftsman building a dry-stone wall will have appreciated another interesting technique; a waller, on picking up a stone, will not put it down until he has found a place for it in his wall. The moment of truth arrives when, on completion of the wall, the waller generally tests his workmanship by taking a flying leap at it with both feet!

Because of the varied nature of the solid geology within the Lake District, the dry-stone walls show marked changes in character from region to region.[9] In the north of the area the so-called Skiddaw Slates and Shales produce not only the smooth, rounded outlines of such well-known mountains as Skiddaw and Blencathra, but also a distinctive type of dry-stone wall, whereas the Borrowdale Volcanic group of rocks which make up the craggy central fells produce more massively built walls with a more rugged appearance (plate 94). In the southern Lake District the Silurian Slates of the subdued, wooded country between Coniston Water and Windermere produce dry-stone walls which are more akin to those of the Skiddaw Slates, for the rock is generally of a fissile nature and often splits along the bedding plane to produce plate-like slabs. Around the Coniston, Hawkshead and Ambleside areas where the Brathay flagstones occur, another distinctive type of wall may be seen composed of large, vertical 'flags' skilfully interlocked edge to edge (plate 93). Along the Cumbrian coasts, close to the shore, another building material and another style prevail; here the rounded, water-worn seashore 'cobbles' are used in the construction of turf and stone dykes, layers of turf alternating with the stone courses in order to provide a bedding for the round stones (plate 96).

Although these differences in material and structure are in themselves fascinating, a closer examination of Lakeland dry-stone walls will illustrate the ingenuity of the craftsmen who built them. At Stephenson Ground, in the Lickle Valley, clever use has been made of hexagonal rhyolitic pillars—smaller versions of the Giant's Causeway columns—in bridging a small stream, allowing the beck to flow through a gap in the wall but preventing animals from straying out of the field (plate 97). 'Hogg-holes' are another ingenious feature which ought not to escape mention; these square holes left in the footing of many Lakeland walls allowed 'hoggs', or yearling sheep, to pass unhindered from one part of the heaf to another, and if necessary they could be closed by rolling a convenient stone slab across the opening. Usually hogg-holes were formed by roofing over a gap in the lowest course of a wall with a large slab capable of supporting the remaining upper courses, but variations on this theme can be observed; one waller in the Lickle valley has clearly indulged his fancy for gable-shaped hogg-holes! (Plates 103–5.) Although not so common as hogg-holes, rabbit 'smoots' (fig. 28) were sometimes built into walls at appropriate places; these small holes allowed unsuspecting rabbits to pass through the wall to a slyly concealed trap-door and stone-lined pit, so ensuring a ready supply of rabbit stew on the farmhouse table! Wall 'heads', common in those walls built during the eighteenth and nineteenth centuries, also served a useful function, for they marked the boundary of lengths of wall belonging to different people. If, for example, a landowner was required under an enclosure award to build one section of a common wall, his neighbour might be required to complete the wall, the junction between the two sections being indicated by a 'head' or vertical clear-cut join in the wall created by a number of large stones one on top of the other (plate 106). In this way the sections for which the landowners had responsibility for upkeep and repair were clearly visible.

Of individual stone-wallers little is known, but certainly their lives were hard and the work was back-breaking. Very often they 'bivouacked' on the fellside for weeks on end, walling from sunrise to sunset and coming down to the valley floor only at weekends. In many cases stone for the walls had to be obtained from specially opened quarries on the fellside and great skill was exercised in the choice of through stones and topstones, as the following extracts from a nineteenth-century walling account[10] for work done at Lanthwaite, near Loweswater, illustrate:

1837 January 6 To 1 Daye work for Getting threwstone . . . at 3/3 per day   3/3
1837 April 10 To 3 Dayes Work for Getting top stones and undersetting at 3/3 per day   9/9
1841 August 5 To 4 dayes Work for Getting settle stones and top stones   14/0

Stones were often carried to the site not on carts, which would have overturned on the steep slopes, but on wooden sleds, and many walling accounts refer to 'the sledging of stones'. Wages were low and in 1794 seven and a half yards of dry-stone wall some five and a half feet high could be built for between 1s. 6d. and 1s. 8d.;[11] however, by 1877 the rate had increased to 6s. 6d. per rood of seven yards.[12] Craftsmen though they were, these wallers were often illiterate, and like Joseph Lancaster, who built the walls at Lanthwaite Green in 1841, they could sign their wage receipts only with a cross (fig. 29), yet these men have, in another way, indelibly written their signatures on the fells for all to see and admire.

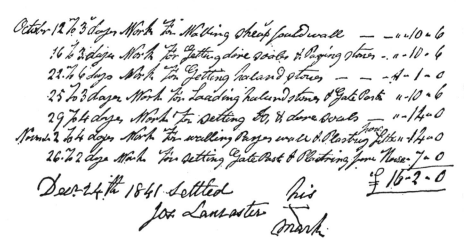

Fig. 29. Part of a wage receipt for work done by Joseph Lancaster, waller, at Lanthwaite Green, Loweswater, in 1841.

11 THE WOODLAND CRAFT INDUSTRIES

Few, if any, of the Lakeland craft industries have had so profound an effect on the rural economy as the woodland industries; and few can equal the long tradition of craftsmanship which began in early medieval times, perhaps even earlier, and has continued until the present. Although these woodland crafts undoubtedly have an ancient history, some of the earliest documentary evidence appears in the certificate of revenues of Furness Abbey drawn up by Henry VIII's commissioners in 1537, the year in which the monastery was dissolved.[1] Here we read that in the Furness Fells

'. . . there ys another yerely profytte commyng and growing of the said Woodes, called Grenehewe, Bastyng, Blecking, byndyng, making of sadeltrees, cartwheles, cuppes, disshes and many other things wrought by Cowpers and Turners, with makying of Coles, and pannage of Hogges, according as hath always been accustomed to be made in the said woodes, to the yerely valewe by estymacyon of xiii£ . . . vis . . . viiid.'

Some of these terms are easily recognizable today, but others require some explanation: 'grenehewe' was the rent paid by the abbey's tenants for the right to lop off branches of ash, holly, and other trees for sheep fodder in winter (*see* page 88), while 'bastyng' means the manufacture of coarse matting from bark peelings and also the making of spelk or swill baskets. 'Blecking' seems to indicate the bleaching or drying of bark, or possibly the making of ashes from which soap was manufactured, and 'byndyng' signifies the making of barrels and hoops; 'sadeltrees' were the frames for the pack-horses which were the most common means of transport in Cumbria until the early nineteenth century, while 'the makying of Coles' is clearly a reference to the manufacture of charcoal.[2] Here, then, in spite of their apparently low value, is the first account of the woodland industries to indicate their range.

All the activities mentioned in this sixteenth-century document have either become extinct or dwindled into insignificance, but as Dr J. D. Marshall has pointed out, local surnames survive to remind us of their former importance. Ashburner is still a common name in Furness, as is Turner, literally one who 'turned' cups and dishes on a primitive lathe. Tobman or Tubman, perhaps derived from the art of coopering, was once common in some parts of west Cumberland, and Cowper, a surname still met with in High Furness, may reflect the same industry.[3] Moreover, there are still retired craftsmen who in their youth made charcoal in the coppice woods of the Furness Fells, or bobbins for the Lancashire cotton mills, and men like Myles Newton of Lowick Green and Wilfred Barker of Broughton-in-Furness, sitting astride their swillers' horses, can produce a spelk basket as fine as any made by the generations of craftsmen before them.* But these men are the inheritors of a dying art, for unless the rural craft organizations are able to train young men to carry on the traditions, these crafts, together with those

*The word 'spelk' is derived from the Old Norse *spelkr*, meaning a splinter. The local term for these baskets, however, is 'swill'.

of stone-walling, wheelwrighting and hoopmaking, will shortly become extinct, and only the neglected coppice woodland of the southern fells (plate 112) will remain as a reminder of a once important industry.

CHARCOAL BURNING

During the pre-industrial period the importance of charcoal to the iron industry cannot be over-estimated for this was the only effective fuel which could be used in the smelting processes of that time. The Cistercian monks of Furness Abbey had their 'colepittes' and 'colepots' in the woods of Low Furness, and these supplied the abbey with sufficient charcoal to smelt the rich red haematite ores; but by the sixteenth century the woodland had been depleted and so ore had to be transported to small 'bloomery hearths' dotted throughout the still thickly wooded High Furness Fells. Since it required five tons of wood to produce one ton of charcoal and eleven hundredweights of charcoal to make three hundredweights of iron from half a ton of ore, it was clearly cheaper to carry the ore to the woodland for smelting rather than *vice versa*. The availability of charcoal, then, became the main locating factor of the early iron industry; for several centuries the pale blue smoke from the pitsteads drifted through the coppice woods and, on still, overcast days, hung like a veil over Coniston Water and Windermere. The turf huts of the 'colliers', located close by the pitsteads, became an integral part of the human landscape of southern Lakeland.

The current meaning of the term 'collier' is unequivocal; it signifies someone who mines coal, but this is a relatively recent definition, for during the centuries which preceded the Industrial Revolution the term was used for anyone who made charcoal. For example, the Ulverston Parish Registers for 1598 record the burial of 'a daughter of a collier of blaw th,' [Blawith],[4] and similarly the Hawkshead Parish Registers for 1701 show the death on 10th December of Clement Holm 'colier de Deal Park'.[5] And even the name of Colton, the small village near Greenodd, may be derived from Coleton or Charcoal-town.[6]

Basically, the craft of making charcoal began with the coppicing of the woods; this involved the felling of 'standards', or trees, just above the ground, thus leaving a stool or bole from which eventually between ten and twenty 'poles' sprouted, fiercely competing for the available sunlight. In some ways the coppice wood was regarded as a crop, utilizing land which could otherwise not be used, and ready for harvesting every fifteen or sixteen years. When the 'poles' attained a diameter of about five or six inches, the copse was cut, usually 'at t'back end', that is, between November and April, for at this time of the year there was little sap in the wood. Only the oak trees were allowed to remain until the spring, for then the rising sap allowed the bark to be peeled away more easily. During the summer the work of cutting, peeling and grading the wood according to size occupied the woodsman, and eventually the larger wood was sent to the bobbin mills (*see* page 146), while the smaller wood, about an inch or two in diameter, was utilized by the colliers.[7] Two sizes of wood were usually 'coaled': the 'shanklings', about three feet long, and the smaller 'coalwood', approximately two feet in length.

The process of converting the wood to charcoal was one which changed little from very early times; a shallow circular pit between fifteen and thirty feet in diameter was dug, and a stake or 'motty peg' was set up in the centre. These 'pit-rings', or 'pitsteads', were usually in level shelter-ed areas with running water close by, but occasionally, when there was little available level land, a small platform was built out of the hillside in order to create the pitstead; there are several fine examples of this latter type in the upper Troutbeck valley (plate 113). Around the stake

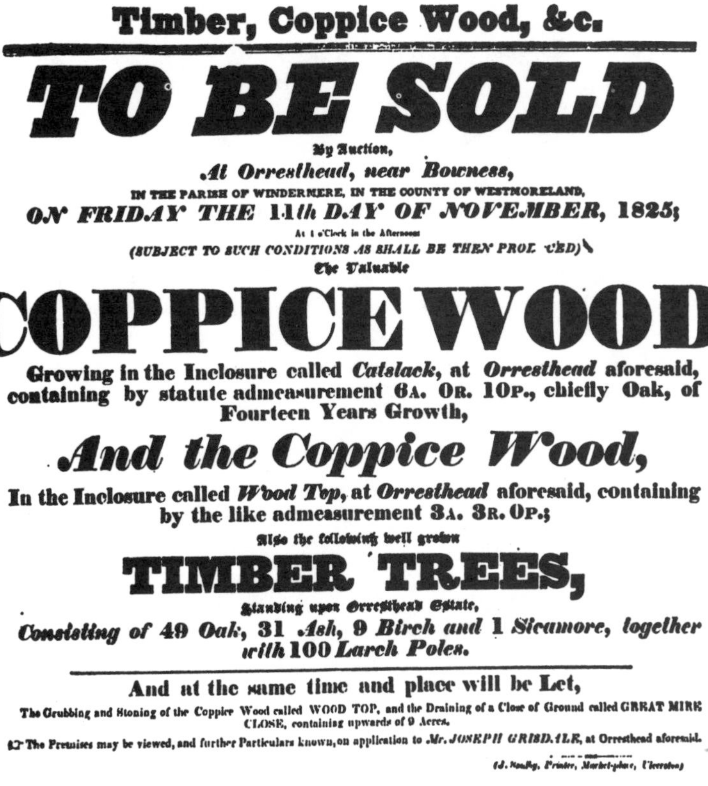

Timber, Coppice Wood, &c.

TO BE SOLD

By Auction,

At Orresthead, near Bowness,

IN THE PARISH OF WINDERMERE, IN THE COUNTY OF WESTMORELAND,

ON FRIDAY THE 11th DAY OF NOVEMBER, 1825;

At 1 o'Clock in the Afternoon

(SUBJECT TO SUCH CONDITIONS AS SHALL BE THEN PRODUCED)

The Valuable

COPPICE WOOD

Growing in the Inclosure called Catslack, at Orresthead aforesaid, containing by statute admeasurement 6A. 0R. 10P., chiefly Oak, of Fourteen Years Growth,

And the Coppice Wood,

In the Inclosure called Wood Top, at Orresthead aforesaid, containing by the like admeasurement 3A. 3R. 0P.;

Also the following well grown

TIMBER TREES,

Standing upon Orresthead Estate,

Consisting of 49 Oak, 31 Ash, 9 Birch and 1 Sicamore, together with 100 Larch Poles.

And at the same time and place will be Let,

The Grubbing and Stoning of the Coppice Wood called WOOD TOP, and the Draining of a Close of Ground called GREAT MIRE CLOSE, containing upwards of 9 Acres.

☞ The Premises may be viewed, and further Particulars known, on application to Mr. JOSEPH GRISDALE, at Orresthead aforesaid.

(J. Soulby, Printer, Market-place, Ulverston)

Fig. 30. Coppice wood was a valuable asset in the eighteenth and nineteenth centuries, and the timber crop was harvested every fifteen or sixteen years.

the pieces of wood, about three or four feet long, were piled concentrically until a beehive-shaped pile was formed, about six feet in height. The whole was then covered with bracken or grass on top of which was spread a layer of finely sifted marl or sods to check any influx of air which might ignite the wood rather than 'coal' it. The pit was further protected from winds by a series of movable screens or hurdles made of interlaced twigs, bracken and bark. Finally, the central stake was removed and glowing charcoal placed in the opening, which was then closed with a sod. Once ignited, the pit required constant attention; parts of the cone would collapse and need to be rearranged, and any indication of a flame had to be smothered with wet turf or water, which was usually held in large barrels close to the pit. The 'coaling' process usually took between twenty-four hours and three days, during which time, it was said, an experienced collier could tell exactly how the pit was faring. When 'coaling' was complete a 'saying' of water was thrown over the pit to create steam, which effectively cooled the charcoal. Traditionally the implement used for this process was a 'say'[8] or shallow dish, but a bucket was equally effective. After an hour or so, the charcoal was raked over to cool it before it was shovelled into sacks. (See plates 114–21.)

The sale of coppice wood and charcoal, together with oak bark for the tanning industry, was quite a profitable business in the eighteenth century. Fig. 31 shows an account for the production of charcoal and bark from a wood near Troutbeck[9] in 1770 and gives us an insight into the costs of making a pitstead, hurdles, and coaling; the amount of charcoal produced is recorded here in dozen sackfuls, an empty sack measuring 2½ yards by 1 yard, and when full, standing four feet nine inches high.[10] In the 1880s it was reckoned that each 'pit' produced two dozen and a half sacks per 'coaling' which were worth £4. 10s. During the early days of the iron industry in the Furness Fells, most of the charcoal produced from the coppices was used in the bloomeries which dotted the woodland, and also in forges, such as those at Cunsey, Force Forge, Hacket in Little Langdale, and the delightfully named Burblethwaite on the River Winster. Later, however, much of the charcoal produced in the Furness Fells was used by the famous Backbarrow Furnace on the River Leven, and boats carried charcoal the length of Windermere to a landing stage at Newby Bridge not far from Backbarrow. The furnace continued to produce high-grade charcoal iron until 1920–1, but even then the demand for charcoal

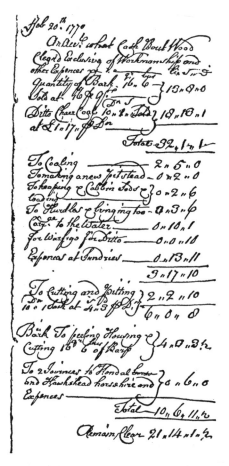

Fig. 31. Charcoal burning and bark peeling near Troutbeck, 1770. This account mentions such activities as coaling, peeling, the making of pitsteads and the construction of hurdles.

did not cease, for it was an important ingredient of gunpowder, which continued to be made in the southern Lake District until 1937[11] (*see* pages 148–50).

Little is known of individual charcoal burners other than the meagre entries in parish records, but one needs only a little imagination to picture the dirty and arduous working conditions. Once one pit was kindled a second, third and fourth followed in succession, and during 'coaling' work went on day and night for seven days a week without respite through the late summer and early autumn. The constant attention which the pits required necessitated the colliers remaining in the woods during this period and consequently they built for themselves turf huts, large enough to accommodate two people. These archaic survivals remained in the woods of the southern Lake District until the early twentieth century and, like the pitsteads themselves, their remains can still be found today. Basically the colliers' hut was circular and built on a tripod not dissimilar to a Red Indian wigwam. The whole structure was then 'thacked' with sods overlapping each other like tiles on a roof. Such huts usually stood about seven or eight feet high, and had no windows or openings other than a door of withies or sacking (plate 122 and fig. 32). Readers of Arthur Ransome's book *Swallows and Amazons* will remember his description of similar charcoal burners' huts in the High Furness woods. Food was prepared and brought to the colliers from neighbouring farmsteads, and therefore there was no need to provide the huts with hearths. The turf huts built by the bark peelers, however, were more sophisticated, for their work was more leisurely, and whereas the colliers' huts stood for only two months or so, the bark peelers' huts were intended to survive longer.[12] Although they were constructed on a light timber frame with a ridge pole and a low encircling wattle-and-turf wall, they were larger than the colliers' huts, accommodating four people. Moreover, because of the more permanent nature of these huts, they often contained a stone-built hearth which projected externally from the walls of the hut.

SWILLMAKING

The making of spelk or swill baskets is another Lake District woodland craft which, unlike charcoal making, has not yet completely died out. Like charcoal-burning, however, this industry also has its roots in antiquity; the term 'bastyng' found in the 1537 revenue accounts of Furness Abbey probably includes the making of swills, and a 1563 inventory of the goods of Matthew Dixon of Brantfell, Windermere, refers to 'iij spelks and iij corves xixd',[13] while the Parish Register of Hawkshead for 1673 records the burial of 'John Harrison, Swiller, who dyed at Grysdall'.[14]

The raw material for swill making was straight-grained oak poles about six inches thick, and naturally the centre of the industry lay in the coppice woods of the Furness Fells. After felling, the poles are riven or split into pieces and boiled in water for several hours in order to make them more pliable. Later, the pieces are further split into 'smarts' with a maul and split-axe, known locally as a 'lat-axe'; these are then shaved and trimmed on a swiller's 'horse'. Although crude and cumbersome in appearance, this is an effective piece of equipment (plate 129 and fig. 32 (1)); the swiller sits astride the 'horse' and with his feet operates a pivoted arm which causes a heavy wooden head to swing down on a platform, thus gripping the 'smart' while it is shaved with a two-handled knife. While the oak is boiling, the 'bools' or oval rims of the shallow coracle-shaped baskets have to be made from hazel or ash withies; these are boiled for about five minutes and then formed into oval frames and nailed. A heavy, wooden, A-shaped 'set-horse' is sometimes used in this process (*see* plate 131). The bowl of the swill is then woven with spells, the short strong cross pieces, and taws, the longer, finer pieces. The photograph of the partly finished swill (plate 134) shows that the spells were put in the frame first, and then the taws, which at the sides were narrower than the spells but in the bottom of the swill they were the same width. So fine was the workmanship in this craft that it was said that the best of these swills would hold water.

The durability of swill baskets is almost legendary; they were used wherever a hard-wearing container was needed, in farming, coal-mining, charcoal-burning (plate 123), urban refuse collecting and on board ships, and thousands of swills were exported from southern Lakeland annually. Swills were made in various sizes ranging from sixteen to thirty-six inches in length, but the most popular size was the twenty-inch basket which was sold in Liverpool for coaling steamers at one shilling a swill. A good workman could make seven of these baskets per day. Seventy years ago almost every village had its swill-maker, but now the art is kept alive by a handful of men, retired or nearing retirement, who know the secrets of the craft.

Allied to swill-making was the craft of hooping, the manufacture of hoops for barrels, kegs and casks. Generally, sap-filled oak and hazel poles were split into three or four 'smarts' which were trimmed on a 'horse' before being coiled on to a frame. This resembled an eight-armed cross which had pegs along each arm so that the size of the hoops could be altered when necessary (plates 126, 127). The hoops were tied with tarred hemp and left to season before being exported in bundles of sixty which were known as 'half-a-hundred'.[15] The main markets were Manchester and Liverpool, where the hoops were used in the coopering trade. Merseyside formed the main market for an off-shoot of the hooping industry—the manufacture of ship fenders from withies; one of the most important centres of production was the water mill at Sunny Bank, Torver, which continued working until the early decades of the present century.[16]

BOBBIN MAKING

As well as charcoal-burning and swill- and hoop-making, the coppice woodlands of southern Lakeland gave rise to another activity, a cross between a skilled craft and an organized industry —bobbin or cotton-reel manufacture. Yet this was an industry which was not conspicuous, for the mills were usually hidden away in the woodlands on one of the many rapidly flowing becks, and being largely water-powered, they did not smudge the surrounding countryside with a pall of black smoke. The fortunes of the bobbin industry have necessarily been linked with those of Lancashire cotton; the first Lakeland bobbin mills were opened in the eighteenth century as a direct response to the demands of the textile plants of south Lancashire. During the cotton famine of the 1860s the bobbin mills were forced to turn to the manufacture of other products such as tool handles, pill boxes and mangle rollers; and with the decline of the cotton industry and the competition from plastic cotton reels so, too, the bobbin industry has declined. The Stott Park Mill at Finsthwaite, originally built in 1835 by John Harrison, a local landed farmer, was finally closed in 1971, but the site has been opened as an industrial museum where bobbins are still turned but for demonstration purposes only. It is one of the few representatives of over 50 such plants once in production in Lakeland. There is, in fact, reason to believe that by the mid nineteenth century the Lake District mills produced about 50 per cent of all the bobbin

Fig. 32. *WOODLAND INDUSTRIES.*
1. Swiller's 'horse'.   2. Two-handled draw knife.   3. A swill or spelk basket.
Below: Plans of woodmen's temporary shelters.

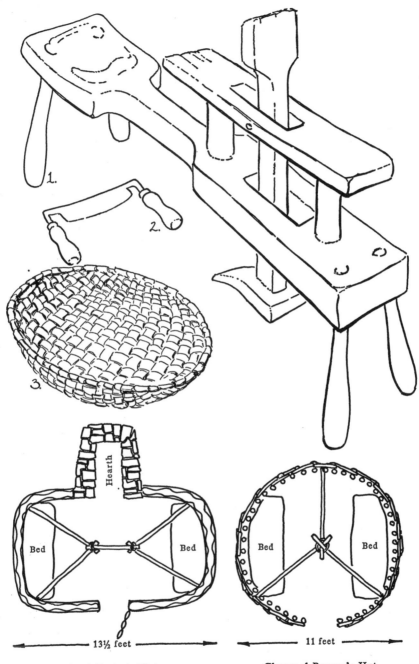

1.

2.

3.

Hearth

Bed · Bed

◄— 13½ feet —►

Bark Peeler's Hut

Bed · Bed

◄— 11 feet —►

Charcoal Burner's Hut

requirements of the British textile industry.

Usually, only the larger poles from the coppice were used in the bobbin mills; after sawing into lengths slightly longer than the finished reels, the bobbins were 'blocked out' and passed through a drying kiln. The next process involved the 'wrincing' of the holes to the exact specification, followed by the finishing lathe which turned out between 1,200 and 2,700 per hour (plate 125). Finally the bobbins were dyed, or waxed by tumbling them in a revolving drum containing lumps of wax.[17] Unlike the crafts of burning charcoal and making swills, the manufacture of bobbins necessitated the use of complicated machinery, and this has been fully described by Dr J. D. Marshall and Mr M. Davies-Shiel in their book *The Industrial Archaeology of the Lake Counties.*

OTHER WOODLAND ACTIVITIES

Closely allied to the coppicing of the woodlands of the southern Lake District was the craft of bark-peeling. Usually carried out between early May and early July, the bark on a 'pole' was carefully ringed and then 'oozed' off in one piece ready for storage (plate 124). Most of this oak bark was used in the tanning industry which flourished in Lakeland during the late eighteenth and early nineteenth centuries; tan pits were active about this period in such places as Ulverston, Greenodd, Penny Bridge, Nibthwaite, Spark Bridge, Barkhouse, and Hyde (hide), Park, both at Lowick, and several more in the Kendal vicinity. Later in the nineteenth century, because of technological changes, many of these small tan pits became obsolete, yet the bark from Lakeland coppice woods continued to be used in the tanning industry of Lancashire and Cheshire.

Visitors to Kendal's Stricklandgate will, no doubt, have wondered at the large beady-eyed, bristly hog which protrudes from the wall of an estate agent's office in this busy street (plate 135). The building dates from the seventeenth century and was known as Blackhall, but the black hog is one of the last surviving relics of the brush industry, a craft which had its origin in Lakeland's woodlands. Birch twig besoms made by women and children had long been used and sold locally, but the commercial manufacture of brushes largely dates from the nineteenth-century development of coppicing. With the exception of oak, almost any coppiced timber could be used in the making of brush handles and stocks—birch, alder, ash, sycamore and beech. Bristles and fibres, however, had to be imported from South America, Africa, Mexico, Poland, Siberia and elsewhere,[18] so, unlike most of the other woodland craft industries, brush-making was not a hundred per cent Lakeland craft. Kendal was not the only town to be involved in the industry, for Ulverston too had several small establishments manufacturing not only complete brushes but also brush sticks and handles. These, and other woodland products, were exported by sea along the canal which connected this small north Lancashire market town with Morecambe Bay. But Kendal remained the centre of the brush industry. The Blackhall works began making brushes in 1869 and continued until 1922, when the firm moved to other premises in the town. The industry finally came to an end in 1963; apart from the wooden hog of Stricklandgate, and one or two exhibits in the Kendal Museum, there is little tangible evidence of this craft which had such close links with the Lakeland coppice woods.

GUNPOWDER MANUFACTURE

Although it cannot be considered as a woodland craft industry, the making of gunpowder was closely associated with the production of charcoal, one of the main ingredients, and therefore gunpowder mills developed in association with charcoal-producing areas of Lakeland.[19] Yet gunpowder making is among the more recent of the 'traditional' Lake District industries, for it was not introduced into the region until 1764, when John Wakefield opened his mill at Sedgwick, south of Kendal. Clearly Wakefield had appreciated the advantages which southern Cumbria had to offer his new venture; first, there was a ready supply of silver birch and alder charcoal, but in particular 'savin coals' or charcoal made from the juniper bushes, which flourished on the lower slopes of the fells and which made the best quality gunpowder. Water power from the fast-flowing Lakeland becks operated the heavy machinery used in the crushing and milling processes, but in addition to these advantages, raw materials such as saltpetre from India and sulphur from Sicily and Italy could be transported from Liverpool to the small port of Miln-thorpe and, similarly, the gunpowder could be shipped to the magazines on the Mersey from the same port. Finally, of course, there was a growing demand for gunpowder in the late eighteenth and nineteenth centuries from the slate quarries, copper and lead mines of the central fells and the coal mines of west Cumberland. Moreover, until slave trading by British vessels was abolished in 1807, there was a tremendous demand for gunpowder from Africa, for it was one of the commodities most required in exchange for slaves.

These then were the main advantages which the Westmorland and Furness coppice woodlands offered to the gunpowder entrepreneurs. The success of Wakefield's initial investment was assured, and by the end of the eighteenth century two more gunpowder works had been built, one at Bassingill near by, the other at Lowwood near Haverthwaite on the River Leven. In 1824 David Huddleston opened his mills at Elterwater in Great Langdale, using power from Langdale Beck, but later he built a dam at Stickle Tarn, below Pavey Ark on the Langdale Pikes, and piped off the water to his works some four miles away. In spite of its comparative remoteness, the Elterwater mill received its raw materials largely by water, for boats brought the sulphur and saltpetre up Coniston Water to Waterhead or along the length of Windermere from Newby Bridge to Brathay, where a small pier was built. During the second half of the nineteenth century three other factories began manufacturing powder in southern Lakeland; in 1852 the Gatebeck works, south-east of Kendal, commenced working, and this was followed six years later by a new plant at Sedgwick, and finally, in 1860, the Blackbeck works near Bouth began operations.

Basically, the making of gunpowder involves the mixing of the three ingredients saltpetre, sulphur and charcoal in the correct proportions; but the various processes are both complicated and dangerous,[20] and at every stage, from incorporating the ingredients to pressing and 'corning' or granulating the powder, and finally packing it, extreme care was necessary. Even in the early days of the Sedgwick plant, protective leather skins and gloves were worn by the workers,[21] and special nail-less boots were used in order to avoid accidental sparks. At the Blackbeck works, which had an unfortunate reputation for explosions, the management provided both overshoes and protective clothing which lacked pockets so that no unnecessary metals should be taken into the plant. Horses were used to haul carts within the works but they were always shod with copper rather than with the usual iron horse-shoes, and in the late nineteenth century, when horse-operated light tramways connected both the Lowwood and Blackbeck works to the then recently opened Ulverston to Lakeside Railway, it is believed that the tramway lines close to the works were of non-ferrous metal.[22] Even the purchase of stone rollers used to incorporate and press the powder required careful selection, for stone containing iron pyrites could produce sparks; the Lowwood Company, after much deliberation, chose rollers made of the so-called Dent marble and limestone from Birkrigg, near Ulverston.[23]

In spite of these precautionary measures explosions were not uncommon; in January 1863 six workers at Lowwood lost their lives in an explosion which was heard at Kendal some thirteen miles away; five years later five more men died in a blast in the corning house, and in 1887 and 1903 there were fatalities. At Blackbeck between 1867 and 1911 there was a total of eight accidents in which twenty-seven people died,[24] and such figures help to emphasize dramatically the dangers of this hazardous industry. Yet, certainly at the beginning of the nineteenth century, wages were not noticeably higher than in other local industries; in June 1808 the Lowwood wage books record that three 'workmen' received the following wages:

David Daw	3/6 per day
Sam Daw	3/- per day
Wm Taylor	2/- per day 'with an extra 1/6 if he works nights'.

The same document gives details of the wages paid to six 'gunpowder makers', Natty Bathrop, John Brockbank, John Harper, Jas. Pearce, John Murphy and Henry Tyson, who received between 2s. and 2s. 4d. per day.[25] At the same time, quarrymen working in equally arduous and dangerous conditions (*see* pages 151–63), could earn between 3s. and 5s. per day, and farm labourers were paid 1s. 6d. per day in winter and 2s. 6d. per day in summer.

By the second half of the nineteenth century the total labour force working in Lakeland gunpowder mills probably numbered about 500,[26] but following the First World War the demand for black powder decreased and mills began to close. In 1928–9 the Elterwater and Blackbeck plants ceased production, to be followed in 1934 by the Lowwood Company, and finally, in 1937, the liquidation of the Gatebeck mill closed another chapter in the history of Lakeland industries.

12 SLATE QUARRYING AND MINING

QUARRYING

One of the most traditional of all Lakeland industries is the winning of blue-grey and sea-green slate from remote quarries on the fellsides. Today, the yawning caverns reverberating to the noise of explosives, compressed air drills and diesel lorries are a far cry from the dripping, silent and abandoned quarries which pock-mark many valleys, yet both are part of the same industry which goes back many centuries. The Romans, with typical astuteness, quickly appreciated the advantage of roofing their granaries at Ambleside, Hardknott and elsewhere with local slate, and later, in the medieval period, when most Cumbrians were living in wattle and daub huts, several monasteries had slated roofs, but these were exceptions rather than the rule. By the seventeenth century, however, there is more definite evidence of the development of slate quarrying as an industry, and craftsmen describing themselves as 'slaters' begin to appear in Lakeland parish registers; for example, in 1689 Christopher, son of Christopher Nicholson, a slater of Monk Coniston, was christened at Coniston, and in 1693 Richard, son of William Rowenson, a slater, was likewise baptized. During the second half of the eighteenth century and into the nineteenth, however, the industry flourished as never before; the demand for slate came from the growing industrial towns of the North and the Midlands; the response came in the form of an expansion of the industry and the opening of hundreds of quarries. large and small, wherever good slate could be worked.

Although there is reason to believe that the famous Honister Quarries were being worked in 1643,[1] output cannot have been great, but by 1753 they were certainly in full operation.[2] The transport of slate from these isolated quarries presented difficulties; pack-horses carried loads of slate by way of the track known as Moses' sled-gate from Honister Crag, along the side of Great Gable to Wasdale Head and on to Drigg on the coast where it was finally loaded onto coasting vessels, yet in spite of the incredible journey, it was still considered profitable to ship slate in this way. In the Coniston area, similar developments were taking place; by 1774 Thomas West was able to record that 'the most considerable slate quarries in the kingdom' were in the Coniston fells,[3] and six years later the artist and writer William Green saw the quarry near the summit of Coniston Old Man 'in high working condition'.[4] Many of these quarries at Coniston were worked by the firm of William Rigge and Son, of Hawkshead, who exported some 1,100 tons a year at the end of the eighteenth century, but here the difficulties of carrying slates were not as great as those encountered at Honister, for the slate was shipped the length of Coniston Water from Kirkby Quay, Waterhead, to Nibthwaite, where it was off-loaded for Greenodd and Ulverston before it was finally shipped to Bristol, Chepstow, London and, during the early nineteenth century, to the West Indies. Similarly, the availability of water transport influenced the development of the great Kirkby slate quarries overlooking the Duddon estuary, and by the end of the eighteenth century small ports such as Angerton and Kirkby Pool were busily engaged in the slate shipping trade.

Elsewhere, other quarries were being worked; in the 1770s George Bownass, the Coniston blacksmith, was supplying and repairing quarrying tools for a variety of customers, and his account books[5] indicate that there was a Company of Slategetters working quarries at Pennyrigg and Hodge in the Tilberthwaite valley, at Blind Tarn and at Goatswater, while other individuals were getting slate from Stang End and Bessy Crag in Little Langdale, from Ashgill near Torver, and from various small quarries on the flanks of the Old Man. At the same time, over in Troutbeck, a number of small quarries had been opened at Troutbeck Park; these were managed on behalf of the owner, R. A. Day of Maidenhead, by William Birkett of Troutbeck, and his careful accounts throw some light on the industry at this time. Traditionally, Lakeland quarries produced four kinds of slate classified according to fineness: 'London', 'Country', 'Tom', the coarsest, and 'Peg', used for cladding walls. At the Troutbeck Park quarries 'London' slate, measuring not less than '10 inches in length under the pin hole nor less than 6 inches in breadth',[6] clearly formed the bulk of the output as the following note shows:[7]

An Acc[t] of what slate weighed since the 28th Sept. 1754 until the 12th July 1755 at the slate quarries at Troutbeck Park.

London slate.	897 Lds		Cash paid for getting.	£97. 13. 4.
Country ditto.	603		do.	£03. 07. 4.
Tom ditto.	86			

[One load of slate = 16 stones weight.]

The slate was taken from Troutbeck by road to the shores of Windermere, where it was shipped down the lake to Waterfoot, then carted overland to Haverthwaite and finally taken by lighter down the River Leven to Ulverston and Greenodd, where ships such as the *Hope*, the *Clifford*, and the *Kendal Merchant* called regularly to carry it to distant markets.

As the momentum of the Industrial Revolution gathered force, and the rash of redbrick building spread, so too the demand for slate increased; by 1792 'London' slates brought between £3 and £4 per thousand, while even the poorer quality 'Toms' sold at £1 10s. to £2 per thousand. Yet the fortunes of the slate industry were not entirely set fair, for there were minor fluctuations; in 1794 the government of the day, in an attempt to increase revenue to continue the French war, imposed a tax of ten shillings on each ton of slate conveyed by sea. The outcome was a slump in trade and the redundancy of many quarry workers.[8] In 1800 quarrymen from Coniston, Tilberthwaite, Torver and Kirkby marched on Ulverston, stormed the flour mills and warehouses, and distributed provisions amongst their families—an early example of Self-help, though Samuel Smiles would hardly have approved! A couple of years later a similar march was organized, though this time the 'rioters' were hotly pursued by the local militia; however, the quarrymen withdrew to the maze of galleries and tunnels of their quarries where inaccessibility was more than a match for the soldiers, and so the uprising petered out.[9] By 1805 the industry had recovered, for in that year Dr William Close claimed that some 25,000 tons of slate were annually produced from the Coniston and Kirkby quarries alone[10] and most of this was exported down the Ulverston Canal, which had been opened to traffic in 1796.

Slate output increased during the nineteenth century, but lists of tonnage exported or profits made can scarcely illuminate the dangers and difficulties which quarrymen accepted as part of their existence. One of the most hazardous of all operations was the transport of the slate from

112. *Coppice woodland in the Furness Fells.*

113. *The floor of an abandoned pitstead in Woundale, Troutbeck, Westmorland.*

114. *Coppice wood being loaded on to a cart.*

115. *Stacking the coppice timber on the pitstead floor.*

116. *Timber stacked around a central stake (motty peg) on a pitstead floor.*

117. *The stack has been turfed, the motty peg withdrawn, and here a collier begins the coaling process by placing glowing charcoal in the centre of the stack.*

118. *Coaling in process. Note the movable screens which shelter the pitstead from the prevailing winds.*

119. *'Saying' with water to end the coaling.*

120. *A final raking to cool the charcoal.*

121. *Clearing the floor of the pitstead and filling the sacks. Note the wooden rakes and the swill baskets.*

122. *Top: A group of 'colliers' and their huts about 1905. These wigwam-like structures were made of poles and withies and 'thacked' with sods.*

123. *Above: Charcoal burners at Kirkby Park about 1905. The large sacks of charcoal are piled high on the cart and in the foreground is a heap of 'bran ends', the unburnt remains of the coaling process.*

124. *Right: Bark peeling was usually carried out between early May and early July. The 'pole' was ringed and then the bark 'oozed' off in one piece ready for storage.*

125. *Finishing bobbins at the Stott Park Bobbin Mill near Finsthwaite, 1971.*

126. *Hoop-making at Hawkshead Field, c. 1910. Here the hooper is splitting a 'pole' with a wedge. Note the coiling frame to the left of the door.*

127. *Trimming 'smarts' for hoop-making. Many of these hoops were used in the manufacture of barrels for the local gunpowder industry, but thousands were sent to Liverpool and Manchester.*

128, 129.
The late Mr Charlie Airey of
Storth, Westmorland, splitting oak
timber into 'smarts' (left), and
shaving smarts with a two-handled
knife.

130. A swiller's tools.

131. Using a 'set-horse' to make an
ash 'bool', the rim of a swill basket.

132. *Mr Hartley repairing a swill in his workshop at Eskdale Green, Cumberland.*

133. *Mr Myles Newton, swiller, of Lowick Green, High Furness, astride his 'horse'.*

134. *A Furness swiller and a partly finished basket. The photograph clearly shows the short cross 'spells' of approximately the same width, and the longer, finer 'taws'.*

135. The Black Hog of Strickland-gate, Kendal, one of the last reminders of the brush-making industry which once flourished in the town.

136, 137. A rural woollen industry. In the sixteenth and seventeenth centuries the Lake District was famous for its coarse woollen cloths, but by the end of the eighteenth century this reputation had declined. In one or two areas, however, spinning and weaving continued; the Moore family of south-west Cumberland continued to work their blanket mill until early this century.

the quarry face to the dressing sheds, for this usually involved a very steep descent. James Clarke, observing the process near Hartsop, in 1787, apparently minimizes the dangers involved but ruefully has to admit that he himself could not complete the manœuvre:

'The slate is laid upon a barrow, which is called a "trail-barrow"; it has two inclining handles or stangs between which the man is placed, going, like a horse, before the weight, and has nothing more to do than keep it in the tract, and prevent it from running too fast. Those who are dextrous will not sometimes set a foot on the ground for ten or twelve yards together; but the barrow will often run away with an unskilful person, which was my case when I made an attempt.'[11]

Seventy-five years later Mrs E. Lynn Linton saw the same method employed on Honister Crag and recorded that a quarryman would make seven or eight such journeys, bringing down a quarter of a ton each time, the descent taking no more than a few minutes but the return trip with the empty sleds occupying half an hour's laborious climbing. Little wonder, then, that she noticed that the men looked 'wan and worn, as if they were all consumptive or had heart disease'.[12] Although such feats appear staggering by modern standards, the Honister quarrymen of the 1860s remembered with awe the legendary deeds of their folk heroes such as Samuel Trimmer, who once made fifteen journeys in a day for a bottle of rum and a small percentage of the slate he had sledged, and Joseph Clarke of Stonethwaite, who travelled seventeen miles in seventeen journeys and transported almost five tons of slate in one day. The sledging of slate at Honister (plate 140) ended in 1881, for in that year a gravitational railway made this hazardous operation unnecessary.

Working conditions at the quarry face were both primitive and dangerous; most of the Lake District quarries were open to the sky and the workers were consequently exposed to the elements, but at Honister the workings were all underground, and these 'closehead' quarries had to be lit by flickering tallow candles even as late as the twentieth century. Accidents were common, and in the first half of the nineteenth century William Green was prompted to suggest that '. . . slate rocks, like the balls from cannon, have prostrated many a brave fellow. . . . A club of all the northern slaters would prove greatly beneficial to widows and orphans, and a donation of even one farthing in the pound, from proprietors or renters, on the annual value of houses covered with slate from the English Lakes, would produce a sum, the interest of which would be very considerable'.[13] Quarry workers, like the dry-stone wallers, often lived during the week in small huts on the fellside, going home only from Saturday night until the following Monday morning. Moreover, wages were low; in the 1830s the best workmen received 3s. 6d. per day or £1 1s. for a six-day week, and for this they were expected to quarry more than a ton of slate each day. Youngsters started at the quarry face for 6d. per day, but apprentice slate dressers were paid more, usually between 1s. and 1s. 6d., and this was increased to 2s. 6d. before their apprenticeship was completed and they were 'out of their time'.[14] Even by the late nineteenth century wages were still low and the working week long. In 1878 the late Mr Peter Hodgson of Little Langdale began work as a slate weigher in the Lingmoor quarries; he was then aged fifteen and the hours were from 7 a.m. to 5.30 p.m. and until 4 p.m. on Saturdays, for which he received 1s. 2d. per day. When, at the age of sixteen, he transferred to Chapel Stile to learn the art of riving and dressing, his wage increased each year by 3d. per day so that in 1883 he was earning 3s. 4d. a day.

The very nature of slate quarrying amid the fells has always meant that transport presented problems. In the eighteenth century water transport was sought wherever possible, but in the

BLUE SLATE

This is to acquaint the PUBLIC,

THAT JAMES CLARKE, has taken A SLATE QUARRY, in PATTERDALE; any Gentleman wanting Blue Slate may depend on the beſt Uſage, by

Their humble Servant,

JAMES CLARKE.

Attendance at Mr Idles, the Griffin, in Penrith, on Tueſdays and at John Marſhalls, Ullswater Foot, all other Days.

PENRITH: Printed by JOHN BELL.

Fig. 33 A handbill of 1773.

nineteenth century railways enabled more slate to be produced from the Kirkby and Coniston areas. In 1846 the Furness Railway Company connected the great Burlington Quarries with the small agricultural hamlet of Barrow on the coast, and the following year the opening of the Windermere–Kendal line meant that slate from Great Langdale could be carted to the railhead by horse and cart, and in 1859 Coniston acquired its line. But none of these improvements affected the remote and isolated Honister quarries; however, in one respect, Honister was able to score over its rivals. The offices of the Buttermere Green Slate Company, which worked Honister Crag, were in Keswick, some six miles away, so carrier pigeons were used to convey urgent messages to the quarries. It was not practicable to use such methods in the Coniston and Langdale areas because of the large numbers of hawks and falcons which infested the vicinity![15] Even as late as 1914, quarrymen who spent their working week at Honister communicated with their wives in Borrowdale by means of carrier pigeons; a message took anything between ten minutes (the record) and a day, according to wind and weather[16]—and perhaps the inclination of the pigeon!

Perhaps because of the nature of their work, quarrymen tended to 'live hard and drink hard', and were sometimes criticized for this; Clarke, writing of Langdale in 1787, notes that the valley was 'as poor as any in these parts, except for the slate quarries and slaters . . . [who] . . . debauch the natives so far that even the poor Curate is obliged to sell ale to support himself and his family'.[17] Wages increased during the twentieth century but the work still remained dangerous and arduous; before 1910 drilling into the rock face preparatory to blasting was done by hand by men known as 'rock-hands', but in that year compressed-air drills were first

used and the old laborious method became obsolete. Even fifty years ago the large blocks
which resulted from a blast had to be reduced to smaller blocks, or 'clogs', by a hammer, a
chisel and the knack of working the slate along the natural grain (plate 143). By the 1930s,
however, diamond-tipped saws had been introduced and these are able to cope with enormous
blocks of slate, cutting through the green rock with the ease of a warm knife through butter.
But two processes have resisted the passage of time and the progress of automation: riving
and dressing, for here lie true skill and craftsmanship. Using a riving hammer and a chisel, the
'river' reduces a clog into a series of smooth slabs about $2\frac{1}{2}$ inches thick, from which about
eight slates about $\frac{1}{4}$ inch thick can be riven (plate 141). These are then passed to the dresser
(plate 144), who uses two tools, a 'brake' and a 'whittle'; the brake is a metal blade about three
or four feet long, rather like an old-fashioned foot scraper, while the whittle is a long, knife-like
implement with a wooden handle. Seated on the ground, with the brake between his outstretched
legs and holding the 'riving' in his left hand across the brake, the dresser deftly trims the edges
of the slate. Finally, the slates are graded according to quality and size; the old nomenclature
has given way to the less colourful 'bests', 'seconds', and 'thirds', but the quality and craftsmanship have remained the same. Although today much of the output from Lakeland quarries is
cladding slate, which does not require the same degree of dressing as roofing slate, it is still
possible to see the 'river' and the 'dresser' working side by side as they have done for centuries.

MINING

Although not a craft industry, mining must be mentioned here as another of the traditional
occupations which were once important but have declined within the present century. The
activities of the German miners of the Company of the Mines Royal operating in the Keswick
area in the sixteenth and seventeenth centuries have been well documented elsewhere;[18] although
the mines were closed by Parliamentary troops during the Civil War, they were later reopened
and continued to be worked intermittently until the nineteenth century, though they never
again reached the importance achieved during the period of the Mines Royal. One mine which
did flourish in the eighteenth and early nineteenth centuries was the Borrowdale Black Lead
mine at Seathwaite; first mentioned in documents in 1555, the black lead, 'wad' or plumbago
was much sought after in the eighteenth century, largely because of its versatility. Used in the
casting of 'bomb shells, round-shot, and cannon balls', it was also employed in the glazing of
pottery, the fixing of blue dyes, the marking of sheep, and in medicine (*see* page 79), as well as
in the manufacture of pencils at Keswick. And even today there must be many women who
remember the drudgery of 'black-leading' cast-iron fire grates. Clearly such a useful mineral
commanded a high price on the open market, so much so that in the middle of the eighteenth
century an Act of Parliament made 'unlawful entering of any mine or wad hole of wad or black
cawke, commonly called black lead, or unlawfully taking or carrying away any wad etc., there-
from, as also the buying or receiving the same, knowing it to be unlawfully taken . . .'[19] a felony,
and the culprit liable to imprisonment with hard labour. But in spite of such dire penalties and
the presence of armed guards at the mine entrance to search miners as they left work, smuggling
increased with the price of graphite. On one occasion armed men raided the offices of the mine
superintendent but—in true wild-west style—they were driven off with musket fire! During the
early part of the nineteenth century several 'pipes' or deposits of graphite were discovered, but
by the 1830s the output declined: in 1836 it was reported that twelve men had been regularly
employed in the mines for fifteen months 'without so much as falling in with even a single sop of

the valuable material',[20] and in that year the workings were closed, though they were reopened for a short period two years later.

The Coniston copper mines have also had a somewhat chequered history; at the end of the sixteenth century and the beginning of the seventeenth, German miners from Keswick began actively to exploit the copper ore on the flanks of the Old Man, the ore being carried on the backs of pack-horses to Keswick for smelting, but after the Civil War mining ceased for a time. Little is known of copper-mining activity in the eighteenth century but by 1802 production had been resumed once again, and by mid century some 400 men were employed and an average of 250 tons of ore per month was being won. During the second half of the century the importance of the Coniston copper mines declined in the face of competition from foreign imported ore, and in spite of a short-lived resurgence during the First World War, the mines were closed soon after.[21] The Greenside lead mine, on the other hand, was one of the few mines to be worked almost continuously from its opening some time in the sixteenth century to 1962 when it was closed, although it was not extensively worked until 1825. Since the closure of the Greenside mine there has been little mining development within the Lakeland fells; although the tungsten ore mine in Mosedale at the foot of Carrock Fell was reopened in 1971, it is currently disused.

Like quarrymen, miners were sometimes shunned by their neighbours. Indeed, James Clarke went so far as to blame miners for the decay of rural society; writing of Patterdale at the end of the eighteenth century he noted that following the introduction of a number of lead miners, '. . . vice and poverty sit pictured in almost every countenance, and the rustic fireside is no longer the abode of peace and contentment. . . . These fellows, who are in general the most abandoned, wicked, and profligate part of mankind no sooner settled here than they immediately began to propagate their vices among the innocent unsuspecting inhabitants. The farmer listened greedily to stories of places he had never seen . . . his daughters, allured by promises, were seduced; even those who withstood promises, and were actually married, were, upon the stopping of the mines, deserted by their faithless husbands and left to all the horrors of poverty and shame.'[22] But such a scurrilous and exaggerated accusation was countered by A. C. Gibson, at one time medical officer in the Coniston copper mines, for he argued that 'they have, like the rest of us, their share of the failings of human nature, and may enjoy themselves rather freely at the month's end when they receive their pay, but open or obtrusive profligacy is very rare amongst them, whilst their ignorance is certainly not equal to that of the pastoral and agricultural population around them.'[23]

Working conditions in Lakeland mines were harsh and dangerous; in the days before gunpowder, 'levels' were cut by hand using picks, hammers and 'stope and feather' wedges, but the ancient method of kindling a fire and then dousing it with a mixture of vinegar and water to shatter the rock was also used in the Coniston copper mines.[24] Later, when blasting with gunpowder became common, the boring of holes to receive the charge became a skilled job, the tools used being a hammer and a 'jumper', a steel rod which was turned slightly after every blow. A. C. Gibson has left one of the few eye-witness descriptions of blasting at Coniston:

'The attitudes of the men as they ply their melancholy toil are rather picturesque, holding up and turning the jumper with the left hand, whilst they keep driving it into the flinty rock with a hammer held in the right. Having bored the holes to a sufficient depth—say about eighteen or twenty inches—they clear out the borings or fragments, proceed to charge with gunpowder and then . . . they light the match and retire to await the results of the "shots". . . . After the explosion the men return to their working . . . breaking up the larger fragments, and carefully beating down any loose pieces lodged about the sides, select the most suitable "lofe" and recommence boring. Three of these borings and blasts are considered a fair day's work in this hard rock, the men working in three shifts of eight hours each.'[25]

Blasting, of course, was one of the most dangerous of tasks, particularly before the introduction of the safety fuse in the 1870s, for the powder was fired by straws filled with fine gunpowder and ignited by touch-paper. Miners were responsible for providing their own straws and usually oat straw was preferred because of the length from the ground to the first joint. Bundles of these carefully prepared straws—each batch tested for running speed—were a common feature in miners' kitchens in the nineteenth century.[26] But in addition there were other hazards to be accepted as part of the miner's lot; ventilation of shafts was primitive, although in some mines falling water created a current of air which was conveyed to the workings by wooden tubes.[27] Tallow candles set in balls of soft clay were commonly used for lighting until the First World War, when acetylene lamps were introduced; in draughty workings a glassless lanthorn known as a 'bug' was used, and in confined spaces miners attached tallow candles to the 'nebs' of their hats. Protective clothing was virtually unknown until the twentieth century, though nineteenth-century miners wore thick woollen trousers and long leather jackets. Clogs with iron caulkers were preferred, for boots were difficult to dry and, moreover, were more expensive. The clogs were often lined with soft straw for warmth, and it is said that experienced miners wore footless stockings so that if they got their feet wet they merely emptied out the wet straw and replaced it with dry which was always carried for this purpose.

Although the wages paid to miners were somewhat higher than those of agricultural workers, the arduous conditions and heavy manual work endured by these men brought premature old age and sometimes appalling injuries for which the extra financial reward was no compensation. Perhaps because of the very nature of the work, these mining communities in the fells remained separate, ostracized almost by their agricultural neighbours; but all this is a thing of the past, for mining has declined to the point of insignificance. Those miners who worked the tungsten mines of the 1970s did not suffer the hardships of the past, for compressed air drills have replaced picks and 'stope and feathers', electric lights have displaced the guttering, acrid, tallow candles, and the remote detonation of dynamite has ousted the powder-filled straw and touch-paper.

13 COCKFIGHTING AND FOXHUNTING

The popularity of the nineteenth-century John Peel ballad might well lead one to believe that foxhunting was the most popular Cumbrian sport, but this was certainly not so. Although foxhunting had many adherents in the Lake counties the most popular blood-sport was cock-fighting, an ancient and traditional northern pastime. Although gamecock fighting was once widespread throughout England—both Henry VIII and James I were passionately fond of the sport—it seems to have taken root firmly in our northern counties. No sport was followed with more zeal and enthusiasm, and until it was made illegal in 1835 'cocking' attracted a wide range of supporters from the squire, schoolteacher and statesman to the hired hand and the village school lads. Indeed, in the eighteenth and early nineteenth centuries 'cocking' gained some of the same mystique which surrounded rugby football in the later nineteenth and twentieth centuries—it was believed that it developed character by providing examples of pluck and 'gameness', and in the eighteenth century most of the public schoolboys were initiated into the mysteries of cockfighting. It was even suggested that 'masters and pupils were often more conversant with the points, qualities and colours of cocks than with grammar and arithmetic'.[1]

The link between the schools and cockfighting is both ancient and interesting; it seems that in London schools during the reign of Henry II it was customary for Shrovetide cockfights to be held under the supervision of the master,[2] and a similar tradition remained in Cumbria for centuries. Moreover, the often meagre salary of the schoolmaster was supplemented by the 'cockpenny' which each pupil provided every Shrovetide. James Clarke, writing in 1787, claimed that in many cases half of the master's salary depended on the cockpennies[3] but the value of these cockpennies appears to have varied. Sir Daniel Fleming annually records in his account book the donations of 'cockpennies' to his sons then at school; when the boys attended the Rydal village school they generally received 6d. each as a 'cockpenny':

1665. Feb. 6. Given unto Will, Harry and Daniel, for their cockpenny.   £00. 01. 06.

But the following year the boys received a bonus:

1666. Feb. 26. Given to the three boyes for cock-pennyes 2s. and to bett, 6d.   £00. 02. 06.

When the children moved to school in Kendal the 'cockpenny' was increased; in 1675 Henry was elected as a captain and Sir Daniel, with obvious parental pride, records:

1675. Jan. 30 Sent by John Banckes to my son William 10s., Henry—being a captaine—a broad 20s. piece in gold and Daniel 5s. for cock-pennyes to the master.[4]

At Cartmel the cockpenny paid to the village schoolmaster varied from one shilling to a guinea, dependent on the wealth of the parents.[5]

Exactly what the cockpennies were intended to provide is uncertain; there is some evidence to suggest that the schoolmaster provided a prize to be fought for—at Wreay and at Bromfield in Cumberland the prize was a silver bell, but elsewhere it seems that the schoolmaster provided cocks to fight the birds brought by his pupils. The 'cocking' on these occasions must have been rather festive affairs: Francis Nicholson has described the preparations at Wreay, near Carlisle:

'About three weeks previous to the eventful day, the boys assembled and selected as their captains two of their schoolfellows whose parents were willing to bear the expenses incurred in the forthcoming contest. After an early dinner on Shrove Tuesday the two captains, attended by their friends and schoolfellows, who were distinguished by blue and red ribbons, marched in procession from their respective homes to the village green, where each produced three cocks, and the bell was appended to the hat of the victor.'[6]

James Clarke remarks that the winner of such contests had 'great honours conferred upon him in the presence of all the neighbourhood, who never fail to assemble on these occasions', and adds: 'When these are the practices inculcated to early youth we need not wonder at that spirit which has so often displayed itself to the terror and destruction of all opposers'.[7] Clearly the cockpits of Cumbria corresponded to the playing fields of Eton.

But the schoolmasters were not the only pillars of the establishment to encourage this blood-thirsty sport, for the Church was often closely involved, and in many of the remote Lakeland dales clergymen actively engaged in 'cocking'. At Burgh-by-Sands and Bromfield the cockpits were located close to the church and at the latter cockfighting was carried on after service on Sundays;[8] at Penrith the cockpit was on the south side of the churchyard,[9] while at Heversham, Westmorland, Ulpha in Dunnerdale[10] and at Warton, north Lancashire, the cockpits were near to the churches and the ancient schools. At Urswick-in-Furness, during the last years of the eighteenth century, the vicar presided at the Shrove Tuesday cockfights, and according to John Bolton, the amateur geologist, he 'might be seen running round the ring, being then a strong and active man, but instead of preaching a sermon, or reciting passages of the Scripture to his unruly parishioners to keep them quiet, he used a more persuasive and irresistible argument —a nice little two-handled cudgel . . .'[11] There is a tradition, too, that a former Bishop of Carlisle had a cockpit at his home, Rose Castle, near Dalston,[12] so clearly the sport appealed to those of both elevated and lowly callings.*

Many hamlets and villages in the Lake District still have their cockpits, though most are overgrown and neglected; in Westmorland there are examples still at Heversham, Orton, Patterdale and Natland, south of Kendal,[13] in Furness at Oxenpark, and perhaps the best of all at Stainton, south-west of Ulverston (see fig. 34 and plate 146). From this we can gain an impression of a typical cockpit: a level area of the village green has been enclosed by a shallow circular ditch, leaving a circular platform about 17 feet in diameter on which the action took place. The upcast from the trench formed a circular enclosing bank on the outer edge of the arena giving a total diameter of 38 feet. Spectators stood on this outer bank but only the only the 'feeders' and 'setters' were allowed beyond the ditch. Not all cockpits were in the open; certainly after 1835, when the sport became illegal, cockfighting went on behind closed doors, often in barns or outbuildings, but even before that, some pits had been constructed indoors. That colourful Scot, John Wilson, while constructing his new house at Elleray on the shores of Windermere had turf laid under his dining-room floor so that he could enjoy a cockfight.[14] 'Closed pits', so called because they were held indoors and an entrance fee was charged, were

* This particular legend was scotched in 1909 by the Bishop's chaplain, who claimed that the so-called cockpit was nothing more sinister than a sunken water garden!

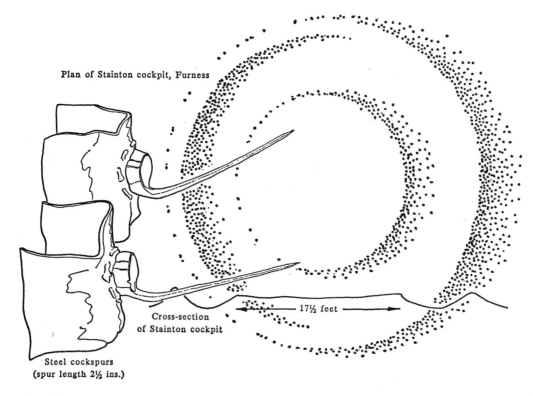

Plan of Stainton cockpit, Furness

Cross-section
of Stainton cockpit

17½ feet

Steel cockspurs
(spur length 2½ ins.)

Fig. 34.

not uncommon, and H. S. Cowper records such meetings at Skelwith Bridge, at Oxenpark, and in an upstairs room at the Brown Cow Inn, Hawkshead.[15]

Fighting cocks were, of course, bred solely for combat which, by all accounts, was a bloody sport. Most cocks ranged in weight from 3 lb. 14 oz. to 5 lb. 6 oz.; the birds were equipped with spurs—steel spikes, slightly curved, mounted on a leather band in which there was a hole which fitted over the bird's natural spur (*see* fig. 34). With such weaponry lashed to its legs the bird could inflict fearsome wounds on its opponent. Cowper argues[16] that with properly made spurs —'fair' spurs as they were called—the wounds inflicted were either fatal or clean and quick-healing, but such reasoning seems to be that of the apologist. Young cocks were known as 'stags', and 'stag mains' or fights were popular; the one-eyed veterans of several 'mains' became 'Blenkards' or 'blanchards'. The most popular form of competition seems to have been the Welch or Welsh 'main' in which a given number of pairs of cocks fought to the death. The remaining half were pitted a second time until only a quarter of the birds survived, and so on. Finally the remaining pair fought until the weaker succumbed (*see* plate 145). The Browne manuscripts from Townend, Troutbeck, Westmorland, throw some light on the sport; as early as 1661 records were kept of mains held in the village and plate 147 illustrates how the rules for a Welsh main were carefully drawn up during the eighteenth century.[17]

A champion cock was clearly a financial asset and much care and attention were devoted to such birds. The precise diet of cocks was often a matter for close secrecy, but generally the birds were fed on fresh, warm milk and 'cock-loaf', a rich bread made from flour, eggs, milk and sugar, and currants, together with the whites of eggs, parched barley, and sometimes sherry. Little wonder, then, that even today the term 'fed like a fighting cock' is in common use in the Lake Counties for anyone in receipt of gastronomic delicacies! The following recipe for cock-feeding was used about 1865—long after cockfighting had been declared illegal—by Miles Birkett[18] of the Blackbeck Gunpowder works near Bouth:

2 oz. cream of Tartar   ⎫
2 oz. candied lemon   ⎬   Boil in 3 pints of water. When cool pour into a Bottle.
1 juice of lemon.   ⎭

Cock loaf:
Wheaten bread without crusts crumbled up, mixed with 3 eggs according to quantity. ½ [lb.?] mutton without fat. 1 glass of port wine all mixed up into a paste ... after a meal of that stuff with two teasponsfull [from the bottle?] With the cock-bread when broken up.

Between times feed with Barley pratched [*sic*] in oven till very dry and beard dries off.

Champion stuff of all the world for feeding.

Many big cockfights often accompanied race meetings, but county mains were attractions in themselves. At Ulverston the annual three days' cockfighting extravaganza was held on a raised pit in the town's Assembly Rooms and drew a large number of spectators. The last of these mains was held in 1828 when it was announced that 'a grand main of cocks will be fought at Ulverston on the 29th, 30th and 31st of May between the gentlemen of Lancashire and Cumberland. William Woodcock feeder for Lancashire and Addison for Cumberland. A pair of cocks to be in the pit each day at ten o'clock.'

There can be no doubt that nearly every village within the Lake District had its own open mains, and it is estimated that within a ten-mile radius of Ulverston thousands of cocks were slaughtered annually. Yet there were voices raised in protest against this ritual killing. William Fleming, a Furness diarist, made the following entries in 1813:[19]

'Thursday, March 11. This Morning the annual Assembly of Blacklegs and Blackguards, Gamesters and Pickpockets commenced at Ulverston with brutal Pleasure to observe the Courage and Ferocity of a few poor Cocks. The Main between the Cumberland and Lancashire Men which commenced this Day was much in the Favour of Lancashire, [and] was attended by many who paid 6*s.* for Admittance into the Pit. Some Men from Liverpool, Newcastle, Carlisle and other Places at a Distance attended, and there is little Doubt they would be amply recompensed for taking so long Journeys at this Season of the Year and for so laudable a Purpose as Cardplaying and Cockfighting, quarrelling, Drinking, swearing, lying and cheating, injuring their Health and in all Probability losing their Money.'

And shortly after, as if to justify his convictions concerning the debauchery of cockfighting, the same writer records:

'Sunday, March 14. John Ashburner, one of the Cockfighters, emerged from the Alehouse this Morning, stood at the Top of the Backlane where it joins Church-walk at Ulverston as the People were going to the Church, hallooed and waved his Hat, uttering many strange Exclamations and insulting many People, but without being noticed. However, just when the Clergyman had taken his Text and begun his Sermon the same Person entered the Church and smacking the small Door too violently he marched up the middle Aisle till opposite the Pulpit; there waving his Hat he interrupted the Preacher and began to harangue the Audience, but was soon disturbed by the Churchwardens and Dogwhipper and committed to the Black Hole.'

Poor John Ashburner! he was a somewhat unlucky character; in 1806 William Fleming recorded a 'Main of cocks' fought at Dalton between Ashburner and a gentleman called Addison, the stakes being 2 guineas per battle and 10 guineas the Main. Ashburner lost and Fleming prophesied: '. . . Ashburner will be a Beggar if he live 10 years from this Time, or his Intellects will be deranged.'

Though cockfighting, together with bull-baiting and badger-drawing, was made illegal in 1835, 'cocking', with its long-standing popularity and traditions, was difficult to kill and for many years mains were held in the remote dales and fells of Cumbria—indeed, there are those who maintain that the sport is still not dead.

H. S. Cowper records a delightful story which has a certain 'wild-west' flavour; after the abolition of 'cocking' the so-called 'gentlemen of the sod' of Hawkshead held their meetings at various spots on the northern boundary of the parish. As soon as the police were reported on their tracks they bagged the cocks and fled across the river Brathay to Westmorland, where the 'main' continued![20] However, although this barbarous pastime is no longer legal, cock-fighting has become a part of Lakeland folk lore celebrated in verse and song. The following is part of the cockfighting song 'The Charcoal Black and the Bonnie Grey';[21] this happens to be a version sung on Walney Island, but the ballad was popular throughout Cumbria, the place-names being altered to suit a particular location:

Come all you cockers far and near
I'll tell of a cockfight when and where,
At Tummerhill I've heard them say,
The North Scale lads had a bonnie grey.

Two dozen lads from Biggar came
To Tummerhill to see the game,
They brought along with them that day,
A black to match with the bonnie grey.

They all went in to take a cup,
The cocks they then were soon set up.
For ten guineas aside those cocks did play,
The charcoal black and the bonnie grey.

When these two cocks came on the sods,
The Biggar lads said 'Now, what odds?',
'No odds, no odds', the rest did say,
'But we'll hold your guineas and beat your grey.'

These cocks had struck but two or three blows,
When the Biggar lads saw they were like to lose,
Which made them all look wan and pale,
And wish they had fought for a gallon of ale.

Now the black cock he has lost their brass,
And the Biggar lads did swear and curse,
And wish they'd never come that day,
To Tummerhill to see the play.

FOXHUNTING

Cockfighting is undoubtedly a bloody business, and so too is foxhunting, but whatever one's views on blood-sports, it has to be acknowledged that foxhunting in the fells is as much a necessity as a sport. Moreover, the Cumbrian hunt bears little similarity to the colourful ritual of the Midlands; few huntsmen wear the 'pink' coat and black hat of the 'squirearchy', and to follow the hounds one requires not a glossy, well-groomed hunter but a stout pair of well-dubbined boots and a stick, for fell-packs are followed on foot. And the huntsmen are the local farmers, intent on killing a predator which has been seizing the newly dropped lambs, rather than the well-heeled sportsmen of the shires. Indeed, foxhunting in Cumbria, it has been said, has none of the 'unspeakable in pursuit of the uneatable' about it—it is altogether a more democratic and homely affair.[22]

However, organized foxhunting on any scale dates only from the middle of the eighteenth century. Before that, farmers and landowners had to kill foxes, ravens, eagles and other vermin however and whenever they could. The registers of several parish churches record the rewards given to those who successfully produced evidence of a 'kill'; at Hawkshead during the early eighteenth century the standard rate was five shillings for a fox, half a crown for a cub and four-pence for a raven if the head was produced,[23] and at Cartmel foxes' heads were impaled on the church gates.[24] At Crosthwaite the parish register records the following payments:

1752. To Wm. Ware for 1 old Eagle.	2s. 0d.
To Jas. Gateskel for 2 young Eagles.	2s. 0d.
1762. For 2 Eagles and 1 Fox.	4s. 4d.
For Eagles and Foxes.	£1. 6s. 6d.

At Keswick during the early eighteenth century cub-hunting was tried for a few seasons;[25] in 1723, for example, thirteen cubs and three old foxes were destroyed, but it was soon found that the killing of cubs was unremunerative, for at this time the Crosthwaite churchwardens were paying only one shilling for a cub but three shillings for a fox, consequently the entries which follow refer to full-grown animals.

During the seventeenth and eighteenth centuries it was common for young men who had killed foxes to take the carcases round to local dignitaries in the hope of a monetary reward—and usually they were not disappointed. The account books of Sir Daniel Fleming record several such rewards:[26]

1673. May 12. Item, to some Ambleside men who had killed a spotted fox.	£00. 00. 06.
1674. May 31. Given to some Ambleside fox-killers.	£00. 00. 06.

While foxes were certainly the most common type of predator, the eagle too was classed as vermin to be destroyed. Two hundred years ago eagles were common in the Borrowdale area and George Smith's curious map of the Black Lead Mines,[27] drawn in 1751, cryptically records in the Buttermere valley 'here eagles build' with the same awe that medieval cartographers used to indicate 'here be dragons'! And at the end of the eighteenth century, a long rope was kept in Borrowdale, by subscription, for the purpose of lowering men down the crags to destroy the eggs and the young. This 'eagle rope' was available for Buttermere, Ennerdale, Langdale and Eskdale, but was kept in Borrowdale where, it is believed, it was used every year.[28] Such birds of prey were very destructive; not only would they seize lambs and the occasional sheep dog, but they had the ability to drive sheep over a precipice in order to kill them. James Clarke, writing in 1787, mentions an eyrie high up on Wallow Crag, Haweswater, which when destroyed was found to contain thirty-five fish and seven lambs in addition to the remains of other prey.[29] The sheer size of these birds certainly commanded respect; Clarke claims that the largest he saw had a wing span of six feet eight inches, and goes on to record how he once tried to shoot one:

'. . . it flew about 90 or 100 [yards], when I got near it and fired at him again, and so a third time, but did not kill it; I had shot No. 4, but durst not attempt it again, for while I was loading my gun the fourth time, it came within six or seven yards of me, so fierce as if to begin an attack, so I left it.'[30]

Not only was Clarke a poor shot, he also clearly believed that discretion was the better part of valour!

By the mid nineteenth century eagles had ceased to be common, and *The Field* sporting journal began to record sightings in the 1860s, an interesting indication of the decline in numbers. After many years' absence from the Lake District hills, the eagles have returned to nest once more, although the ornithological fraternity have gone to great lengths to ensure that the eyries are kept secret—a far cry from the days of the Borrowdale 'eagle rope' and nest raiding.

Although, as we have seen, eagles could be destructive, in terms of impact and scale the fox had no equal. The trapping of foxes was once common: vicious steel-jawed spring traps were used, but a fascinating and perhaps older 'mechanism', the so-called goose bield, was sometimes employed. This curious and ingenious device was basically a beehive hut made of dry-stone walling, with the walls overhanging on the inside, the only opening being the hole in the top (fig. 35). The setting of the trap was relatively simple—a plank with a goose or chicken dangling from the end like the clapper inside a bell was carefully balanced on the rim of the bield; the fox then literally walked the plank towards the bait until his weight overbalanced the plank and tipped him into his dry-stone prison. Because of the overhanging walls and the skilful way in which every foothold on the inside wall was carefully filled with small stones, escape was difficult. Thomas Hay has pointed out a good example of a goose bield on Great Borne, Ennerdale, at a height of about 1,300 feet,[31] but there is an even better one on the crags overlooking Levers Water on the Coniston Old Man range at a height of approximately 1,700 feet (plate 148). I am particularly grateful to the late Mr R. G. Plint of Kendal for drawing my attention to this bield.[32] Here the walls are still standing to a height of about five feet, and although much of the corbelling has fallen in, there is still an overhang of fifteen inches. The whole structure is roughly circular, measuring between ten and twelve feet in diameter. Such fox traps can never have been very common, but there must be several undiscovered examples still hidden away amongst the crags and screes of the fells.

But to most people foxhunting in the Lake District means only one thing—the John Peel saga, the legend which has become not only part of Lakeland folk lore, but part of our national folk lore. The tales about John Peel are legion, some of them no doubt true, others apocryphal, but for all that 'D'y ken John Peel?' is sung wherever the English language is spoken, there are some remarkable discrepancies. Peel was born at Caldbeck, amid the wild country 'back o' Skidda', in 1777—not in Troutbeck; moreover, his coat was not 'gay' as some versions have it,

CROSS SECTION OF A GOOSE BIELD

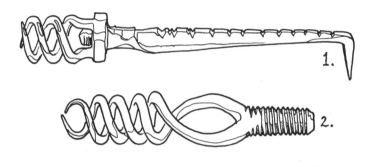

FOX SCREWS FROM GREAT LANGDALE

Fig. 35., 1. Length $4\frac{1}{2}$ inches. 2. Length $3\frac{4}{5}$ inches.

but grey—'hodden grey' in fact. By all accounts he was 'terrible lang in t' leg and lish, with a fine girt neb [nose] and grey eyes that could see for ivver', and most portraits show a rather sour-faced, square-jawed individual wearing a battered top-hat and holding his 'laal bugle horn'. However, although John Peel may be popularly regarded as the father of Lakeland foxhunting, detailed examination shows that organized packs were operating on the fells even before he was born.

One of the earliest reports of organized foxhunting comes from the parish of Watermillock in 1759; it appears that although the Bailiff of Gowbarrow received a rate of 'forty quarts of oats' from each farmer in return for which he kept hounds to suppress foxes, he had failed to do this. At a vestry meeting held in that year it was decided to 'hire men to destroy the Vermint',[33] consequently the members of the vestry 'procured the swiftest fox hounds from the mountainious enoersons [*sic*] of Keswick etc.' Men were also hired 'to attend with guns and every other engine' for the destruction of foxes, eagles, martens, wild cats and ravens. James Clarke was an eye-witness to the ensuing hunt held during Whitsun Week, 1759, and claims that 'the sum-total of vermin destroyed, were fifteen foxes, seven badgers, twelve wild cats and nine marterns (called here, by way of distinction, Clean Marts) besides a prodigious number of foulmarts, eagles, ravens, gleads, etc.'[34] A fine bag by any standard.

Anyone who has ever witnessed a Lakeland foxhunt will surely appreciate the difficulties which both hounds and men experience; in the Midlands it is usual to go in search of the fox in some covert about midday, but here in the dales, 'dragging' to locate the scent is an early morning preliminary to the hunt. Having once picked up the scent, the hounds will follow the fox over the most difficult and hostile terrain, though the result is not always a 'kill', for the wiles of the fox are both legendary and very real. Foxes can run with ease along the top of a dry stone wall, using their brushes for balance, so confusing the hounds; similarly they have been known to follow stream beds to conceal their tracks or run amongst sheep in order to mask their scent. And, of course, they can cover enormous distances; in March 1818 John Peel's hounds ran fifty miles in a day, and on another occasion they covered sixty miles, but one of the most strenuous runs occurred in the middle of the last century when the Blencathra pack followed a large dog fox from the slopes of Skiddaw through Portinscale, along the western shores of Derwentwater, up the Borrowdale valley and over Sty Head Pass where, under cover of darkness, it eventually escaped! The hounds were discovered the following morning in the Coniston area, having travelled, with deviations, about fifty miles over some of the roughest country in the Lake District.[35] If very hard pressed, the fox can always go to earth in a 'borran', a pile of loose boulders commonly found in areas of scree. If the hunt is unable to winkle him out by creating a din close by, then the terriers are put in the borran—but there is no guarantee who will be the victor in such an encounter! In the nineteenth century a vicious instrument known as a fox screw was used to extract foxes which had taken refuge in borrans; essentially, this consisted of an iron double corkscrew fixed to the end of a pole which was then inserted into the borran and screwed into the body of the fox or into its mouth if it happened to snap it.[36] The two examples illustrated in figure 35 both come from Great Langdale and are now preserved in the Barrow-in-Furness Museum. If the fox cannot find a borran he will sometimes take refuge on a 'bink' or narrow ledge on a crag-face; in this event he must be dislodged by stones from above or one of the hunt may be lowered on a rope in order to knock the animal off his perch. There is a much-told tale of one man who successfully removed a fox from a 'bink' and then was left dangling at the end of his rope as the rest of the hunt went off in hot pursuit![37] These methods, and the fox screw which is no longer used, may seem unsporting, but it must be remembered that the fox is the shepherd's natural enemy, and for him any method of destroying this predator is considered justifiable.

Foxhunting in Cumbria has been followed with something approaching fanaticism—it is said that most dalesmen love the hunt better than marriage! This is perhaps why it has its own folk heroes, its songs and its own legends. The foxes, and the hounds which hunted them, were of tough and hardy constitution, but so too were the huntsmen, and none more so than an eighteenth-century Kentmere farmer named Dixon. James Clarke relates how this man fell from Blea Water Crag when out hunting with a pack on the High Street range. Although he broke no bones he was severly bruised and completely scalped; however, such was his devotion and perseverance that before he fell down unconscious he was able to give these directions to the others about the fox: 'Lads, t' fox is gane out at t' hee end; lig t' dogs on and I'll come syun.'[38]

The story of John Peel and the man who wrote the words of the famous song, John Woodcock Graves, is too well known to bear repeating here: the song certainly made Peel the best-known huntsman in England for, as Graves is reported to have told Peel, 'you'll be sung when we're both run to earth', and such was the case. However, there have been other famous huntsmen. Joe Bowman, himself celebrated in song, was huntsman with the Ullswater hounds almost continuously from 1879 until 1924, and anecdotes told about him are almost as many as those told of John Peel. Tommy Dobson, a bobbin turner, founded the Eskdale and Ennerdale Farmers' Hunt in 1857 and served it until 1910; his tombstone in the tiny graveyard of St Catherine's chapel in Eskdale bears not only a carving of the huntsman's genial features but the head of a hound and a fox (plate 152). But even in the days before the formation of the recognized packs, huntsmen were still popular folk-heroes; the *Carlisle Journal* for 10th January 1829 recorded that

'. . . the shepherds and others resident at Crosthwaite, Watermillock, Patterdale and Martindale, presented a handsome silver cup to John Taylor Esq., of Baldhow, for his indefatigable exertions in destroying foxes by his excellent pack of hounds. In the course of the last two years these dogs have killed fifty-six foxes.'

The spirit and traditions of Peel, Bowman and Dobson live on in the present Lakeland packs, the best known of which are the Coniston, the Mellbreak, the Eskdale and Ennerdale, the Ullswater, the Lonsdale and the Blencathra. These packs are maintained by the subscriptions of local farmers, and for the summer months the hounds are fed and housed by these farmers, meeting together in kennels only during the hunting season. Foxhounds were not the only packs kept for hunting purposes; terriers were bred for foumart or polecat hunting and similarly packs of otterhounds were kennelled in some valleys. In other areas, particularly in the Barton region, wild cats were killed in considerable numbers; the Barton Parish Registers record the killing of forty-eight wild cats in Martindale alone between 1706 and 1755. The wild cat is now, or course, extinct within Lakeland. In Troutbeck, and no doubt in other dales too, hare coursing was a popular eighteenth-century pastime and harriers were kept for this purpose.[39] But it was the fox who merited most attention, and it was the foxhunters who were praised in the dozen or so rousing hunting songs which still enliven many a Cumbrian 'Merry Neet'.

Although in no sense to be regarded as hunting, bull-baiting must be mentioned here, since it certainly constituted a 'blood-sport'. This barbarous practice was carried on in several places in Cumbria until it was finally abolished, along with cockfighting and badger-baiting, in 1835. In Keswick market place bulls were fastened to a large iron ring fixed in a stone block and then baited with dogs until they were exhausted, after which they were killed. Such baitings often attracted large crowds of spectators, many of whom sat on the roofs of houses overlooking the market place in order to get a better view.[40] As well as providing a spectacle for the mob, it was argued that baiting the bull improved the quality of the beef, but one suspects that this was little more than an apology for a cruel and degenerate custom, the passing of which few will regret.

14 SPORTS, PASTIMES AND ENTERTAINMENTS

MERRY NEETS AND AULD WIVES' HAKES

Opportunities for social gatherings were not common in the remote Lakeland dales even in the late nineteenth century, so when the chance presented itself it was eagerly seized. 'Auld Wives' Hakes' were eagerly awaited as an occasion when the farmers' wives could get together over a cup of tea and generally catch up with local gossip. At Troutbeck the 'hake' was generally held on Old Christmas Eve at the Mortal Man Inn, but elsewhere it was often timed to coincide with events which involved the menfolk. As well as the annual festivities at Christmas, clipping time and harvest, when a 'kern supper' usually took place, there were other, though less regular, excuses for 'merry neets'. When a new house was built and the roof completed, a 'timber raising' could be expected, and all the neighbours were 'lated' to a supper and a 'carding do', or a card party in the newly completed house; similarly, when a farmer took on a new farm, a day would be set aside when friends and neighbours would come with horses and ploughs to give him a day's work or 'boon ploughing', and this would generally be followed by a tatie-pot supper. cards for the elderly folk, and dancing in the barn for the youngsters. The most popular card games in the nineteenth century were 'three card lant', whist, and the unsophisticated 'brag' and 'nap', and the prizes were fittingly a goose, a leg of mutton, or sometimes a whole sheep! But there were those who were content to spend a 'merry neet' listening to the music, watching the dancing, consuming ale possets and the aptly named 'humming grog', or merely having a 'crack' with the neighbours.

The dances performed at these merrymakings were usually a mixture of traditional and modern; the traditional country dances usually included the Cumberland Square Eight, the Long Eight, Ninepins Reel and the Circassian Circle, dances which in some respects resemble Scottish country dances, a point which did not escape the poet John Keats when he witnessed a dance at the Tun Inn at Ireby in 1818:

'. . . they kickit and jumpit with mettle extraordinary, and whiskit and friskit, and toe'd it and go'd it, twirled it and whirled it, and stamped it and sweated it, tattooing the floor like mad. The difference between our country dances and these Scottish figures is about the same as leisurely stirring a cup o' tea and beating up a batter pudding'.[1]

Yet, in spite of the obvious rustic quality of these country dances, It was considered an important social grace to be able to participate. The sons and daughters of yeomen farmers were therefore sent for dancing instruction to schools held in the Assembly Rooms in Ulverston, Ambleside, Keswick and elsewhere; very often the task must have smacked of silk purses and sows' ears, as this description of one such class held in Bowness in 1802 shows:

'We went up a flight of stone stairs to a large room where we were not a little amused by the essay of the lads and girls of Bowness—a more awkward squad can scarcely be imagined—and

138. *The stone-breaker in a Cumberland quarry,* c. *1895.*

139. *Circular saw at work on Lakeland greenslate.*

140. *Above: Sledging slate with a trail barrow, Honister. Slate is no longer transported in this hazardous manner.*

141. *Above right: Mr Rex Barrow riving a 'clog' of greenslate at the Tilberthwaite quarry of the Lakeland Greenslate Co.*

142. *A river's tools—a mell and a chisel.*

143. *Splitting slabs of greenslate by hand before the introduction of the circular diamond-tipped saw. Tilberthwaite quarries, c. 1880.*

144. *The slate dressing floor at Tilberthwaite, c. 1880. The man in the foreground is using a brake and whittle.*

April 4th. 1771.

Cocks enter'd to fight in the
Welshmain at Geo. Tyson's
in Troutbeck, for a Silver Watch
Valued at ———— £ 3 . 16 . 0
Landlord's Gift ———— 0 . 5 . 0
                    £ 4 . 1 . 0

The 8 loosing Cocks the 2d } X 0 . 12 . 0
time over to have each 1/6 }

The 4 loosing Cocks third } X 0 . 10 . 0
time over 2/6 each ———— }

The 2 . fourth time. 5. each X 0 . 10 . 0

The Last Loosing Cock X 0 . 10 . 0

The Wining Cock ———— X 1 . 19 . 0
                    £ 4 . 01 . 0

The Winner to Chuse Watch or Money

145. *Prize money for fighting cocks competing
in a Welsh main at Troutbeck, 1771.*

146. *The cockpit on the Green at Stainton-in-
Furness. The ditch and circular embankment can
be clearly seen in the foreground.*

50ls. worth of Malt.

The Property of Mr. JOHN THOMPSON, of Stainton, Maltman.

WILL BE FOUGHT FOR,

In WELCH MAINS, at the cover'd PIT, in PENRITH.

On Thurfday the 26th, and Friday the 27th, Days of APRIL, 1787.

IN Sixteens, Eights, & Fours, as they may fall in Weight. Cocks of all weights will be taken in, and one ounce & half allowed to Stags, and two ounce to Blenkards ; to Fight in Steel.

The Owner of each Cock to pay 18s. being the value of Half a Load of MALT, and to Fight Win and Draw; to fhew and weigh the Monday before fighting : Cocks brought in to feed the 17th of April.---The Money for each Day's Main to be paid before the Cocks are fet down. The Owner of each Cock admitted into the PIT GRATIS.

Feeders { Bownefs, at the Angel. / Thompfon, at the Duke's Head. / Brownrigg, at the Golden Fleece. } PENRITH.

❖❖❖❖❖❖❖❖❖ BELL, PRINT, PENRITH. ❖❖❖❖❖❖❖❖❖

147. *A Penrith cockfight poster, 1787.*

148. *A fine 'goose bield' overlooking Levers Water, Coniston. These ingenious fox traps were often baited with a dead goose, hence the name.*

149. *West Cumberland fox hounds on the packhorse bridge at Wasdale Head.*

150. *The hunter—and the hunted, a fine dog fox.*

151. *John Peel's Day celebrated in traditional style at the Oddfellows Arms, Caldbeck, Cumberland.*

152. *Tommy Dobson's gravestone at St Catherine's Chapel in Eskdale. The inscription is flanked by the heads of a fox and a hound, and below there are a whip, a hunting horn and a brush.*

153. *Sheepdog trials at Wasdale Head.*

154. *The start of the hound trail at Rydal 'dog day'.*

the rough and brawling voice of the Master promised but an ill omen for the graces and manners of his pupils. However, let me not undervalue praiseworthy and innocent endeavour in the Parent to educate the minds and assist the sympathy and graces of his little ones—and worthy of commendation.'[2]

Music for these merry neet dances was usually provided by a fiddle—most dales could boast at least one fiddler—and perhaps by a tin whistle, though these were sometimes augmented by a melodeon. In certain dales the music was provided by a most unconventional 'instrument'— a metal coffee pot which emitted a sound not unlike that of a piccolo. However, the lack of musical accompaniment was not always the major deterrent it would be today, for in south Cumberland, and no doubt in other areas, the winnowing machine was pressed into service to beat out the rhythm of the dances. The popularity of these dances remained throughout the early decades of this century, although their form and organization remained virtually unchanged since Keats's time; the Vicar of Patterdale, W. P. Morris, writing in 1903, conveys something of the warmth and spirit of the local 'hop':

'The floor is polished, made up-to-date and slippery with bits or scrapings of wax candles, and if the room gets very dusty by midnight, the M.C. or deputy produces a jug of water and profusely sprinkles the floor. The dancers go through the old-fashioned tripping of the light fantastic toe with great enthusiasm. If the atmosphere of the room gets very close, the young men at once take off their coats and "go" with gusto. To strangers it is a wonderful sight to see them swing round in the six reel, long eight, square eight, valse, varso vienna, schottische, polka etc.'[3]

Although village dances, socials and whist drives still continue, particularly during the winter months, they are but a pale shadow of the noisy, boisterous 'merry neets' which were once an important part of Cumbrian folk culture; although kept alive by dedicated folk groups, on the whole the fiddle and the tin whistle have been replaced by the amplified sounds of the electronic guitar, and merry neets have been superseded by the 'discos' and clubs of Keswick, Kendal and Cockermouth.

THE THEATRE

In spite of its remoteness from the centres of theatrical life there existed in Cumbria what we would now call 'folk theatre', and no doubt this tradition was encouraged by the age-old mummers' plays held at Christmas and Easter. In the Westmorland Troutbeck the tradition was particularly strong; in the seventeenth century a band of players from the village regularly performed at Christmas before Sir Daniel Fleming at Rydal Hall, and his account books[4] record such items as:

1661 Dec. 27	Given to Troutbeck players for acting here 'The Fair Maid of the West'	£00. 10. 00
1686 Dec. 28	Given to Troutbeck players, being little boyes	£00. 05. 00

The Troutbeck players usually performed 'play-jiggs', short dramas in verse, specially written for them by local 'rhymers'. Foremost among these was Thomas Hoggart, the village carpenter;* what he lacked in learning 'Ald' Hoggart made up for in enthusiasm and he turned out such epics as *The Siege of Troy* and *The Lascivious Queen*. The latter play was performed in the open

* Thomas Hoggart's nephew was William Hogarth, the satirical artist.

on St James's Day, 1693, on a special stage in a field near the church, but *The Siege of Troy* was a much more ambitious production involving the wooden horse, Hector dragged by the heels of Diomede, the flight of Aeneas and the burning of the city.[5] Clearly this untutored Cumbrian had the panache of a Hollywood film director! As well as writing 'play-jiggs', Thomas Hoggart was often asked to compose epitaphs, several of which are rather amusing. One of his less reverent efforts runs:

> '*Here lies a woman*
> *No man can deny it.*
> *She died in peace although she lived unquiet.*
> *Her husband prays if e'er this way you walk*
> *You would tread softly—if she wake she'll talk.*'

Even after Thomas Hoggart's death in 1709 his plays continued to be performed and the acting tradition continued; indeed, the Troutbeck company were confident enough to give a performance of *Hamlet* in the Jolly Dragoon Inn on 29th December 1786.[6] By this time, however, travelling companies were entertaining rustic audiences in barns and make-shift 'theatres' in various parts of the Lake District. Joseph Budworth visited one of these travelling theatres in Keswick in 1792 and has left us a lively description:

'In the evening we went to see the Merchant of Venice in an unroofed house. The sky was visible through niches of boards laid across the upper beams. The walls were decorated, or rather hid, with cast-off scenes, which shewed in many places a rough, unplastered wall. . . . Between the acts a boy, seated upon an old rush chair in one corner of the stage, struck up a scrape on a fiddle. . . . The house was as full as it could possibly cram, and my friend counted but thirty-six shillings' worth of spectators in the pit, at eighteen pence a head, including a young child that squealed a second to the Crowdero of the house. Perhaps, as the actors were so near the audience, it was frightened by Shylock's terrific look. Whilst I remained, not even the "Hush a be babby" of its mother had any effect.'[7]

Often these travelling companies performed in barns, bales of straw serving as seats for the patrons; J. Mawman, passing through Penrith in 1805, noted a barn with 'Theatre' inscribed in large letters over one door, 'stage' over another, and 'Entrance' over a third, where the manager sat anxiously awaiting an audience which did not materialize.[8] But in Penrith about this time it was common to hold theatrical performances in the Assembly Rooms of the George Inn.

Elsewhere, however, more permanent homes were found for touring companies. The first theatre to be built in Kendal was erected in 1758 in the north-east corner of the market place; this building, later destined to become the Working Men's Institute, still stands. In 1789 a larger theatre was opened in the Woolpack Yard which, after 1818, assumed the grandiose name of Theatre Royal; in 1824 the opening of a theatre in the Crown Inn Yard was announced and the public were assured that it '. . . will be found fitted up in the best style the limits of the place will admit'. Five years later the theatre behind the Shakespeare Inn opened its doors, but within five years opposition from the religious community in Kendal resulted in its conversion to a hay loft and warehouse, though even today something of its original function can be seen in its Georgian architecture. Ulverston, that 'pocket edition of the metropolis, mimicking its dissipation and copying its manners',[9] boasted three theatres, though one was a barn behind an inn. The Theatre Royal, which opened in 1796, became the focus of social life of this thriving north Lancashire market town and its boards were trodden by many well-known actors of the day, including J. P. Kemble, who was a great favourite with Ulverston audiences.[10] (See plates 164–9.)

The taste of theatre-going Cumbrians was, to say the least, catholic; in 1854 a Kendal audience watched scenes from such tear-jerkers as *The Outlaw of Sicily*, *A Murderer's Grove*, and *Richard III*, but a footnote to the playbill cheerfully announced that 'parties desirous of Dancing betwixt each part will be allowed if they choose'. 'Spectaculars' were great crowd-pullers; during the early nineteenth century 'The Real Phantasmagoria (from 28 Haymarket, London)' toured Lakeland theatres with hair-raising representations of 'Louis XVI which changes to a skeleton, Lord Nelson, Paswan Oglou, the Turkish Rebel, the Bleeding Nun from "The Monk", and a striking likeness of His Majesty etc., etc.'. But for those who feared that they might be shocked by such a programme, the playbill hastened to add that the audience 'may rely on the utmost decorum during the whole Performance'. The popular melodrama entitled *The Pilot or A Storm at Sea* flooded the stage with water to the delight of the audience and, no doubt, the consternation of the theatre management!

Characteristically these northern audiences demanded value for their money—and value they certainly got. An Ulverston audience on Christmas Eve, 1808, sat through a performance of *Macbeth*, a comic song entitled 'Country Joe or Down with Bonaparte', a recitation 'Britannia, a Vision', a hornpipe 'performed by Master Meadows', another comic song called 'A medley of Beggars', and finally a performance of a musical farce entitled *The Adopted Child*. Yet all was not sweetness and light, for occasionally there occurred incidents which we would now politely describe as 'audience participation'. In a submission, or printed public apology, dated 21st November 1806, one Richard Cousen, a mariner, of Bouth in High Furness, confesses that 'being in liquor' he

'. . . did on Thursday Evening the 20th November Instant, throw a certain Glass Bottle out of the Gallery of the Theatre at Ulverston, to the imminent Danger of the Audience and Performers for which offence I have been apprehended and ordered to be prosecuted but on account of my general good Character, at the Instance of Mr Butler, the Manager (whose pardon and that of the Public at large, I humbly solicit), I have been set at Liberty'.

It is often argued that television has killed live theatre in our provincial towns and this may well be so, but there are heartening signs of a revival of interest in live entertainment within the Lake District. The theatre at Rosehill in West Cumberland has established itself as a major cultural centre in the north-west, and more recently the exciting development of a 'Theatre in the Forest' at Grizedale, south of Hawkshead, presents a programme ranging from folk music to poetry evenings, while the Renaissance Theatre Trust, based in Ulverston, presents a lively programme in south Cumbria. And at Keswick the long tradition of travelling theatre is still maintained, for the Century Theatre has its mobile headquarters here and entertains residents and visitors alike, certainly with more support, and undoubtedly with more success, than the travelling company which Joseph Budworth patronized in 1792.

REGATTAS AND FAIRS

During the eighteenth century regattas were held on several of the larger Cumbrian lakes; one of the earliest of these was in August 1780 on Bassenthwaite Lake, when a large crowd lined the shores to see the 'entertainments'. The main 'spectacle' involved several horses which were towed out into the lake on rafts which were then allowed to sink, forcing the animals to swim for the shore—wagers being placed on the first horse home and dry! Not to be outdone by the success of the Bassenthwaite regatta, that great eccentric Joseph Pocklington, who owned Pocklington's Island in Derwentwater, organized the Keswick Regatta, the highlight of which was a mock 'sea battle'. The report in the *Cumberland Pacquet* newspaper in 1782 gives some idea of the scale of such manœuvres:

'The fleet (consisting of several barges armed with small cannon and musquetry) retired out of view behind Friar-Crag to prepare for action; previous to which a flag of truce was sent to the Governor, with a summons to surrender. . . . A defiance was returned; soon after which, the fleet was seen advancing with great spirit before the batteries . . . a terrible cannonade began on both sides, accompanied with a dreadful discharge of musquetry. This continued for some time, and being echoed from hill to hill in an amazing variety of sounds, filled the ear with whatever could produce astonishment and awe.'

The festivities ended with dancing, fireworks and illuminations. In the face of such unashamed showmanship, the Windermere Regatta, held at the Ferry, seemed but small beer, for the programme included such comparatively innocuous amusements as sailing, rowing, leaping and wrestling (plate 170). However, the Keswick Regatta was clearly designed to appeal to the tourists, who were just beginning to explore the Lakes in search of the picturesque, whereas the programme of the Windermere Regatta seemed arranged so as to interest local people rather than 'off-comers'.

In spite of regattas and wrestling matches, shepherds' meets and merry neets, opportunities for holidays were, until fifty years ago, virtually non-existent; however, fair days were the exception, for they were widely regarded as occasions for making merry. Although many of these fairs are still held—the Egremont Crab Fair and the Appleby Horse Fair are two of the most famous—others have been allowed to lapse. One of the most important in the Western Lake District was Ravenglass Fair. The charter, originally granted in 1209, conferred the right to hold a fair on the festival of St James the Apostle, and by the beginning of the eighteenth century the fair was widely known and extended over three days. It was attended by people from Wigton, Kendal, Ennerdale, Wasdale, and Keswick—and even the boys of St Bees School claimed a day's holiday for the fair, but their claim was suppressed. By the early nineteenth century the fair had shrunk to a two-day event and by mid century, like so many local fairs, it had ceased to be a commercial gathering and had become a sports meeting, the 'St Jam Races', with trotting contests along the foreshore, wrestling bouts and blind wheelbarrow races. The same was true of the Egremont Crab Fair, and though this is now really an excuse for side-shows and catch-penny amusements, it still retains something of the flavour of a rustic fair. Spectators are showered with crab-apples—hence the name—from lorries and trailers, but the highlight of the fair is the World Championship gurning contests. 'Gurning through a braffin', grimacing through a horse collar, has long been a favourite Cumbrian pastime and was once common at many country gatherings, although it now seems to flourish mainly in west Cumberland (plate 159). Considerable effort and much practice go into these competitions—though one recent World Champion gurner is alleged merely to have been expressing sympathy with a friend who was competing at the time!

Of all these country fairs, however, none was more eagerly awaited than the twice-yearly hiring fair held at Whitsun and Martinmas. Within the Lake District the most important were held at Cockermouth, Kendal (plate 156), Keswick, Penrith and Ulverston (plate 155), and here those servants and farm hands who were not 'stopping on' for another six months gathered to be hired. A straw stuck in a hat or from the corner of the mouth indicated that a labourer was for hire and on completion of negotiations between master and man hands were struck and the hired man received a shilling as 'arles', or earnest money, as a token of his hiring. Early last century women 'in service' were hired in this way, but later propriety dictated that female servants should gather in some nearby hall rather than on the streets. In 1836 men were hired at between £8 to £10 per half-year with board, lodging and washing included, and the highest wages paid to women servants were £6 to £7 per half-year. By 1900 the rate had gone up to £15 to £20 for men and £13 to £18 for women. Hiring often occupied more than one day; at Ulverston, for example, there were three fairs on consecutive Thursdays, the last being known as 'the runaway fair' because some men who did not like the job they had accepted, ran away to try their luck again. Readers of Melvyn Bragg's novel, *The Hired Man*, will find a vivid and authentic description of a Cockermouth hiring fair at the end of the nineteenth century. It was not until after the Second World War that the system of hiring labour in this manner died out.

The hiring of farm servants could be a risky business—for both the farmer and the hired man. In Kendal in 1909 it was agreed that 'character references' should be given but the experiment was not entirely successful, and the story is told of a lad who agreed to hire with a farmer who then sought a 'character'; this being satisfactory, he returned to the lad and reported 'I'se gitten thee character and it's aw reet me lad'. 'Aye, an I'se gitten thine, and I'se nut gaan', was the reply!

The period of the hiring fair was generally regarded as holiday and a respite from the drudgery of farm labour. For many it presented a rare opportunity for visiting parents and friends, but above all it was a festival for the masses; a lad of sixteen or seventeen with his wages and 'earnest money' in his pocket could rightly feel that the fair, if not the world, was his oyster. There was a wide variety of entertainments: wrestling, slack-wire balancing, performing bears and monkeys, freaks such as the pig-faced lady and the hairy man from Morocco. Travelling 'quacks' sold elixirs, the celebrated 'Balm of Gilead' and 'Reverend John Wesley Pills', so-called because they were alleged to have aroused the liver of that eminent gentleman; 'tooth-pullers' plied their art, often accompanied by a small brass band to drown the distress signals emitted by the patients, and at night the theatre—albeit a barn—offered entertainment and the ale-house provided the liquid refreshment in which many found solace and the encouragement to work for a further six months. Few will regret the passing of this system of hiring of farm labourers, but with it has gone one of the most colourful of the Cumbrian rural festivals.

SOME SPORTING OCCASIONS

One of the oldest of the traditional Lakeland competitive sports is wrestling—not the 'all-in' wrestling which is so frequently featured on television, but the infinitely more skilful 'Cumberland and Westmorland' style which can still be seen at local sports throughout Cumbria. Moreover, this is a sport which has its own distinctive costume, a sleeveless vest, long drawers, tucked into stockings, and velvet trunks which are often finely embroidered with flower motifs (plate 163). Basically the contestants stand facing each other, each grasping the other with locked hands around the body, each one's chin on the other's right shoulder. When both men have 'teken hod', the bout begins, slowly at first as the competitors move crab-like, sizing each other up, but suddenly with a flurry of legs there is action as one man is thrown. If any part of his body other than his feet touches the ground, the bout is lost; similarly if a competitor loses his hold he forfeits the bout. Clearly such a sport calls not only for great reserves of strength but also for skill, stamina and physical fitness; spectators hoping for the shows of feigned anger or pain which so characterize 'all-in' wrestling will be disappointed. The origin of Cumberland and Westmorland wrestling is unknown; some authorities believe that it was introduced into the area by the Norse-Irish colonists in the tenth century, but there is little supporting evidence. Neither is there much verification of the story of the legendary Troutbeck 'giant', Hugh Hird, who supposedly threw Edward VI's wrestling champion and who, on being questioned about his diet, explained that he ate porridge and milk 'that a mouse might walk dryshod on' for breakfast, and the 'sunny side of a wether' (sheep) for dinner. Nevertheless, true or false, these are legends on which wrestling folk lore is firmly based.

There is no doubt, however, about the popularity of wrestling in the eighteenth and nineteenth centuries. One of the earliest recorded matches took place in 1785 on the frozen surface of Windermere near to Rawlinson's Nab; here, with refreshments provided by an ox-roasting, and with music supplied by the Kendal Town Band, spectators witnessed the unusual spectacle of wrestlers competing in clogs! By this time, too, the famous sports at Stone Carr, near Greystoke, had become firmly established, and the wrestling contests formed a popular part of the programme, though the rewards were not great:

For the Horses:
   For the first, a Bridle   value 1s. 6d.
   For the second, a pair of Spurs   „   0s. 6d.
For the Wrestlers   A Leathern Belt
For the Leapers   A pair of Gloves
For the Foot Racers   A Handkerchief
For the Dog Courses   A Pewter quart pot.

Of all the prizes, however, the leather belt was the object of much admiration and the victor's prestige was greatly increased; on the Sunday following his victory, the champion usually wore his trophy to church, and on the next Sunday he might be found displaying it at a neighbouring church, to the admiration of the ladies—and the annoyance of the men.[11] At other contests, too, the rewards were hardly lavish by later standards; in 1809 the Duke of Norfolk gave prizes of buckskin breeches to winners of wrestling bouts held at Greystoke Castle, while at the informal contests held after shearing at Park Farm, Troutbeck, the winner walked off with the best fleece.[12] By the middle of the last century, wrestling had become something of a spectator sport, and certain rings attracted spectators and competitors from a wide area—Melmerby and Langwathby in east Cumberland, Carlisle in the north, Greystoke in the Ullswater area, and Windermere Ferry and Flan How, Ulverston, in the southern Lake District. At this latter ring in 1851 there occurred a wrestling match for the championship of England between Robert Atkinson of Sleagill, Westmorland, and William Jackson of Kinneyside, near Ennerdale. The contest, for a prize of £300, attracted one of the largest crowds ever to witness a wrestling bout, for some 10,000 people arrived from London, Liverpool and Manchester, as well as from towns and villages in Cumbria. The result was a win by three falls to one for Atkinson.[13]

Every sport has its heroes and champions and wrestling is no exception: 'Belted Will' Richardson of Caldbeck, Tommy Longmire of Troutbeck, Ralph Powley of Longlands, and Professor Wilson of Elleray, who did much to popularize the sport in the Ambleside area, all have left their mark in the annals of 'wruslin'; but few can equal the record of George Steadman of Asby near Appleby who, between 1865 and 1900 became a national sporting figure. In 1900, aged fifty-four, he decided to retire from the ring, having won the Heavyweight Championship at Grasmere Sports on seventeen occasions. Grasmere Sports (plate 162) remains as one of the most important fixtures in the Lakeland sporting calendar; it seems to have had its origin in wrestling contests which took place in a field next to the Red Lion on the evening of the annual rushbearing procession, but by 1852 when the first official records of the sports begin other events such as the guides' race and the hound trail had been introduced. Later the sports moved to its present site, east of the village, and here thousands of people gather in August to watch the wrestling, pole vaulting, sprinting, hound trailing, and, for most spectators, the event of the day, the race to the summit of Butter Crag and back (plate 161). Yet the pattern of fell racing is changing and a new breed of folk heroes is emerging; the Grasmere Guides' race was once regarded as one of the most testing mountain events within the Lake District and as a competitive race it still ranks high, but Jos Naylor, a young Wasdale shepherd, racing against the clock, has recently established a record which will certainly be hard to beat—a round of sixty-one summits, a distance of ninety miles and an ascent of 34,000 feet, in twenty-four hours! As for wrestling, the popularity of the sport has certainly declined since the beginning of this century, and the heroes of the ring have been replaced by the pampered superstars of First Division football. However, there is still a lively interest in this most indigenous of all Cumbrian sports and there seems little danger of its dying out completely.

HOUND TRAILING

Only one other fellside sport can be said to challenge wrestling for the affection and loyalty of Cumbrian dalesmen—the sport of hound trailing. Rarely seen outside of Cumbria, hound trailing has no long history, for it seems to have developed during the second half of the nine-teenth century, yet it has come to be regarded as one of the most characteristic of all Lakeland sporting events (plate 154). In some ways, trailing seems to have taken the place of cocking in its popular appeal, and today hound trails are supported by the same cross-section of the community which once supported cockfighting. Before 1906 hound trailing was open to much roguery and corruption; there are many tales of dogs being 'kidnapped'; false trails being laid, or the scent being foiled—and at least one wily trailsman has been known to smear his boots with bacon fat to encourage his hound to take a short cut on a familiar scent! Since 1906, however, the opportunities for irregularities have been reduced, for in that year the Hound Trailing Association was established in order to organize the sport. Many of the early trails were probably laid by dragging the carcase of a freshly killed fox over the course but later, when it was appreciated that a foxhound would eagerly follow a trail of rags soaked in aniseed and oil, this was substituted. The laying of a trail is now carefully supervised by H.T.A. rules; generally, two men drag the trail, both starting at the half-way point, 'the split', and then walking back to the start. The hounds are held until the man laying the first half of the trail comes into sight, then they are slipped. Shortly after, the 'heel', the second trail-layer, arrives back to complete the circuit. Under H.T.A. regulations, a senior hound trail of ten miles must be accomplished within strict maximum and minimum time limits; if any hound finishes in under twenty-five minutes or over forty-five minutes, the trail is declared void.

Trail hounds are both lighter and faster than the more sturdy foxhounds. Bred more for speed than stamina, they can average speeds of 20 m.p.h. over scree, crag and fellside, taking becks, bracken and dry-stone walls in their stride, intent on following the aniseed trail. Weather conditions can affect the performance of a trail hound; for example, damp, cool conditions will usually encourage a faster time than on a warm, dry day. Similarly a trail can be completely upset by the unscheduled appearance of a fox, whereupon the hounds have been known to follow a natural trail rather than an artificial one! Rabbits too can cause something of a diversion, but there is at least one recorded occasion of a hound finishing amongst the leaders with a rabbit clenched firmly in its mouth!

Much of the mystique of hound trailing is concerned with the way in which the animals are fed. Surprisingly, trail hounds are often fed on specially made cock-loaf, identical to that which was once fed to gamecocks (*see* page 169). Though most cock-loaves contain eggs, raisins, sherry, and sometimes port wine, individual recipes are jealously guarded and passed on from one generation to the next—understandably so, for many regard these recipes as the formula for success. But special diets and ingredients are only a part of the mystique, for the way in which an animal is trained is of equal importance. The most successful trainers are those who can discourage their hounds from stopping to drink when following a trail, for many a race has been lost because of this. At the same time, hounds must be taught to respond to a whistle, a signal or a call, as anyone who has witnessed the finish of a hound trail will know. As soon as the hounds are within earshot their trainers break into cries and calls of encouragement, some using whistles, others bells, anything to attract and cajole the hound across the finishing line. The sight of an excited line of owners frantically calling in their hounds is one of the highlights of such meetings as Grasmere Sports or Rydal 'Dog Day'. Certainly the prestige of winning the hound trail at one of Lakeland's big shows or sporting occasions is as great as anything that gamecock fighting had to offer, and it seems that, like wrestling, this most popular of Cumbrian sports will continue for many years to come.

15 LAKELAND TRANSPORT

COACHES, CARS AND CHARABANCS

Within the past two hundred years the winds of change have wrought considerable modifications in the Lakeland dales, changes in farming practice, economics, building techniques and standards of living, yet none was greater in magnitude than the transport 'revolution', for in effect it opened up Cumbria to outside influences, and in so doing hastened the decline of folk culture and folk traditions. However, the improvements in communications were late in coming; even by the middle of the eighteenth century there were few wheeled vehicles within the district and most people travelled on horseback, the women usually seated on pillions behind the men.[1] In 1730 Benjamin Browne, the High Constable of Kendal Ward, undertook a survey of the roads in his area, the results of which are typical of eighteenth-century conditions in Cumbria, for all are described as 'bad' or 'narrow' or 'covered with ye hedges'.[2] The Garburn road, connecting the Troutbeck and Kentmere valleys, was said to be '. . . soe much out of repair and in decay, that a great part of it is not passable for either man or Horse to travel through the said ways without danger of being bogged in moss or lamed among the stones'. The same road has changed little apart from the enclosure walls; it still remains unsurfaced and badly eroded by fellside becks (plate 178), providing us with a marvellous example of what eighteenth-century roads were like.

By mid century strings of pack-horses traversed the fells, linking Whitehaven, Cockermouth, Penrith, Ulverston, Hawkshead and Cartmel with Kendal, which soon became the most important pack-horse station between Wigan and Scotland, and from the cobbled yards of this grey Westmorland town clattered and jingled the weekly trains to York, Barnard Castle, London and elsewhere. Such pack-horse gangs long remained a feature of Cumbrian rural life; in 1868 A. C. Gibson recalled that '. . . there are many of the old inhabitants in Langdale who remember the gangs of pack-horses on their way from Kendal to Whitehaven over Hardknott and Wrynose, one especially, led by a sagacious old black stallion; their master and only attendant rode a pony and had a habit of taking his ease at . . . several inns along the route, following and overtaking the horses between his stopping places and riding on to the next, where he would rest and drink until they had plodded patiently past, when, at his own good time, he would follow and repeat the process'.[3] It is believed that this was the last route in Lakeland to be regularly used by pack-horses.

By 1752, however, the Turnpike movement began to improve Cumbrian roads; first, the road from Kendal to Kirkby Lonsdale and Keighley, then the road from Heron Syke through Kendal to Shap and Eamont Bridge, and later, in 1759, the road from Kendal through Levens to the port of Milnthorpe. By 1763 roads connecting Kendal with Appleby, Ambleside, Keswick, Cockermouth and Ulverston had all been turnpiked, emphasizing the importance of this market town. The effects of such improvements were immediate; carriers' wagons were introduced in 1753[4] (*see* fig. 37) and, for those who could afford them, stage coaches rejoicing

193

in fanciful names such as 'The Flying Machine' (1763), 'The Royal Pilot' (1815) and 'The True Briton' (1817) made incredible journeys at average speeds of between five and six miles an hour. Yet there were those who remained sceptical about such enterprises and, we are told, 'some learned doctors warned people from travelling by the wild and whirling vehicle, as the rate at which it went would bring upon them all manner of strange disorders, chief among which was apoplexy.'[5] The doctors need not have worried overmuch, however, for the introduction of stage coaches barely affected the lives of the vast majority of dalesfolk, and most Lakeland valleys remained remote and isolated. Writing in 1872, James Stockdale remarked '. . . there was not, until some little time before the end of the last century, a four-wheeled carriage of any kind in the whole parish of Cartmel, excepting at Holker Hall and Bigland Hall', and in 1801 Dorothy Wordsworth, living at Dove Cottage, Grasmere, on the Ambleside to Keswick turnpike road, considered it sufficiently noteworthy to record in her diary 'Today a chaise passed', for most people travelled on foot or on horseback.

Much has already been written about Lakeland travelling arrangements and the turnpike roads[6] which broke down the isolation of Cumbria, but it is worth mentioning again the ancient cross-sands route into the district from Lancaster across the sands of Morecambe Bay at low tide. This was certainly one of the most unusual roads in the kingdom, used by locals and visitors alike, and many of the early tourists gained their first glimpse of the Cumbrian mountains reflected in the wet sands of the bay. Although this route had certainly been used from early medieval times, and probably earlier, it was not until 1781 that a public coach service commenced running across the sands; it was a 'diligence' or light coach carrying three passengers and the driver, and it ran from Lancaster every Monday, Wednesday and Friday and returned from Ulverston on Tuesdays, Thursdays and Saturdays, timing, of course, being dependent on tides. The proprietors of the venture assured the public that '. . . they have procured a sober and careful driver, who is well acquainted with the sands, and humbly hope their plan will meet with due encouragement as this is the most cheap, safe, and expeditious method of crossing the

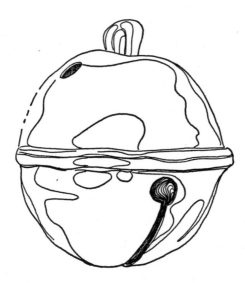

Fig. 36. Pack-horse bell from Kendal.

sands. . .'.[7] Yet, in spite of the company's optimism and the 'brobbing'* of the changing route through the channels of the Kent and the Leven by the guides, the cross-sands route was not without a certain amount of danger, particularly in fog or mist, and there are spine-chilling stories of coaches going round in circles until the tide finally engulfed them. Similarly, the quick-sands regularly claimed victims; in 1821 a post-chaise was lost in the quicksands, and in 1828 the over-sands coach from Lancaster vanished, while in 1846 nine people returning from Ulverston hiring fair were drowned and seven more perished in the same way in 1857. However, it must be said that the early tourists to the Lake District magnified the dangers of the cross-sands road, just as, for that matter, they exaggerated the steepness of the Cumbrian hills, for one local writer in 1810 stated that '. . . in fine weather, along with the attending guides, there is no more danger in a journey across the estuaries than in any other road'. Generations of Cumbrians have used this route southwards to Lancaster; and even when the turnpike road around the estuaries was completed in 1820 local people continued to use the traditional routeway, and the regular coach service remained in operation until 1857 when the Ulverston to Lancaster railway line was completed. Today the cross-sands road is again increasing in popularity, and every year hundreds of enthusiastic walkers trek across the sands in company with 'the attending guide' (plate 188).

As road improvements continued, so too traffic within Lakeland increased and local coach services came into operation; in 1822, for example, Mr Banks, a Keswick tanner, ran a daily coach from Keswick to Cockermouth over the Whinlatter pass,[8] and two years later one intrepid gentleman, Jack Cawx, penetrated the depths of Borrowdale in a chaise, the first to be seen in the valley. The road was so bad, however, that the carriage almost overturned at Grange Bridge, though the driver escaped without injury. With more wheeled vehicles using the roads, the inevitable road accidents occurred; in 1840 Wordsworth and his son, John, narrowly escaped injury on a journey along the turnpike road from Whitehaven to Grasmere. Two or three miles from Keswick their one-horse gig was hit by an approaching mailcoach which flung the gig, the horse, the two Wordsworths and part of a wall into a field. Years later, the coach driver, David Johnson, relating the story of how he had 'spilt the Wadsworths', confessed that he had 'never heard a body's tongue sweer gladlier, though, for I thowt we'd kilt the poit'.[9]

During the mid nineteenth-century period, tourists flocked into Lakeland in their thousands, the age of mass tourism dawned, and transport facilities were expanded to meet the demand. This increase in tourist traffic is reflected in the returns of the Ambleside Turnpike Trust for 1855 when 21,480 carriages passed and repassed Troutbeck Bridge between Ambleside and Windermere, and a further 15,240 paid the toll on the Grasmere to Keswick section of the road[10] where only fifty-four years earlier the passage of a single carriage was something of an event. Undoubtedly one of the reasons for such development was the opening of the Kendal to Windermere railway line in 1847, and from that year onwards the small hamlet of Birthwaite, later to become Windermere, became the centre of the coaching trade. In 1851 *Black's Picturesque Guide to the English Lakes* announced that '. . . on the arrival of the trains, coaches leave the station at Windermere for Ambleside and Keswick and the mail proceeds by this route to Cockermouth, and thence by railway to Whitehaven. Coaches also travel daily between Winder-mere and the towns of Hawkshead and Coniston'. Foremost amongst the private concerns organizing coach services was Mr Richard Rigg of the Windermere Hotel, who built the largest and most successful coaching business in the Lake District. His Royal Mail coaches, pulled by

* 'Brobbs' were small branches from trees which were used to mark the safe routes across the river channels at low water.

Kendal and Ulverstone
COMMON CARRIER.

JOHN CLARKE,
of Haverthwaite, near Ulverstone,

BEGS LEAVE TO INFORM HIS FRIENDS AND THE PUBLICK IN GENERAL, THAT

HE HAS ESTABLISHED

a regular Conveyance for forwarding Goods betwixt

KENDAL AND ULVERSTONE,
BOOTLE, RAVENGLASS,
EGREMONT, WHITEHAVEN,

AND ALL THE INTERMEDIATE AND ADJACENT PLACES.

*** All Goods consigned to him, the Publick may depend will be delivered with the utmost Care and Dispatch.

Leaves the New Inn, *Kendal,* every Wednesday and Saturday at Noon, and arrives at *Haverthwaite* in the Evening; and is at the Brown Cow Inn, *Ulverstone,* every Monday and Thursday Morning, and returns to *Haverthwaite* the same day.

J. C. hopes, by his due Attention to Business, to merit a Share of Publick Support.

October 7th, **1811.**

[Soulby. Printer Ulverston]

Fig. 37. A handbill of 1811.

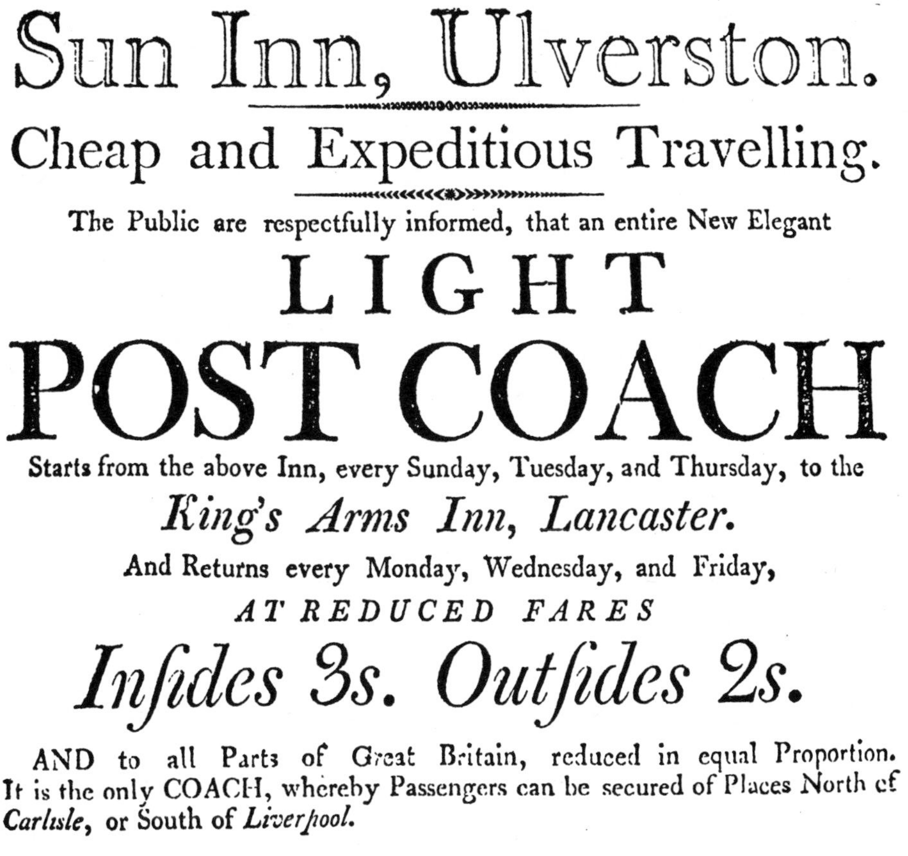

Sun Inn, Ulverston.

Cheap and Expeditious Travelling.

The Public are respectfully informed, that an entire New Elegant

LIGHT
POST COACH

Starts from the above Inn, every Sunday, Tuesday, and Thursday, to the

King's Arms Inn, Lancaster.

And Returns every Monday, Wednesday, and Friday,

AT REDUCED FARES

Infides 3s. Outfides 2s.

AND to all Parts of Great Britain, reduced in equal Proportion. It is the only COACH, whereby Passengers can be secured of Places North of *Carlisle*, or South of *Liverpool*.

Fig. 38. Cross-sands coach poster, early nineteenth century.

three horses and driven by scarlet-coated, white-top-hatted drivers, became part of the Lakeland scene until the 1920s, when the regular coach service was withdrawn and replaced by the buses of the Lake District Road Traffic Company. The introduction of surfaced roads was a further blow to some coach services; although a Keswick–Honister Pass–Buttermere run was successfully initiated in the 1860s, it was found in 1934 when the road over the pass was surfaced that the horses could not restrain a laden coach on a gradient of 1 in 4 and consequently the service was withdrawn.[11]

Coaching, however, was clearly for the tourists who could afford to pay the prices demanded, and the dalesfolk continued to rely on horses and gigs and traps even in the 1920s (plate 184). In some valleys horse-drawn waggonettes established a semi-public service before the First World War; in Borrowdale, for example, a monthly waggonette ran from the Scafell Hotel to Keswick on 'quarry pay Saturday', when the return fare was 3s. 6d. Visits to Keswick at other times meant travelling with Ned White, the postman, in his dog-cart and an overnight stay.[12] In 1896 a two-horse waggonette service ran from Patterdale to Penrith but later this was expanded and four-horse 'charabancs' were used. The service left Patterdale at 7.15 a.m. and

ASKEW'S

KESWICK *AND* BORROWDALE
❧ COACH. ❧

Leave Grange.	Leave Keswick Market-place
9 0	10 15
12 45	2 15
5 0	6 15

The drive between Keswick and Borrowdale, along the margin of Lake Derwentwater, is one of the prettiest in the Lake District. The Bowder Stone (supposed to be the largest piece of detached rock in the world), is within 15 minutes' walk of Grange.

FARE - 9d.

W. ASKEW, Proprietor.

Fig. 39. A handbill of 1909.

reached Penrith at 10.00 a.m., returning at 3.30 p.m. and arriving at 7 o'clock, heralded by a post-horn[13] (plate 185). The Lake District Road Traffic Company began a modest motor service between Bowness, Windermere, Ambleside and Grasmere in 1904, but it was not until the 1920s that motor transport began to penetrate the dales, although by 1915 the Ullswater (Royal Mail) Motor Service was running twice daily between Penrith and Patterdale (plate 186). In Borrowdale, however, Mr John Woodend of Seatoller operated a chain-driven Daimler car between Seatoller and Keswick before 1914, but it ceased running during the period of the First World War. In 1920 Mr W. F. Askew bought a Ford chassis and attached to it the body from an old horse-drawn waggonette—an appropriate fusion of old and new methods of travelling—and about the same time Mr Woodend put into service a fourteen-seater vehicle. By 1926 the road to Keswick had been widened and improved, and two years later five services were operating over the route. Similarly, in 1923, James and Fred Airey ran an eight-seater car between Ambleside, Hawkshead and the Windermere ferry, which proved so successful that in the following year a fourteen-seater bus was brought into service, followed in 1933 by two larger vehicles. Also in the early 1920s the Lake District Road Traffic Company began the so-called 'Yellow Peril' buses, solid-tyred, chain-driven Thorneycroft coaches which ran from Ambleside to Coniston, to Windermere and to Keswick at a maximum speed of 12 m.p.h., slow by modern standards but no doubt then considered to be the acme of rapid transport.

In spite of the increase in car ownership during the past two decades, there is still a need for public transport in the remote dales of Lakeland; indeed, the wheel has gone full circle, for a private enterprise company, The Mountain Goat, runs a minibus service over Kirkstone Pass between Glenridding and Bowness, and even over the hair-raising Hardknott Pass, routes which are not considered profitable for large coaches. And it is still possible in Cumbria to 'ride the Mail', no longer on one of Rigg's Royal Mail coaches but in a special vehicle carrying both passengers and mail which runs from Penrith to remote Martindale east of Ullswater, and between Broughton and the Duddon valley.

Although the days of horse-drawn carriages, carts and waggonettes have long since gone, something of the spirit of pioneer motoring lingered in the Keswick area until recently, for occasionally Mr Edwin Quirk proudly drove his gleaming 1904 8-h.p. single-cylinder Darracq along the Borrowdale roads, recalling a more leisurely age when congestion and traffic jams were unheard of, and when parking presented no problems (plate 177).

THE WINDERMERE FERRY

The fact that there has been a public ferry across the middle 'cubble', or division, of Windermere for at least five hundred years emphasizes the importance of a service which has traditionally linked the market towns of Hawkshead and Kendal. Windermere, the largest 'standing water' in England, is ten miles long and clearly presents a considerable natural barrier to east–west communications, for unless the ferry is used long detours north or south are necessary, and in former times the inconvenience must have been accentuated by the lack of roads. South of the largest island in the lake, Belle Isle, Windermere is barely 560 yards wide and here the main ferry service has operated for centuries, although there is a suggestion that there may have been a minor ferry between Miller Ground and Belle Grange.[14]

The right of ferriage was a prized and jealously guarded privilege which in the seventeenth and early eighteenth centuries belonged to the Braithwaite family. Theirs was the responsibility of providing the 'Great Boat' in which men and horses were rowed across the lake; in 1699 Thomas Braithwaite built a new boat and as a result proposed to increase the toll, a suggestion which sparked off considerable protest, for it was argued that 'itt hath beene ussed and Accustomed . . . time beyond the memory of man' for anyone who wished '. . . to pass repass & travell over Windermer Watter Att the fferry boate on the King's hyeway there to pay only one penny and noe more ffor their soe passing and repassing'.[15] Such was the pressure of public opinion and the law that Thomas Braithwaite was obliged to continue to charge only one penny, though by 1830 the toll had been increased to 2d. for foot passengers, 3s. for a post-chaise, 3s. 6d. for a gentleman's 'chariot', and 4s. for a carriage, though no charge was made for vehicles returning the same day. No regular time-table was used; the boat was normally moored on the Lancashire shore so that travellers approaching from Kendal had to hail the ferryman, and Wordsworth in *The Prelude* recalled

> '. . . *shouting amain*
> *A lusty summons to the farther shore*
> *For the old Ferryman* . . .'

By 1831 two boats were kept in repair, for Thomas Cloudsdale's lease charges him with the upkeep of 'the Little Boat and the Great Boat'. The increase in traffic, and particularly wheeled vehicles, in the late nineteenth century meant that man-powered ferry boats became inadequate and consequently, in 1870, a steam-powered ferry was launched. The *Westmorland Gazette* noted with satisfaction that '. . . the steamer and chains, which have taken the place of the old lumbering row-boat, completes the crossing and return in much less time than the old boat took to go one way. The men employed are also prompt and obliging, so much so that they hurry across the lake on hearing the first intimation of a passenger'.[16] The steam ferry could carry a coach-and-four or two coaches if the leaders were detached, and the Hawkshead to Kendal carriers' carts made the trip across the lake three times a week while Rigg's Coniston coach made a daily journey in summer. The first steam ferry remained in service until 1915, when a larger vessel was commissioned and this, in turn, was replaced by the present ferry, *The Drake*, in 1954 (plate 193).

The Windermere ferry has clearly played an important role in the economic life of this part of Cumbria, but in addition it is closely associated with folk culture and legend, and in particular with the doleful story of 'the Fatall Nuptual'. On 19th October 1635, some forty-eight or forty-nine wedding guests returning from a celebration in Hawkshead were drowned when the ferry capsized. All were buried in Windermere parish churchyard at Bowness. There is, however, no suggestion that the bride and groom were on board the doomed vessel, and therefore they probably escaped the fate which overwhelmed their relatives and friends.[17] Incidentally, perhaps the reason for the tragedy was overcrowding, for almost fifty people, together with eight horses, packed onto the ferry which can hardly have been a large boat. An equally spine-chilling and oft-repeated tale concerns the ghostly 'Crier of Claife', a misguided and troublesome creature who, especially on stormy nights, urgently hailed the ferry from the Westmorland shores. One of the ferrymen who answered the weird summons apparently returned with an empty boat, horror-stricken and dumb, and remained so until he died several days later.[18] Present-day travellers on the ferry need have no apprehensions, for the story has a happy ending—apparently the monks of Furness Abbey were able to exorcise this annoying night walker and he supposedly lies buried on Claife Heights.

SOME EARLY LAKE STEAMERS

The first regular passenger boats on any of the Cumbrian lakes were not, in fact, steamships; they were barges propelled by long oars and supplemented by sails. In 1836 or 1837 Mr James Gibson of Ambleside and Mr White of Newby Bridge initiated a passenger service on Windermere which, until 1845, was the only regular communication up and down the Lake. Mr White's boat operated on the section between Newby Bridge and the Ferry and connected with Mr Gibson's boat, which ran from Waterhead to the Ferry. In the latter case the townsfolk of Ambleside were notified of the imminent departure by a lad who blew a horn in the market place. Although the journey was a slow one—it took three and a half hours to complete the full single journey of fourteen miles—the fares were cheap, for it cost 1s. from Ambleside to Bowness, 1s. 6d. to the Ferry, and 3s. to Newby Bridge.[19]

In 1845 the first steamship began to ply the length of Windermere; she was the *Lady of the Lake*, an 80-foot-long paddle ship owned by the Windermere Steam Yacht Company. Initially, however, there was some opposition to this new form of transport. Writing in 1846, the Rev. Charles Mackay commented that '. . . the inhabitants . . . of Bowness, Lowwood, Ambleside,

Ulverston
CATTLE FAIR,

SHEW OF HORSES,
AND SERVANTS' HIRING.

The Annual Fair for Cattle,
WILL BE HOLDEN
AT ULVERSTON,
On THURSDAY *the* 5th *Day of* OCTOBER, 1809,
WHERE A LARGE QUANTITY OF CATTLE,
Suitable for all descriptions of Buyers, as
GENTLEMEN FARMERS, GRAZIERS, BUTCHERS,
&c. &c.
WILL BE SHEWN.

The flattering encouragement this FAIR has received from the
Grower and Grazier,
PROMISES A VERY FINE FAIR.

A SHEW OF HORSES
In the Afternoon, well worthy the Attention of the Publick.

MALE AND FEMALE
SERVANTS TO BE HIRED.

J. SOULBY—Printer—*Ulverston,*

155. 'Male and Female Servants to be Hired', a poster for the annual Ulverston Fair, October 1809.

156. Kendal Hiring Fair, 1899. The booth on the right is showing scenes from the Transvaal War.

157. *Bowness musicians about to give an* al fresco *performance to celebrate Queen Victoria's Diamond Jubilee in 1897.*

158. *A High Furness sports day, c. 1895. The tug-of-war at Satterthwaite.*

159. *Mr T. Thomas 'gurning through a braffin' at Egremont Crab Fair. Gurning was once a popular pastime throughout Cumbria—now it seems to be largely confined to west Cumberland. One hesitates to suggest a reason . . .*

160. *Skating on Windermere, 16th February 1895.*

161. *The senior guides' race at Grasmere Sports. This is regarded as one of the most gruelling of all Lakeland fell races.*

162. *'Tekin' hod' at Grasmere Sports.*

163. *What the best-dressed wrestlers wear. Mr Roger Wilkinson of Staveley was the winner of the 1972 Grasmere Sports Wrestlers' costume competition.*

Kendal 27th Jan'y 1787. being last day

Robert & William Knight — 6.9

THE UNPARALLELED
IRISH GIANTS.
THE MOST SURPRISING GIGANTIC
TWIN BROTHERS,

Who had the Honour to be seen by their Majesties, and the Royal Family,
at Windsor, in the Year 1784, with great Applause; being the only Tall
Men that his Majesty ever honoured with that Compliment,

ARE JUST ARRIVED,

And to be seen at the *Golden Lyon in Kendal*,
These truly amazing Phænomena are indisputably the most astonishing Production of the human Species ever beheld since the Days of

GOLIAH;

As has been sufficiently demonstrated from the repeated Approbation of
the first Personages in this Kingdom, as well as Foreigners of Distinction,
from several of whom they have had the most pressing Invitations to visit their
respective Courts.

THESE AMAZING
COLOSSUSES

Are but TWENTY-FOUR YEARS OF AGE,
AND VERY NEAR

EIGHT FEET HIGH.

Nor does that amazing Size more agreeably surprise the curious spectator,
than their Proportion in every Respect to their stupendious Height; a Cir-
cumstance so seldom to be found in any extraordinary Production of Nature.
Ladies and Gentlemen are respectfully informed, that the Hours of Admittance are from Ten in the Morning till Two in the Afternoon, and from
Three to Nine at Night.—Their Stay will be but *six* Days.

ADMITTANCE, Ladies and Gentlemen 1s.—Servants, &c. 6d.

LAST NIGHT THIS SEASON.

Mr. BUTLER's humble respects to the Ladies and Gentlemen of Ulverston, and
its Vicinity, returns them Thanks for Favours conferred on him and Company this Season,
and assures them he shall ever make it his Study to merit their future Support.

FOR THE BENEFIT OF

Mr. KEMBLE.

THEATRE-ROYAL, ULVERSTON.

SATURDAY Evening, the 10th of JANUARY, 1807,
Their Majesties' Servants
Will perform a favourite COMEDY, written by Shakespeare, called, The

Merry Wives of Windsor.

Sir John Falstaff, - Mr. KEMBLE.

Fenton,	Mr. JEFFERSON,	Nym,	Mr. WORRALL,
Shallow,	Mr. SMITH,	Robin,	Master H. MEADOWS,
Slender,	Mr. DAVIS,	Simple,	Mrs. DAVIS,
Mr. Page,	Mr. BEVERLEY,	Jack Rugby,	Master MEADOWS.
Mr. Ford,	Mr. CLIFTON,		
Sir Hugh Evans,	Mr. MEADOWS,	Mrs. Page,	Miss CRAVEN,
Doctor Caius,	Mr. DUNNING,	Anne Ford,	Mrs. BUTLER,
Host of the Garter,	Mr. WATSON,	Anne Page,	Miss JEFFERSON,
Bardolph,	Mr. MARTIN,	Mrs. Quickly,	Mrs. FILDEW.
Pistol,	Mr. GEORGE,		

In the course of the Evening, Mr. KEMBLE will deliver

A CENTO,

Selected by himself from the works of Shakespeare
ADDRESSED TO
The Volunteers of the United Kingdom,
And which he had the honour of delivering repeatedly last Summer before
Their MAJESTIES, at the Theatre-Royal, Weymouth.

To which will be added a Musical FARCE, called

The SPOIL'D CHILD

Little Pickle,	Miss JEFFERSON,	Maria,	Mrs. DAVIS,
Old Pickle,	Mr. MEADOWS,	Susan,	Mrs. CRAVEN,
Tagg,	Mr. DUNNING,	Margery,	Mrs. MURRAY,
John,	Mr. GEORGE,	Miss Pickle,	Miss FILDEW,
	Mr. DAVIS.		

IN ACT THE SECOND,

Kelly and Crouch's favourite DUET,
By Mr. DAVIS, and Mrs. FILDEW.

BOXES 3s.—PIT 2s.—GALLERY, 1s.—To begin at Seven o'Clock.
* Tickets Delivered where places for the BOXES are Taken, at Mr. Soulby's shop, King-street.
TICKETS to be had of Mr. Kemble, at Mr. Cassel's, the Buddyill's Arms, and of Mr. Ashburner, Printer.
Servants will be sent to keep Places.

J. Soulby, Printer, Ulverston.

FOR THE BENEFIT OF
Mr. and Mrs. JEFFERSON

THEATRE-ROYAL, ULVERSTON.

On THURSDAY Evening DECEMBER 22d 18
THEIR MAJESTIES' SERVANTS,
Will perform a favourite Comedy, called,

THE WAY TO G
MARRIED

Written by T. Morton, Esq. Author of A Cure for the Heart Ache, Speed the P

Tangent,	Mr. JEFFERSON,	Ned,	Mr
Toby Allspice,	Mr. FINN,	Caustic's Servant,	
Captain Faulkner,	Mr. SMITH,	Bailiff,	
Caustic,	Mr. DAVIS,		
Dicky Dashall,	Mr. MORTIMER,	Julia Faulkner,	
Mac Query,	Mrs. BLACKETT,	Lady Sorrel,	
Landlord,	Mr. GEORGE,	Clementina Allspice,	
Shopman,	Mr. DUNNING,	Fanny,	

A HORNPIPE by Mrs. Je
"The GREAT BOOB
By Mr. DAVIS.

A PLOUGHING MA
IN WHICH THIRTY MOVING FIG
Will be seen in the Act of
PLOUGHING Extensive

With a correct representation of the Ploughs and Horses belonging to respectable Fa
Neighbourhood of ULVERSTON, particularly of
Dalton	Colton,
Lindale,	Arrad,
Ureswicks,	Lowick,
Bardsea,	Gleaston,
Penny-bridge,	Scales,
Bouth,	Aldingham,

Bayclift, Nether Houses, Thurston-ville,
Broughton-beck, Hollow Mire, Mountbarrow,
Scathwaite, Mannrigg, Low Greaves,
Swarthmoor, Torp, Glascow,
Bridgefield, Routhwaite, Plumpton,
Newby Bridge, Summer-hill, Flann,

In the course of the Exhibition will be introduced Mr. HANDY's new in
CURRICLE-PLOUGH in MOT
An Address to the Ladies & Ge
Of ULVERSTON, (Written by Mr. Jefferson,) to be spoken by Mrs. Jeff
To which will be added a FARCE, called

RAISING the WIN

Plainway,	Mr. SMITH,	Waiter,	Mr
Fainwould,	Mr. DAVIS,	Richard,	
Diddler,	Mr. JEFFERSON,	Messenger,	
Sam,	Mr. DUNNING,	Peggy,	
John,	Mr. MARTIN,	Miss Laurelia Durable,	

* Tickets to be had of Mr. Jefferson, at Miss Towers, Fountain Street, and of M
Ashburner, Printers.

G. Ashburner, P

BY PERMISSION,
And particular Desire.

Theatre-Royal, Ulverston.

On Friday Evening, August 18th, 1809,
will be presented a favourite DRAMATIC Entertainment,
Written by DIBDIN, COLLINS, STEVENS, COLMAN, and others,
CALLED

A Banquet
OF MIRTH;
OR,
TWO HEADS are better than ONE.

CONSISTING OF
LECTURES, RECITATIONS, PUNS,
COMIC SKETCHES,
AND LAUGHABLE BLUNDERS.

The above ENTERTAINMENT will be interspersed with a Number of

COMIC SONGS,
and
PASTORAL AIRS.

I. P. PATEFIELD takes this opportunity of
returning most sincere and humble thanks
to the LADIES and GENTLEMEN, who honor-
ed him with their Patronage on TUESDAY
Evening; and pledges himself to the Ladies
and Gentlemen to give an ENTIRE CHANGE of
ENTERTAINMENTS for FRIDAY Evening.

BOXES 2s.—PIT 1s. GALLERY 6d. To begin at 8 o'Clock.
Tickets to be had of Mr. Soulby, King-street.

J. SOULBY, PRINTER.

LAST WEEK.

By Permission of the Worshipful the Mayor.

THEATRE, CROWN INN, KENDAL.

By Desire & under the Patronage
of the Stewards of the Races.

ON WEDNESDAY EVENING, AUGUST 2nd, 1826,
Will be performed the fashionable Comedy of

CHARLES II.
OR THE
Adventures of the Merry Monarch.

King Charles	Mr. HALL	Captain Copp, Landlord of the	
disguised as Jack Mizen	Mr. HALL!	Grand Admiral, at Wapping	Mr. BOWMAN
	Mr. HAMILTON!		
Rochester	disguised as Tom Tofril	Mr. HAMILTON!!	Lady Clara	Mrs. HAMILTON
Edward, a Page	Mr. MELVILLE!	Mary, niece of Captain Copp	Mrs. BOWMAN
Music Master	Mr. MELVILLE!!		

A FAVOURITE SONG—BY Mrs. HAMILTON,
" Love's a Tyrant."—by Mrs. Bateman.

To conclude with the laughable farce of the

HEN-PECKED HUSBAND.

Sir Jacob Jollup	Mr. HALL	Roger	Mr. SMITH
Major Surgeon	Mr. HAMILTON		
Gregory Snack	Mr. BOWMAN	Mrs. Snack	Mrs. BOWMAN
Bruin	Mr. MELVILLE	Mrs. Bruin	Mrs. BATEMAN

BOXES 3s.—PIT 2s.—GAL. 1s.

Doors open at 7, and performance to begin at 8.
Tickets to be had of Mr. Bowman, and of the Printer's, and Crown Inn.

Printed by M. and R. Branthwaite, Kendal.

Theatre, Kendal.

On Saturday Evening, July 14th, 1838,
Will be performed the Tragedy, of

HAMLET
PRINCE OF
DENMARK.

Hamlet,	Mr. DARLEY	Laertes,	Mr. JONES	King, Mr. BANKS
Osric,	Mr. MONTAGUE		Horatio, Mr. L. BANK
Bernardo,	Mr. STEVENS	Polonius, Mr. CLARKE
Mrs. MONTAGUE	Ophelia, Miss TANNETT	Player Queen, Miss DEANS

END OF THE TRAGEDY

A Comic Song by Mr. MACKERALL

The whole to conclude with the laughable Farce of

NO!
OR THE
GLORIOUS MINORITY.

Sir George Doubtful,	Mr. STANLEY	Frederic, (his nephew)	Mr. DARLEY	Smart Mr L. BANK
	Mr. MACKERALL	John,	Mr. STEVENS	Thomas, Mr. JONES
		Commodore Hurricane,	Mr. MONTAGUE	
Lady Doubtful,	Mrs. BANKS	Maria Miss TANNETT
		Deborah,	Miss DEANS

Boxes, 2s. Pit, 1s. Gallery, 6d.

Doors open at Seven,—commence at half-past Seven precisely.
Tickets to be had of the Booksellers, and of Mr Martin, at Mrs Clark's
Confectioner, Highgate.
Mr Martin will feel obliged by Shopkeepers allowing the Bills to be seen in
their windows.

On Monday Evening, July 16th, 1838
FOR THE BENEFIT OF
MR. MARTIN,
(MANAGER,)
A NEW LOCAL DRAMA CALLED
Kendal Castle,
AND THE AFTERPIECE OF THE
BOTTLE IMP,
Which will be revised with great splendour having been some time in preparation

---

164–9. *Although Lakeland was remote from the centres of theatrical life,
visiting companies performed in barns, inns and, later, in specially constructed
theatres. These handbills from Kendal and Ulverston show something of their
repertoire.*

WINANDERMERE REGATTA.

WINANDERMERE REGATTA,

Will take Place at the Ferry House,

On Wednesday the 25th July, 1810,

WHEN THE FOLLOWING

MATCHES,

WILL BE SAILED FOR.

1. Mr. Bolton's Schooner, the *VICTORY*.
   Mr. Wilson's Schooner, the *ENDEAVOUR*.
   Mr. Pedder's Schooner, the *EXPERIMENT*.
   To start at eleven o'Clock.
2. Mr. Pedder's Schooner, *ROVER*.
   Mr. Wilson's Cutter, *ELIZA*.
   Mr. Wilson's Latine Sailed Vessel, *PALAFOX*.
3. Mr. William Jernett's, *LIVERPOOLIAN*.
   Mr. Smith's, *KITTY*.

ROWING MATCHES.

1. Mr. Francis Astley's Wherry, *MARY*.
   Mr. Wilson's Wherry, *SWIFT*.
2. A Prize of one Guinea, to the best *Fishing Boat* on the Lake.
3. A Prize of one Guinea, to the best *Boat* kept by an Innkeeper.
4. A Gown to be rowed for by *Women*.
5. A Prize of two Guineas, for the best *Boat* on the Lake; Wherries excepted.

RUNNING.

1. One Guinea to the best *Runner*, distance two Miles.
2. A Gown to be run for by *Women*, distance one Mile.
3. A Hat to the best Runner, *(Man or Woman)* blindfolded, distance one hundred Yards.

LEAPING.

One Guinea to the best *Leaper*.

WRESTLING.

One Guinea to the best *Wrestler*.

A Variety of other Amusements will take place.

Dinner on the Table at four o'Clock.

There will be a BALL at the Salutation Inn, Ambleside, on Thursday the 26th.

JOHN WILSON, Esq. of Elleray, Steward.

170, 171. *Two nineteenth-century social gatherings.*

BATTALION DRILL.

The First Administrative Battalion of Westmorland Rifle Volunteers will meet for Drill

On MONDAY, MAY 9th, 1864,

AT CALGARTH PARK.

AN

Auld Wife Hake

Will take place on the Evening of that day,

AT THE SUN HOTEL,

TROUTBECK BRIDGE.

April 27th, 1864.

172, 173. *Walking geese to market . . . or (below left) taking them on horseback; in the 1880s.*

174. *Packmen, commonly known as 'Scotchmen', regularly visited Lakeland farms selling ribbons, pins, needles and thread. Here a bowler-hatted packman displays his goods at the home of Mr and Mrs Revel of Newby Bridge, c. 1910.*

175. *Horse power at Caldbeck,*
c. *1900.*

176. *Fruit and vegetable delivery in*
south-west Cumberland, c. *1920.*

177. *Admiring glances for Mr E.*
Quirk's 1904 8-h.p. single-cylinder
Darracq, still to be seen on the roads of
Borrowdale.

178. *The badly eroded, unsurfaced Garburn Road between Troutbeck and Kentmere. In 1730 the High Constable of Kendal Ward described it as '. . . soe much out of repair and in decay, that a great part of it is not passable for either man or Horse to travel through the said ways without danger of being bogged in moss or lamed among the stones.'*

179. *The Kirkstone Pass Inn, c. 1860. This bleak and exposed hostelry once served refreshment to weary travellers journeying over the pass; it now caters for the coach-confined tourist.*

180. *A steep section on the 'Buttermere Round', c. 1890. The road was not surfaced until 1934.*

181. *Four-horse charabancs descending Kirkstone Pass. Note the early motor-car; c. 1900.*

182. *The Ullswater coach at the Sun Hotel, Pooley Bridge, c. 1890, with Mr Richard Bell driving. This service operated from Penrith Railway Station to Pooley Bridge ('for Lake Ullswater') twice daily.*

183. *Coaches at Thirlspot, Thirlmere, c. 1890.*

184. *A light trap c. 1920s. Vehicles like this were in common use in the Lake District until the 1940s.*

Patterdale to Penrith.

A CHAR-A-BANC

Will leave Crook-a-beck Posting Establishment, every **Tuesday, Thursday and Saturday morning,** arriving at Penrith Station at 10 a.m., and returning from Borrowdale's Central Hotel, at 3-30 p.m.

FARES:	Single.	Return.
Patterdale to Penrith.. ..	2/=	3/=
Pooley Bridge to Penrith ..	1/=	1/6

PRIVATE CONVEYANCES ON HIRE.

R. PEARS, Crook-a-beck, Proprietor.

185. A charabanc poster, 1895

186. The Ullswater (Royal Mail) Motor Coach on its twice-daily run between Penrith and Patterdale, 1915.

187. *Crossing the sands of Morecambe Bay; an engraving based on the painting by J. M. W. Turner.*

188. *Modern cross-bay travellers fording the Leven at Canal Foot, Furness.*

189. *The first* Swan *at Waterhead, Windermere, c. 1895. Launched in 1869, she was withdrawn from service in 1938 and broken up.*

190. *The* Gondola *at the head of Coniston Water.*

191. *The Boot Express. Originally constructed in 1875, the Ravenglass–Boot railway line carried iron ore and passengers down Eskdale to the sea. In 1915 the track was re-laid using a fifteen-inch gauge and today the line, affectionately known as 'l'ile Ratty', carries thousands of holiday-makers. The engine shown here is a pre-1915 model, the* Nab Gill.

192. *The Windermere steam ferry about the time of the First World War with two of Rigg's Windermere–Coniston coaches on board.*

193. *The present Windermere ferry, the* Drake.

and generally the gentry of the neighbourhood set their faces against it and would not use it . . . even for the conveyance of a parcel—so annoyed were they that their darling lake should be so disturbed by the evolution of the paddle, or their clear atmosphere contaminated by the smoke of a funnel'.[20] Yet in spite of such opposition from an early conservationist lobby, it was appreciated that in the absence of good roads the new service was a great convenience to visitors and residents alike, and in her first short season the 'Lady' carried 5,000 passengers.[21] Moreover, the speed and cheapness—2s. on deck and 3s. in the saloon from Ambleside to Newby Bridge— were further recommendations. The success of the service encouraged further expansion, and in 1846 a sister ship, the Lord of the Isles, was launched, but soon there was a competitor; in 1849 the Windermere Iron Steam Boat Company launched its first vessel, the Fire Fly, followed in the next year by the Dragon Fly. The cut-price competition which resulted would have formed an excellent plot for a Gilbert and Sullivan comic opera! In July 1850 the Lady of the Lake and Fire Fly were damaged in an attempt to hinder each other; and when the Steam Yacht Co. offered trips round the lake for a maximum fare of 6d. (cabin) and 3d. (deck), and included a bottle of porter, the rival Iron Steam Boat Co. countered by advertising free excursions. Economic disaster was eventually averted when, in 1858, the two companies amalgamated, forming the Windermere United Steam Yacht Company, and eight years later the united company launched the Rothay, the last of the Windermere paddle steamers. By this time it was clear that, like the coaches, the steamer service had become something of a tourist attraction catering for visitors rather than residents, and this undoubtedly encouraged the Furness Railway Company to build a passenger line from Ulverston to Lakeside, where a new landing stage was incorporated into the station. The opening of the branch line in 1869 was closely followed by the launch of a new steamer, the Swan (plate 189), and in 1871 the Furness Railway Company assumed control of the Windermere United Steam Yacht Co. Since privatisation in 1985 the company has reverted to its earlier name, the Windermere Iron Steam Boat Company.

Like Windermere, Ullswater still retains a passenger service, but its history is not as rich as the Windermere fleet's. In 1859 a paddle steamer, the Enterprise, was launched at Pooley Bridge, though little is known of her,[22] but in 1877 the Ullswater Steam Navigation Company commissioned their Lady of the Lake, the success of which motivated the building of the Raven in 1899. This latter vessel carried Kaiser Wilhelm II in 1900 when he was the guest of Lord Lonsdale at Lowther Castle.

Like the larger lakes of Windermere and Ullswater, Coniston Water also has an honourable tradition of steam boats, beginning in 1855 when a small steamer, owned by a Mr James Sladen, started a service from the Waterhead Inn calling at Nibthwaite and Lake Bank.[23] The timetable allowed three trips every day including Sundays, and the fare for the round trip was 1s. 6d. first class and 1s. second class. Mr Sladen's enterprise was not rewarded, however, for within weeks of commencement the service was withdrawn because of lack of support. This inauspicious beginning did not discourage the Coniston Railway Company from launching, in 1859, the Gondola (plate 190) which operated a popular service until 1908 when yet another Lady of the Lake, a larger and more powerful steamer, replaced her, although the Gondola continued in service intermittently until the Second World War. In 1950 the 'Lady' was broken up, and until recently the Gondola lay half submerged in the reeds at the foot of Coniston Water. Happily, she has been restored by the National Trust and now once again proudly carries passengers on the lake.

In 1844 Wordsworth, fearing the imminent violation of his native Lakeland by the proposed Kendal to Windermere railway, complained of this new invasion and recorded his displeasure at '. . . the directors of railway companies . . . always ready to devise or encourage entertainments for tempting the humbler classes to leave their homes'.[24] Yet, in spite of the Laureate's verbal attack, the line was completed in 1847 and the tiny hamlet of Birthwaite grew into the town of Windermere, as much a creation of the railways as Swindon or Crewe. In 1859 the Foxfield Junction to Coniston line was opened for traffic, followed some six years later by the Penrith to Cockermouth railway through Keswick. But not all the proposed railway schemes were successful; that doyen of the Victorian intellectuals, John Ruskin, lent his considerable weight to the campaign against a line through Dunmail Raise, and similarly there was opposition to proposals for a line from Braithwaite to Buttermere and a line into Ennerdale.

By the end of the nineteenth century, though, the flood-gates were open; the process started by the turnpike roads of the eighteenth century was accelerated by the railways of the nineteenth, and the Lake District dales were opened up not only to visitors but to the *nouveaux riches* settlers who built mock-gothic turreted fantasies along the shores of Windermere, in Keswick, in the Vale of Grasmere, and in Borrowdale. This was, however, more than merely a change in transport and architectural styles; it was an alteration of a whole way of life, the inexorable march of Progress superimposing new ideas and new techniques against which the age-old manners, customs and traditions were powerless.

'And now you've a swatch o' them good oald days,
'At fwoak brags on as hevvin lang sen;
And you know summat now o' their wark and their ways;
Wad ye swap eb'm hands, good men?'

William Dickinson, 1876.

GLOSSARY

Adits: Horizontal mining tunnels cut into the hillsides.

Arles or earnest money: Money paid to farm servants on hiring as a token of their hire.

Arvel bread: Wheaten bread distributed to mourners at a funeral to be taken home with them.

Bakstone: Slate or iron plate on which oatbread was baked.

Bears: Crude matting made from the peelings of rushes.

Beltane fires: Bonfires lit on the eve of May Day.

Bink: A narrow ledge used by a fox as a refuge.

Blenkard, Blanchard: One-eyed cock, veteran of several fights.

Bloomery hearths: Iron-ore smelting hearths.

Borran: A pile of stones.

Bower or Chamber: The bedroom of the master and mistress.

Braffin: Horse-collar.

Brake and Whittle: Tools used in the dressing of roofing slate.

Brandreth, Brandiron: Iron tripod used in cooking.

Brands, Brand ends: Unburnt wood remaining after charcoal burning.

Bread cupboards: Carved oak cupboards, often forming part of a clam-staff and daub partition separating the 'house' from the chamber and buttery. Many bear a seventeenth-century date and the initials of the owner and his wife. Traditionally, clap bread (q.v.) was stored in these cupboards, which were sometimes known as court cupboards.

Brobbs: Small tree branches used to mark the fords across the Kent and Leven channels on the cross-sands road over Morecambe Bay.

Cams: Stones which surmount a dry-stone wall.

Catmallison: A recess shelf or carved cupboard, often above the fire window, which contained the family Bible.

Clap bread, Haver bread: Oat bread.

Clog-wheels: Solid wooden wheels fixed to an axle which turned under the cart.

Cockpenny: Money contribution paid to the schoolmaster by his pupils partly towards the financing of a cockfight.

Colliers: Charcoal burners.

Corpse ways: Traditional routes along which funeral processions made their way to the church.

Crucks: Pairs of naturally arched timbers, pegged together at the apex to form a frame for a house or barn. Sometimes called 'siles'.

Deeting: Winnowing of grain in a through-draught of wind.

Dobbie stones: Holed stones hung in byres to protect animals from sorcery.

Down-house: The service area of a farmhouse.

Elding: Wood or peat fuel.

Fire-house, house: The living accommodation in a farmhouse.

Fire window: Small window which illuminated the hearth.

Fleam: A blood-letting instrument used in veterinary medicine.

Flourice: Iron striker used with flint to light fire.

Gimmer: A yearling ewe.

Goose bield: Fox-trap made of dry-stone walling and baited with a goose.

To Grave: To dig (usually peats).

'Gurning through a braffin': Grimacing through a horse-collar.

Hake: Auld Wives' Hake: By some authorities (e.g. S. H. Scott) described as an 'assembly of old dames', but by others as merely a rustic gathering.

Hallan: A passage running from the front to the back of a farmhouse.

Hallan-drop: A black, sooty liquid which fell down the open chimneys, often on the heads of those seated below.

Haver bread: *See* Clap bread.

Heaf: Sheep pasture.

Hearting: Small stones used as in-filling in a dry-stone wall.

Heck: Partition which formed one side of the mell (q.v.). See footnote on page 23.

Hodden grey: A grey woollen cloth made of a mixture of black and white wool.

Hogg, hogget: Male or female lamb before shearing.

Hogg-holes: Square holes left in the base of a dry-stone wall to allow hoggs (q.v.) to pass through.

Kern supper: Harvest supper.

Kists, arks: Chests, usually of oak, used for storing oatmeal.

Lat-axe: An axe used in the splitting of timber.

Ley: A scythe.

Lish: Agile.

'London', 'country', 'tom', 'peg': Classification of slates according to fineness; used in the eighteenth century.

Mash vat: Vessel for brewing ale.

Mell: Short passage leading from the hallan (q.v.) into the fire-house (q.v.).

Merry neet: Social get-together.

Motty-peg: Stake around which a charcoal pitstead was built.

Naffs: Naves or hubs of a cart-wheel.

Nag-rake, Donkey-rake, T'o'd Meare: Drag-rakes used in haymaking.

Piggins: Stave-built wooden vessels from which liquid foods were consumed.

Pitsteads, Pit-rings: Charcoal burning floors.

Push-plough, Breast-plough: A cutting spade used to remove shallow turf prior to cultivation.

Rabbit-smoot: A form of rabbit trap consisting of a small hole in a dry-stone wall and a pit.

Rannel-balk, Randle-tree: Wooden beam fixed across the open hearth from which the ratten-crooks hung.

Ratten-crooks, Racken-crooks: Adjustable pot hangers suspended from the rannel-balk.

Ruddle: Dye for marking sheep.

Rush bark: Cylindrical metal box for rush-lights.

Say: A shallow dish used to hold water for quenching charcoal pitsteads.

Sconce: A fixed wooden bench under which kindling or elding was stored.

Scummer: Long-handled spoon for skimming off the salt meat boiling in cauldrons.

Seeves, Sieves: Rushes, usually *Juncus conglomeratus*, from which rushlights were made.

Shanklings: Wood used in charcoal making, usually about 3 feet in length.

Shelvings: Moveable frames added to a cart to extend its length and increase its capacity.

Smart: Oak lath used in the manufacture of swill baskets.

Smit-books: Books showing 'smits' or marks used to identify sheep.

Sonks: Green turf sods often used as substitute saddles.

Souse tub: Vessel holding brine or sour whey used for pickling meat.

Stag: Young cock.

Stang: Shaft of a cart; a pole. See 'riding the stang', page 68.

Strickle: Instrument for sharpening scythes.

Swill-basket, Spelk-basket: Woven oak basket.

Swiller's 'horse' or 'mare': A foot-operated vice and seat used by swill-basket makers.

Tatie-pot: The traditional fare at hunts, merry meets and kern suppers. It consists of black puddings, Herdwick mutton, onions and potatoes, and beside it the Lancashire hot-pot pales into insignificance!

Threshwood: A wooden doorstep.

Thrinter: 'Three-winter' sheep.

Throughs: Stones which help to tie the two faces of a dry-stone wall together. They often project through the wall on each side, hence the name.

Trail barrow: Wheel-less wooden barrow used to convey slate down a mountainside.

Tumble-tom: A hay sweep.

Tummel cars: Single-horse, two-wheeled-carts made entirely of wood. The wheels were usually clog-wheels (q.v.).

Tup: A ram.

Twinter: 'Two-winter' sheep.

Wall head: A visible boundary built into a dry-stone wall to indicate ownership or responsibility for repair.

Wangs: Leather thongs, hence 'wangy' cheese, a tough blue milk cheese.

Weyt: A shallow sheepskin dish used in deeting (q.v.) or winnowing grain.

NOTES

Chapter 1.

FARMS AND FARM BUILDINGS

1 Partington, 1960.
2 W. G. Hoskins, The Rebuilding of Rural England, 1570–1640, in his *Provincial England*, London, 1963.
3 Rollinson, 1967.
4 For an analysis of the dates of 'the Great Rebuilding' *see* Brunskill, 1970.
5 R. W. Brunskill, in Bouch and Jones, 1961.
6 Hodgson, 1822.
7 Gough, 1812, p. 11.
8 Hodgson, 1822. Similar wicker and lath-and-plaster chimney hoods were common in Ireland.
9 Gough, 1812, p. 12.
10 Evans, 1957, p. 68.
11 Hodgson, 1822, p. 290.
12 Wilson, 1887, p. 74.
13 Gough, 1812, p. 12.
14 Clarke, 1787, p. xx.
15 W. Wordsworth, *Guide to the Lakes*, 1810 (1951 reprint), p. 114.
16 Marshall, 1971, p. 37.
17 Brunskill, 1970, p. 135.
18 *See* J. Walton, Upland Houses, *Antiquity*, vol. 119, 1956.
19 Brunskill, 1970, p. 139.
20 Armitt, 1916, p. 324.
21 RCHM, 1936, p. 193.
22 J. Walton, Upland Houses, *Antiquity*, vol. 119, 1956.
23 Fair, 1922, p. 98.

Chapter 2.

HEARTH AND HOME—SOME FARMHOUSE EQUIPMENT

1 Gibson, 1865–6a, p. 173.
2 Evans, 1957, p. **59**.
3 Evans, 1957, p. **66**.
4 Browne Manuscripts, vol. 2, p. 176. Westmorland Record Office, Kendal.
5 Peate, 1972, p. 42.
6 Evans, 1957, p. 77. For an account of the manufacture of oat bread in the West Riding of Yorkshire *see* M. Hartley and J. Ingilby, *Life and Tradition in the Yorkshire Dales*, pp. 21–8; London 1968.
7 Armitt, 1916, p. 398.
8 C. Fiennes, *The Journeys of Celia Fiennes*, ed. C. Morris. London, 1947, pp. 193–4.
9 Manuscript notes, Barrow-in-Furness Public Library.
10 Gough, 1812, p. 14.
11 Cowper, 1895a, pp. 253–68.
12 Hodgson, 1822, p. 289.
13 Evans, 1957, p. 74.
14 Hodgson, 1822, p. 292.
15 Cowper, 1893, p. 109.
16 *ibid*. H. S. Cowper's extensive collection of Cumbrian candle and rushlight holders is now in the Barrow-in-Furness Museum.
17 Hodgson, 1822, p. 289.
18 Greenop, 1907, pp. 206–8.
19 Cowper, 1899b, p. 258.
20 Cowper, 1899a, p. 298.
21 Cowper, 1895a, p. 265.
22 W. Close, *Furness Agricultural Implements*, Manuscript with drawings, z2293/1–2. Barrow-in-Furness Public Library.

Chapter 3.

CUMBRIAN FARE AND FOLK DRESS

1 W. Dickinson, quoted in Garnett, 1912, p. 8.
2 Fleming, 20th August 1801.
3 Clarke, 1787, p. 75.
4 Hodgson, 1822, p. 252.
5 Scott, D., 1899, p. 174.
6 Eden, 1797, vol. 1, p. 501. *See also* Bouch and Jones, 1961, p. 243.
7 Garnett, 1912, p. 10.
8 Armitt, 1916, p. 287.
9 Clarke, 1787, p. 115.
10 Fleming, 8th May 1810.
11 Cowper, 1897, pp. lxxxvii–lxxxviii.
12 Gough, 1812, p. 21.
13 Gibson, 1857–8, p. 104.
14 Fleming, 14th April 1810.
15 The full text of the Furness pace-egg play is given in Cowper, 1899a, pp. 334–38.

16 Scott, S. H., 1904, p. 137.
17 T. K. Fell, *Legendary and Folk Lore in Furness*. Manuscript z2606. Barrow-in-Furness Public Library.
18 Clarke, 1787, p. 32.
19 Fleming, 1st February 1818.
20 Budworth, 1795 (1810 edn.), pp. 289–90.
21 Clarke, 1787, p. 45.
22 Budworth, 1795 (1810 edn.), p. 39.
23 Garnett, 1912, p. 5.
24 Gough, 1812, pp. 9–10.
25 Hodgson, 1822, p. 291.
26 Gough, 1812, p. 10.
27 Hodgson, 1822, p. 291.
28 Scott, S. H., 1904, pp. 91–3.
29 *Gentleman's Magazine*, vol. 60, pp. 505–6.
30 West, 1774 (1805 edn.), p. 17.
31 Gough, 1812, p. 10.

Chapter 4.

SOME CUSTOMS AND TRADITIONS

1 Hodgson, 1822, p. 377.
2 Evans, 1957, p. 285.
3 Hodgson, 1822, p. 377.
4 Cowper, 1899a, p. 322.
5 See example in Keswick Museum.
6 Thomas Hardy, *The Mayor of Casterbridge*, 1886; Hugh Walpole, *Rogue Herries*, 1930.
7 Fleming, 27th and 28th January 1812.
8 Hodgson, 1822, p. 379.
9 Gibson, 1857–8, p. 106.
10 Evans, 1957, p. 289.
11 Hodgson, 1822, p. 377.
12 Barber, 1894, p. 354.

13 Scott, S. H., 1904, p. 134.
14 Parker and Collingwood, 1926, p. 77.
15 Historic Manuscripts Commission, 1890.
16 Bolton, 1869, p. 123.
17 T. Pennant, *Tour in Scotland*, London, 1769, vol. 2, p. 49.
18 Gibson, 1857–8, p. 105.
19 Evans, 1957, p. 297.
20 Collingwood, 1895, p. 405.
21 Fleming, 24th May 1801.
22 Clarke, 1787, p. 124.
23 Armitt, 1912, p. 219.
24 Rawnsley, 1902, pp. 7–10.

Chapter 5.

FOLK MEDICINE

1 Barnes, H., 1895.
2 Historic Manuscripts Commission, 1890.
3 Cowper, 1899a, p. 314.
4 Scott, S. H., 1904, p. 130.
5 Elizabeth Birkett, manuscript commonplace and

recipe book. Browne MSS., Westmorland Record Office, Kendal.
6 Cowper, 1899a, p. 317.
7 Scott, S. H., 1904, p. 132.
8 Gibson, 1857–8, p. 107.

9 H. S. Cowper, A Commonplace Book for the Parish of Hawkshead. Manuscript z292. Barrow-in-Furness Public Library.
10 Elizabeth Birkett, manuscript commonplace and recipe book. Browne MSS., Westmorland Record Office, Kendal.
11 Fleming, 15th March 1816.
12 Fisher, 22nd December 1834. *See also* Rollinson, 1966.

13 Hall, 1787.
14 Fleming.
15 Robinson, 1819.
16 Kipling, 1961.
17 Thomas Short, quoted in Kipling, 1961.
18 Clarke, 1787, p. 83.
19 K. Rawnsley, *Lakeland Rambler*, No. 32, Whitehaven, 1971.

Chapter 6.

EARLY VETERINARY PRACTICE

1 Historic Manuscripts Commission, 1890.
2 Hall, 1787.
3 Rawnsley, 1911, p. 58.
4 I am indebted to Mr Paul Boyle, B.V.S.C., for this information.
5 Hall, 1787.
6 Fleming, 11th June 1819.
7 Sullivan, 1857, p. 153.
8 *Troutbeck*, 'by a member of the Scandinavian Society', Kendal, 1876.

9 Beaumont, 1863, p. 18.
10 Wilson, 1887, p. 85.
11 Armitt, 1916, p. 260.
12 Historic Manuscripts Commission, 1890.
13 Garnett, 1912, p. 167.
14 Garnett, 1912, p. 167.
15 T. Harrison, manuscript account book. Westmorland Record Office, Kendal.

Chapter 7.

MOUNTAIN SHEEP

1 Cowper, 1899a, p. 262.
2 Bouch and Jones, 1961, p. 348.
3 Clarke, 1787, p. 98.
4 P. Crosthwaite, manuscript notes in his copy of Clarke, 1787. Barrow-in-Furness Public Library.
5 Webster, 1868, p. 13.
6 Armitt, 1906, p. 10.
7 West, 1774 (1805 edn), pp. 40–1.

8 Rollinson, 1967, pp. 54–73.
9 Ellwood, 1899, p. 6.
10 Clarke, 1787, p. 41.
11 Linton, 1864, pp. 113–14.
12 Webster, 1868, p. 15.
13 Mrs S. J. Bulman, Federation of Women's Institutes Essay Competition, 1969. Westmorland Record Office, Kendal.

Chapter 8.

SOME AGRICULTURAL TOOLS AND TECHNIQUES

1 Clarke, 1787, p. 75.
2 Bailey and Culley, 1794, p. 31.
3 Bailey and Culley, 1794, p. 31.
4 Stockdale, 1872, p. 570.
5 W. Close, *Furness Agricultural Implements*. Manuscript with drawings, z2293/1–2. Barrow-in-Furness Public Library.
6 Dickinson, 1850, p. 63.

7 Dickinson, 1876.
8 Stockdale, 1872, p. 571.
9 Dickinson, 1850, p. 63.
10 Cowper, 1895b, p. 95.
11 Collins, 1969, p. 7.
12 W. Close, *Furness Agricultural Implements*. Manuscript with drawings, z2293/1–2. Barrow-in-Furness Public Library.

13 Garnett, 1912, p. 205.
14 Rollinson, 1967, p. 107.
15 Cowper, 1895a, p. 258.
16 Garnett, 1912, p. 205.

17 Mrs Finch Dawson, Federation of Women's Institutes Essay Competition, 1969. Westmorland Record Office, Kendal.

Chapter 9.

WEATHER LORE

1 Clarke, 1787, p. 37.
2 Walker, 1792, p. 101.
3 W. Gell, *A Tour in the Lakes made in 1797*, ed. W. Rollinson, Newcastle, 1968, p. 38.

4 Allen, 1880, p. 34.
5 Palmer, 1948, p. 86.

Chapter 10.

DRY-STONE WALLS

1 Rollinson, 1972, p. 3.
2 Palmer, 1937, p. 74.
3 Otley, 1850, p. 123.
4 *Furness Abbey Coucher Book*, vol. 2, part 2, pp. 565–6. Chetham Society, Manchester, 1916.
5 B. L. Thompson, *The Troutbeck Hundreds and the Common Lands of Troutbeck*. Privately printed, Kendal, pp. 6–7.

6 Westmorland Record Office, Kendal.
7 Ward, 1929, p. 63.
8 Cumberland Record Office, Carlisle.
9 Rollinson, 1972, pp. 10–17.
10 Leconfield Estate Papers, Cockermouth Castle (Marshall Documents, D/Lec/ATK).
11 Pringle, 1794, p. 36.
12 Garnett, 1912, p. 57.

Chapter 11.

THE WOODLAND CRAFT INDUSTRIES

1 Beck, 1844, p. lxvi.
2 Cowper, 1899a, p. 275.
3 Marshall, 1971, pp. 24–5.
4 Bardsley and Ayre, 1886, p. 119.
5 Cowper, 1897, p. 386.
6 Fell, A., 1908, p. 129.
7 *North Lonsdale Magazine*, vol. 3, 1898–1900, pp. 80–4.
8 Fell, A., 1908, p. 134.
9 Browne Manuscripts (unbound MSS. F. 216). Westmorland Record Office, Kendal.
10 Barnes, F., 1968, p. 76.
11 Marshall and Davies-Shiel, 1969, pp. 75–88.
12 Cowper, 1901, pp. 141–3.
13 Marshall and Davies-Shiel, 1969, p. 175.
14 Cowper, 1897, p. 302.
15 *North Lonsdale Magazine*, vol. 3, 1898–1900, p. 84.
16 White, 1930, p. 85.

17 *North Lonsdale Magazine*, vol. 3, 1898–1900, p. 81.
18 *Cumbria*, July 1955, p. 134.
19 P. N. Wilson, The Gunpowder Mills of Westmorland and Furness. *Transactions of the Newcomen Society*, vol. 36, 1964.
20 Marshall and Davies-Shiel, 1969, pp. 78–85.
21 A. Palmer, *The Lowwood Gunpowder Co., 1798–1808*. Typescript, Lancashire Record Office, Preston.
22 J. Melville, *North Western Evening Mail*, 22nd January 1971.
23 Records of the Lowwood Gunpowder Works, Lancashire Record Office, Preston.
24 J. Melville, *North Western Evening Mail*, 22nd January 1971.
25 A. Palmer, *The Lowwood Gunpowder Co., 1798–1808*. Typescript, Lancashire Record Office, Preston.
26 Marshall and Davies-Shiel, 1969, p. 87.

Chapter 12.

SLATE QUARRYING AND MINING

1 Sutton, 1961, p. 14.
2 Postlethwaite, 1913, p. 135.
3 West, 1774, p. xxxv.
4 Green, 1819, vol. 1, p. 90.
5 Quoted in Collingwood, 1906, pp. 65–6.
6 Browne Manuscripts. Westmorland Record Office, Kendal.
7 *ibid.*
8 J. Melville, *North Western Evening Mail*, 20th June 1969.
9 Gibson, 1868–9, pp. 45–54.
10 W. Close, in West, 1774 (1805 edn), p. 411.
11 Clarke, 1787, p. 154.
12 Linton, 1864, p. 197.
13 Green, 1819, vol. 2, p. 190.
14 Collingwood, 1906, p. 67.
15 Mrs M. B. Park, Federation of Women's Institutes Essay Competition, 1969. Westmorland Record Office, Kendal.
16 Price, 1914, p. 179.
17 Clarke, 1787, p. 154.
18 Collingwood, 1912; Postlethwaite, 1913.
19 25th George II, cap. 10.
20 Quoted in *Mackereth's Furness Year Book*, Ulverston, 1900, p. 294.
21 Shaw, 1972, p. 12.
22 Clarke, 1787, p. 33.
23 Gibson, 1857, p. 115.
24 Gibson, 1857, p. 110.
25 Gibson, 1857, p. 114.
26 Shaw, 1972, p. 23.
27 Postlethwaite, 1913, p. 71.

Chapter 13.

COCKFIGHTING AND FOXHUNTING

1 F. Nicholson, Gamecock Fighting, in *V.C.H. Cumberland*, p. 475.
2 J. Strutt, *Sports and Pastimes*, London, 1833, p. 281.
3 Clarke, 1787, p. 40.
4 Historic Manuscripts Commission 1890.
5 Bouch and Jones, 1961, p. 200.
6 *V.C.H. Cumberland*, p. 476.
7 Clarke, 1787, p. 40.
8 *V.C.H. Cumberland*, p. 476.
9 Ferguson, 1888, p. 375.
10 Cowper, 1895b, p. 98.
11 Bolton, 1869, p. 123.
12 Scott, D., 1899, p. 194.
13 RCHM., 1936.
14 *V.C.H. Cumberland*, p. 477.
15 Cowper, 1899a, p. 220.
16 Cowper, 1899a, p. 119.
17 Browne Manuscripts. Westmorland Record Office, Kendal.
18 Barrow-in-Furness Public Library, z2497.
19 Fleming, March 1813.
20 Cowper, 1895b, p. 98.
21 Barrow-in-Furness Public Library, z2496.
22 Rice, 1969, p. 61.
23 Cowper, 1899a, p. 217.
24 Stockdale, 1872, p. 573.
25 Macpherson, 1892, pp. 13–14.
26 Historic Manuscripts Commission, 1890.
27 *Gentleman's Magazine*, 1st June 1751.
28 Dickinson, 1876, p. 189.
29 Clarke, 1787, p. 189.
30 Clarke, 1787, p. 189.
31 Hay, 1943, pp. 28–31.
32 See also Plint, 1972, pp. 332–3.
33 H. Maclean, *The Watermillock Parish Registers, 1579–1812*, Kendal, 1908, p. XIV.
34 Clarke, 1787, p. 30.
35 Lady M. Howard, Fox Hunting, in *V.C.H. Cumberland*, p. 425.
36 Cowper, 1899a, p. 218.
37 Clapham, 1920, p. 106.
38 Clarke, 1787, pp. 41–2.
39 Scott, S. H., 1904, p. 105.
40 Wilson, 1887, p. 83.

Chapter 14.

SPORTS, PASTIMES AND ENTERTAINMENTS

1 Quoted in W. and C. Jerrold, *Cumberland in Prose and Poetry*, London, 1930, p. 121.
2 Quoted in M. Storey, *Associations of Clappersgate and Ambleside*, Ambleside, 1958, p. 32.
3 Morris, 1903, pp. 145–6.
4 Historic Manuscripts Commission, 1890.
5 Scott, S. H., 1904, p. 166.
6 Scott, S. H., 1904, p. 121.

7 Budworth, 1795, pp. 210–11.
8 Mawman, 1805, pp. 199–200.
9 Bardsley, 1885, p. 8.
10 Rollinson and Twyman, 1966.
11 Clarke, 1787, p. 51.
12 *Troutbeck*, 'by a member of the Scandinavian Society', Kendal, 1876, p. 35.
13 *V.C.H. Cumberland*, p. 488.

Chapter 15.

LAKELAND TRANSPORT

1 Gough, 1812, p. 33
2 Browne Manuscripts, vol. 1, p. 220. Westmorland Record Office, Kendal.
3 Quoted in Garnett, 1912, p. 34.
4 Bouch and Jones, 1961, p. 280.
5 Watson, 1894, p. 24.
6 Melville and Hobbs, 1946. Also Hobbs, 1955.
7 Fell, J., 1884, p. 6.
8 W. Wilson, 1885, p. 15.
9 Quoted in Palmer, 1946, p. 23.
10 Williams, L. A., *The Development of Road Transport in Cumberland, Westmorland and Furness District of Lancashire*, Ph.D. thesis, Leicester University, 1967, p. 268. Copy in Westmorland Record Office, Kendal.
11 Palmer, 1946, p. 23.
12 Sutton, 1961, p. 23.
13 Little, 1972, p. 25.

14 B. L. Thompson, *The Windermere Ferry*. Privately printed, Kendal, 1971, p. 3.
15 Quoted in Cowper, 1899a, p. 526.
16 *The Westmorland Gazette*, 12th November 1870.
17 *See* W. G. Collingwood, *Transactions of the Cumberland and Westmorland Antiquarian and Archaeological Society*, vol. 13 1913; and B. L. Thompson, *The Windermere Ferry*, Kendal, 1971.
18 Gibson, 1865–6b, pp. 159–160.
19 Cowper, 1899a, p. 249.
20 Mackay, 1846, pp. 46–7.
21 Hobbs, 1957, pp. 342–6, 398–401.
22 L. Speller, English Lake Steamers. *Sea Breezes*, April 1957, p. 283.
23 Hobbs, 1960, pp. 199–202.
24 Letter to *The Morning Post*, 9th December 1844.

BIBLIOGRAPHY

ALLEN, J., 1880. The Early Registers and Parish Accounts of Hawkshead. *Transactions of the Cumberland and Westmorland Antiquarian and Archaeological Society*, vol. 4 (Old Series).

ARMITT, M. L., 1906. Ambleside Town and Chapel. *Transactions of the Cumberland and Westmorland Antiquarian and Archaeological Society*, vol. 6 (New Series).

1912. *The Church of Grasmere*, Kendal.

1916. *Rydal*, Kendal.

BAILEY, J., and CULLEY, G., 1794. *A General View of the Agriculture of Cumberland*. London.

BARBER, H., 1894. *Furness and Cartmel Notes*. Ulverston.

BARDSLEY, C. W., 1885. *Chronicles of the Town and Church of Ulverston*.

BARDSLEY, C. W., and AYRE, L. R. (eds.), 1886. *Ulverston Parish Registers*. Ulverston.

BARNES, F., 1968. *Barrow and District*. Barrow.

BARNES, H., 1895. On Touching for the King's Evil. *Transactions of the Cumberland and Westmorland Antiquarian and Archaeological Society*, vol. 13 (Old Series).

BEAUMONT, T., 1863. *The Complete Cow Doctor*. Halifax.

BECK, T. A., 1844. *Annales Furnesienses*. London.

BOLTON, J., 1869. *Geological Fragments*. Ulverston.

BOUCH, C. M. L., and JONES, G. P., 1961. *The Lake Counties, 1500–1830*. Manchester.

BRUNSKILL, R. W., 1970. *Vernacular Architecture*. London.

BUDWORTH, J., 1795. *A Fortnight's Ramble to the Lakes*, 2nd edn. London; and 3rd edn. 1810.

CLAPHAM, R., 1920. *Foxhunting on the Lakeland Fells*. London.

CLARKE, J., 1787. *A Survey of the Lakes of Cumberland, Westmorland and Lancashire*. London.

COLLINGWOOD, W. G., 1895. Some Manx Names in Cumbria. *Transactions of the Cumberland and Westmorland Antiquarian and Archaeological Society*, vol. 13 (Old Series).

1906. *The Book of Coniston*. Kendal.

1912. *Elizabethan Keswick*. Kendal.

COLLINS, E. J. T., 1969. *Sickle to Combine*. Reading.

COWPER, H. S., 1893. The Domestic Candlestick of Iron in Cumberland, Westmorland and Furness. *Transactions of the Cumberland and Westmorland Antiquarian and Achaeological Society*, vol. 12 (Old Series).

1895a. A Grasmere Farmer's Sale Schedule in 1710. *Transactions of the Cumberland and Westmorland Antiquarian and Archaeological Society*, vol. 13 (Old Series).

1895b. On Some Obsolete and Semi-Obsolete Appliances. *Transactions of the Cumberland and Westmorland Antiquarian and Archaeological Society*, vol. 13 (Old Series).

(ed.), 1897. *The Oldest Register Book of the Parish of Hawkshead in Lancashire, 1568–1704*. London.

1899a. *Hawkshead*. London.

1899b. Illustrations of Old Fashions and Obsolete Contrivances in Lakeland. *Transactions of the Cumberland and Westmorland Antiquarian and Archaeological Society*, vol. 15 (Old Series).

1901. A Contrast in Architecture. *Transactions of the Cumberland and Westmorland Antiquarian and Archaeological Society*, vol. 1 (New Series).

DICKINSON, W., 1850. *Essay on the Agriculture of West Cumberland*. London and Whitehaven.

1876. *Cumbriana*. London and Whitehaven.

EDEN, F. M., 1797. *The State of the Poor*. London.

ELLWOOD, T., 1899. The Mountain Sheep, their origin and marking. *Transactions of the Cumberland and Westmorland Antiquarian and Archaeological Society*, vol. 15 (Old Series).

EVANS, E. E., 1957. *Irish Folk Ways*. London.

FAIR, M. C., 1922. A Relic of Pack-horse Days in Eskdale. *Transactions of the Cumberland and Westmorland Antiquarian and Archaeological Society*, vol. 22 (New Series).

FELL, A., 1908. *The Early Iron Industry of Furness and District*. Ulverston.

FELL, J., 1884. The Guides over the Kent and Leven Sands. *Transactions of the Cumberland and Westmorland Antiquarian and Archaeological Society*, vol. 7 (Old Series).

FERGUSON, R. S., 1888. Ἀλεκτρυονων Ἀγων. *Transactions of the Cumberland and Westmorland Antiquarian and Archaeological Society*, vol. 9 (Old Series).

FISHER, W., 1811–59. Manuscript diary and commonplace book of William Fisher of Barrow village, 1811–1859. (By kind permission of Mr R. Rowlandson, Ulverston.)

FLEMING, W., 1798–1819. Manuscript diary and commonplace book of William Fleming of Pennington, Furness. Microfilm in the Cohen Library, Liverpool University. (See also *The Countryman*, vol. 55, 1958.)

GARNETT, F. W., 1912. *Westmorland Agriculture, 1800–1900*. Kendal.

GIBSON, A. C., 1857. *The Old Man*, 2nd edn. Windermere.

1957–8. Ancient Customs and Superstitions in Cumberland. *Transactions of the Historic Society of Lancashire and Cheshire*, vol. 10 (1st Series).

1865–6a. Hawkshead Parish. *Transactions of the Historic Society of Lancashire and Cheshire*, vol. 6 (2nd Series).

1865–6b. The Lakeland of Lancashire. *Transactions of the Historic Society of Lancashire and Cheshire*, vol. 6 (2nd Series).

1868–9. The Last Popular Risings in the Lancashire Lake Country. *Transactions of the Historic Society of Lancashire and Cheshire*, vol. 9 (2nd Series).

GOUGH, J., 1812. *The Manners and Customs of Westmorland and Adjoining parts of Cumberland, Lancashire and Yorkshire*. Reprinted 1827.

GREEN, W., 1819. *Guide to the Lakes*. Kendal.

GREENOP, J., 1907. A Contrivance for producing Fire, formerly used in the English Lake District. *Transactions of the Cumberland and Westmorland Antiquarian and Archaeological Society*, vol. 7 (New Series).

HALL, J., 1787. Manuscript commonplace book. Westmorland Record Office, Kendal.

HAY, T., 1943. The Goose Bield. *Transactions of the Cumberland and Westmorland Antiquarian and Archaeological Society*, vol. 43 (New Series).

HISTORIC MANUSCRIPTS COMMISSION, 1890. *12th Report, Appendix, Part VII, Manuscripts of S. H. le Fleming Esq.* London.

HOBBS, J. L., 1955. The Turnpike Roads of North Lonsdale. *Transactions of the Cumberland and Westmorland Antiquarian and Archaeological Society*, vol. 55 (New Series).

1957. The Story of the Windermere Steamers. *Cumbria*, Jan.–Feb. 1957, pp. 342–346, 398–401.

1960. The Story of the Coniston Steamers. *Cumbria*, Sept. 1960, pp. 199–202.

HODGSON, J., 1822. *Westmorland As It Was*. Reprinted in *The Lonsdale Magazine*, vol. 3, 1822, with additional notes by J. Briggs.

KIPLING, C., 1961. A Salt Spring in Borrowdale. *Transactions of the Cumberland and Westmorland Antiquarian and Archaeological Society*, vol. 61 (New Series).

LINTON, E. LYNN, 1864. *The Lake Country*. London.

LITTLE, E. A., 1972. *The Chronicles of Patterdale*. Penrith.

MACKAY, C., 1846. *Scenery and Poetry of the English Lakes*. London.

MACPHERSON, H. A., 1892. *Fauna of Lakeland*. Edinburgh.

MARSHALL, J. D., 1971. *Old Lakeland*. Newton Abbot.

MARSHALL, J. D., and DAVIES-SHIEL, M., 1969. *The Industrial Archaeology of the Lake Counties*. Newton Abbot.

MAWMAN, J., 1805. *An Excursion to the Highlands of Scotland and the English Lakes*. London.

MELVILLE, J., and HOBBS, J. L., 1946. Furness Travelling and Postal Arrangements in the 18th and 19th Centuries. *Transactions of the Cumberland and Westmorland Antiquarian and Archaeological Society*, vol. 46 (New Series).
MORRIS, W. P., 1903. *Records of Patterdale*. Kendal.

OTLEY, J., 1850. *A Descriptive Guide to the English Lakes and Adjacent Mountains* (8th edn). Keswick.

PALMER, W. T., 1937. *Odd Corners in English Lakeland*. London.
  1946. *Wanderings in Lakeland*. London.
  1948. *More Odd Corners of English Lakeland*. London.
PARKER, C. A., and COLLINGWOOD, W. G., 1926. *The Gosforth District*. Kendal.
PARTINGTON, J. E., 1960. *Rural House Types prior to the Early 19th Century in the English Lake District*. Unpublished Ph.D. thesis, Manchester University School of Architecture.
PEATE, I. C., 1972. *Tradition and Folk Life, a Welsh View*. London.
PLINT, R. G., 1972. The Coniston Goose Bield. *Transactions of the Cumberland and Westmorland Antiquarian and Archaeological Society*, vol. 72 (New Series).
POSTLETHWAITE, J., 1913. *Mines and Mining in the Lake District*. Whitehaven.
PRICE, N., 1914. *Vagabond's Way*. London.
PRINGLE, A., 1794. *A General View of the Agriculture of the County of Westmorland*. London.

RAWNSLEY, H. D., 1902. *Life and Nature at the English Lakes*. Glasgow.
  1911. *By Fell and Dale at the English Lakes*. Glasgow.
RICE, H. A. L., 1969. *Where Rise the Mountains*. Newcastle.
ROBINSON, J., 1819. *A Guide to the Lakes*. London.
ROLLINSON, W., 1966. The Diary and Farm Accounts of William Fisher, a Low Furness Yeoman Farmer, 1811–1859. *Transactions of the Cumberland and Westmorland Antiquarian and Archaeological Society*, vol. 66 (New Series).
  1967. *A History of Man in the Lake District*. London.
  1972. *Lakeland Walls*. Clapham.
ROLLINSON, W., and TWYMAN, M., 1966. *John Soulby, Printer, Ulverston*. Reading.
ROYAL COMMISSION ON HISTORICAL MONUMENTS, 1936. *Westmorland*. London.

SCOTT, D., 1899. *Bygone Cumberland and Westmorland*. London.
SCOTT, S. H., 1904. *A Westmorland Village*. London.
SHAW, W. T., 1972. *Mining in the Lake Counties*. Clapham.
STOCKDALE, J., 1872. *Annals of Cartmel*. Ulverston.
SULLIVAN, J., 1857. *Cumberland and Westmorland, Ancient and Modern*. Kendal.
SUTTON, S., 1961. *The Story of Borrowdale*. Keswick.

Victoria County History of Cumberland. 2 vols, 1905. London.

WALKER, A., 1792. *A Tour from London to the Lakes*. London.
WARD, E. M., 1929. *Days in Lakeland*. London.
WATSON, J., (ed.), 1894. *The Annals of a Quiet Valley*. London.
WEBSTER, C., 1868. On the Farming of Westmorland. *Journal of the Royal Agricultural Society of England*, vol. 6 (2nd Series), pt. 1, No. 7.
WEST, T., 1774. *Antiquities of Furness*. Ulverston; and 1805 edn., with additions by W. Close.
WHITE, W., 1930. *Furness Folk and Facts*. Kendal.
WILSON, W., 1885. *Coaching Past and Present*. Windermere.
  1887. Former Social Life in Cumberland and Westmorland. *Transactions of the Cumberland and Westmorland Association for the Advancement of Literature and Science*, No. 12.

INDEX

Agues, 74, 78
Ale, 45, 176
Ambleside, 71, 72, 176, 194, 195, 198, 200
Ambleside Turnpike Trust, 195
Arvel bread, 47, 69
Auld Wives' Hakes, 176

Backbarrow, 144
Bakstones, 34, 36; *9*; pl 30
Bark peelers, 145, 148; *32*; pl 124
Barns, 29–30; *7*; pls 4, 5, 6, 7
Barring out, 69
Barrow, 77, 162
Bassenthwaite regatta, 187
Beltane fires, 70
Bewitched cattle, 83
Bidden weddings, *see* Wedding customs
Birth and christening customs, 47–8
Black Combe, 124
Black lead, 79, 163
Blackbeck gunpowder mills, 149–50
Blencathra foxhounds, 174
Blood-letting, 77–8, 81
Bloomeries, 140, 144
Bobbin making, 146–8; pl 125
Bolton, Col. John (of Storrs Hall), 118
Bolton, John (of Urswick), 69, 167
Boon ploughing, 176
Borrowdale, 113, 126, 127, 172, 195, 198, 199
Borrowdale 'sop', 125
Bottom winds, 126
Bowman, Joe, 174
Bowness (Westmorland), 176
'Braffins', 115, 188
Bread cupboards, 23–4, 37; pls 24, 25, 26
Bromfield, 167
Brotherilkeld Farm, 128; pl 19
Brough, 70
Browne family of Troutbeck, 24, 37, 40, 47, 168, 193
Brownrigg, George, 122
Brunskill, R. W., 28
Brushes, 148; pl 135
Budworth, Joseph, 48, 186

Building materials and geology, 20
Bull-baiting, 175
Burnmoor, 69
Buses, 198–9
Butter, 41, 43
Buttermere valley, 172
Buttery, 41

Caldbeck, 45, 172
Calf immolation, 83
Candlemas, 125
Candles, *see* Rushlights
Card games, 176
Carling Sunday, 46
Cart wheels, 116; pls 89, 90, 91
Cartmel, 115, 166, 171, 193, 194
Carts, 113–16; *23*
Catmallison, 23
Cattle, 81–4
Char, 45; *28*
Charcoal, 141, 142–5; *31*; pls 114–21
Charcoal burners, 142, 145; *32*; pls 122, 123
Cheeses, 41
Chimney hoods, 22, 24
Chimneys, 27
Cholera, 77
Churns, 41; *13*
Clap bread, 34–7, 44
Clarke, James, 24, 44, 45, 48, 71, 79, 87, 113, 124, 161, 162, 164, 166, 167, 172, 173, 174
Clearance cairns, 127
Clipping, 92, 94; *21*; pls 61, 62, 63, 64, 65, 67, 68, 69
Clogs, 65
Close, William, 41, 76, 115, 152
Clothes, 48, 65
Coaches, 193–9; *37*; pls 180, 181, 182, 183, 185, 186
Cockermouth, 188, 189, 193, 195
Cockfighting, 166–71; pls 145, 146, 147
    and the Church, 167
    and schools, 166–7
Cock-loaf, 168–9, 192
Cockpennies, 166
Cockpits, 167, 169; *34*; pl 146
Cocks and cockspurs, 168; *34*

'Colliers', *see* Charcoal burners
Collingwood, W. G., 70
Collop Monday, 46
Colton, 142
Coniston, 84, 151, 152, 162, 164, 199, 200
Coniston copper mines, 164
Coniston Old Man, 151, 164, 172
Coniston Water, 151, 217
Cooking utensils, 34, 40; *8*
Coppice woods, 142; *30*; pl 112
Corn-drying kiln, 30; *7*
Corpse-ways, 69
Country dances, 176, 185
Court cupboards, *see* Bread cupboards
Cowper, H. S., 169, 170
Crakeplace Hall, 31
Crosthwaite, Peter, 88
Crosthwaite (Westmorland), 73, 86
Crowdy, 44
Cruck timbered buildings, 19, 28, 30
Cult objects, 70

Dairy equipment, 41; *13*
Dalton, 47, 71
Date stones, 31; pls 10, 11, 12, 13, 14, 15, 16, 17
Davies-Shiel, M., 148
'Deeting', 120–1
Derwent Farm, Grange-in-Borrowdale, 27–8; *5*
Dialect names for sheep, 89
Dickinson, William, 113, 118
Dobbie stones, 43, 83
Dobson, Tommy, 174–5
Down-house, 22, 24, 40
Drink, *see* Food and drink
Dry-stone walls, 127, 128, 137–40; *28, 29*; pls 92–109

Eagle rope, 172
Eagles, 171–2
Earnest money, 189
Egremont Crab fair, 188
Elding, 22
Elterwater gunpowder mills, 149, 150
Enclosure, 137
Ennerdale, 127, 172
Eskdale, 95, 118, 128, 172, 175
Eskdale Tup Show, 95
Evans, Professor E. Estyn, 22, 32, 37, 70

Fairs, 188–9. *See also* Hiring fairs
Far Orrest Farm, 19; *2*
Farm buildings, 28–30
Farm carts, 113–16
Farmhouses, 19–28
Fiennes, Celia, 35
Fig Sue, 46

Finsthwaite, 84
Fire cranes, 32, 34; *8*
Fire window, 23
Fisher, William (of Barrow), 77, 78, 82
Flails, 120; pl 78
Flan How, Ulverston, 190
Fleming, William, of Pennington, 46, 47, 68, 76, 83, 169
Flemings of Rydal, 46, 69, 73, 74, 77, 81, 84, 94, 166, 171, 185
Flint and striker, 32, 38; *11*
Floods, 126
Folk medicine, 73–80
Food and drink, 44–8
Food and folklore, 46–8
Fox screws, 174; *35*
Foxhound packs, 175
Foxhunting, 171–5
Funeral customs, 47, 68–9
Furness Abbey, 128, 141, 142, 145
Furness pace egg mummers' play, 47; pl 42
Furniture, 37; *10, 12*; pl 31

Garburn Road, 193; pl 178
Gatebeck gunpowder mills, 149, 150
Geology and dry-stone walls, 139
Gibson, A. C., 32, 164, 193
Glencoyne Farm, Ullswater, 27; *4*; pls 1, 18
Goose bield, 172; *35*; pl 148
Gough, John, 65, 66
Graphite, *see* Black lead
Grasmere, 71, 72, 74, 122, 124
Grasmere Sports, 191, 192; pls 161, 162, 163
Green, William, 151, 161
Greenside lead mines, 164
Greystoke, 48, 190
Grizedale, High Furness, 187
Groaning cheese, 48
Gunpowder manufacture, 148–50
'Gurning through a Braffin', 188; pl 159

Hackthorpe Hall, 120
Hall, John (of Leasgill), 78
Hallan, 20, 22, 24
Hallan-drop, 22, 40
'Harden' cloth, 65
Harrison, Thomas, 'cow doctor', 86
Hartsop, 30, 161
Haver bread, *see* Clap bread
Haweswater, 172
Hawkshead, 46, 70, 75, 126, 142, 145, 151, 168, 171, 193, 199
Haymaking, 122–3; pls 80, 81, 82, 83, 84
Hearth cults, 32
Hearths, 22, 23, 32, 40
Herb pudding, 45

Herdwick sheep, 87–8
Heversham, 167
Hewthwaite Hall, 31; pl 10
High Yewdale Farm, 28, 30; 6; pl 2
Hird, Hugh, 190
Hiring fairs, 188–9; pls 155, 156
Hodden grey, 48
Hogg-holes, 139; pls 94, 103, 104, 105
Hoggart, Thomas, of Troutbeck, 186
Honister Pass, 197
Honister quarries, 151, 161, 162
Hooping wheels, 146; pls 126, 127
Horning of cattle, 81
Hound trailing, 191–2
House, fire-house, 22–4, 32–40
Hunting, 171–5; pls 149, 150
Hutton Moor End farm, 31; pl 14

Ireby, 176
Iron utensils, 32, 34; 8; pls 27, 29

Keats, John, 176
Kendal, 48, 65, 125, 148, 149, 186–7, 188, 189, 193
Kent river, 124
Kentmere, 174
Kern supper, 176
Keswick, 84, 121, 124, 126, 162, 163, 164, 171, 175, 176, 186, 188, 194, 195, 199
Keswick regatta, 188
King's Evil, 73–4
Kirkby-in-Furness, 31 (footnote), 151, 152
Kirkstone Pass, 199
Knitted stockings, 48, 65

Lake steamers, 200, 217; pls 189, 190
Lambing, 92
Lancaster, 194, 195
Langdale (Great Langdale), 127, 162, 172, 174
Langdale (Little Langdale), 161
Lanthwaite, 140
Ley, see Scythe
Lickle Valley, 139
Linton, E. Lynn, 94, 161
Lofts, sleeping accommodation, 24
Lorton, 67
Lowwood gunpowder mills, 149–50
Lug marks, see Sheep marks
Lyth Valley, 120, 121

McKay, Charles, 200
Manesty salt spring, 79
Marshall, J. D., 28, 141, 148
Martindale, 199
Martineau, Harriet, 84
Mell, 22

'Merry Neets', 176, 185
Milnthorpe, 149
Miners, 164–5
Mining, 163–5
Morecambe Bay cross-sands road, 194–5; 37; pls 187, 188
Morris, Rev. W. P., 185
Murrain, 83–4
Music, 185

Naylor, Jos., of Wardale, 191
Needfire, 84
Nibthwaite, 151

Oat bread, see Clap bread
Oatmeal, 44. See also Clap bread
Orton, 48
Otley, Jonathan, 127
Oxen Park, High Furness, 31, 167; pl 15

Pace eggs, 47. See also Furness pace egg mummers' play
Pack horses, 193; 39
Partington, J. E. 24 (footnote)
Patterdale, 164, 167, 185, 198
Peat, 121–2; 24; pls 87, 88
Peat spades, 122; 24
Peel, John, 172, 173, 174; pl 151
Pennant, Thomas, 70
'Penny-fairs', 45
Penrith, 167, 186, 188, 193, 198, 199
Piggins, 37; 8
Pitsheads, 142–4; pl 113
Ploughs, 116–18; 25; pls 70, 71, 72
Pocklington, Joseph, 188
'Public' weddings, 67
Push-ploughs, 118; 24

'Quack' doctors, 80

Rabbit smoots, 139; 28
Railways:
  Coniston Railway Co., 162, 217, 218
  Furness, 162
  Kendal–Windermere, 162, 195, 217–18
  Penrith–Cockermouth, 218
  Proposed: Dunmail, 218; Ennerdale, 218
  Ulverston–Lakeside, 217
  Ulverston–Lancaster, 195
Rainfall, 126
Ralph, Samuel (of Sebergham), 79
Randle How, Eskdale, 31; pl. 16
Rannel-balk, randle-tree, 22, 32
Ransome, Arthur, 145
Ratten-crooks, racken-crooks, 22, 32; 8
Ravenglass Fair, 188

Rawnsley, H. D., 72
Reaping machines, 120
Regattas, 187–8
Rigg's Royal Mail Coaches, 195, 197, 200
Roads, 193, 199
Rose Castle, Dalston, 167
Rowan tree, 43, 70
Rowelling, 81
Rum butter, 48
Rushbearing, 71–2; pls 39, 40, 41
Rushlights, 37–8; *11*; pls 34, 35, 36, 37
Ruskin, John, 218
Rydal, 166. *See also* Flemings of Rydal

Salving, 84, 86, 94
Satterthwaite, 47, 70
Sawrey, 84
'Scotchmen', pedlars, 65; pl 174
Scythe, 120; *25*
Seathwaite (Borrowdale), 79, 163
Seatoller, 198
Sebergham, 79
Sedgwick, 149
Shearing, *see* Clipping
Sheep, 82, 84, 86, 87–96; *18, 21*; pls 47, 69. *See also* Herdwick sheep
Sheep marks, 89–91; *19, 21*; pls 53, 54, 56, 66
Sheep-scoring numerals, 91
Shepherd's Guide, 91; pl 52
Shepherds' meets, 91–2
Sickle, 120; *25*; pl 76
Sieves, seeves, *see* Rushlights
Skelwith Bridge, 74, 168
Slate:
  classification, 152
  dressing, 163
  quarrying, 151–2, 161–3; *33*
  'trailing', 161
  workers, 152, 161–3; pls 111, 140, 141, 142, 143, 144
Sleds, 113; *23*; pl 82
Smallpox, 76–7
Smit marks, *see* Sheep marks
Smoked meat, 44–5
'Sonk' saddles, 115
Spark Bridge, 36
Spelk baskets, *see* Swill baskets
Spice cupboards, 22; pls 21, 22, 23
Spinning galleries, 30; pls 8, 9
Stainton, Furness, 167
Stalkers of Penrith, 118
Stang, riding the, 68
'Statesman' farmhouses, 20–8; *3*
'Statesmen', 19–20
Steadman, George, 190
Steamers, *see* Lake steamers

Stephenson Ground Farm, 139
Stockdale, James, 115, 118, 194
Stone Carr sports, 190
Strickle, 120; *25*
'Sturdy', 82
Surnames, 141
Swill baskets, 141, 145–6; *32*; pls 128–34
Swiller's 'horse', 145; *32*; pl 133

Tan pits, 148
Tarn Hows Farm, 19; *1*
Tea, 46
Theatre, 185–7; pls 164–9
Threshing machines, 121; *26*; pl 79
Threshwood, 20, 22
Tilberthwaite, 152; pl 23
Timber raising, 176
Toothache cures, 75, 79
Torver, 146, 152
Townend, Troutbeck, 24, 30; pl 13
Transport, 193–200, 217–18
Tree worship, 70
Troutbeck, 34, 35, 47, 65, 69, 75, 83, 122, 128, 137, 144, 152, 168, 175, 176, 185, 186, 190. *See also* Browne family
Troutbeck Painable Fence Book, 137; *27*
'Tummel cars', 113
Turnip bread, 44
Turnpike roads, 193–4, 195

Ullswater, 124, 199, 217
Ulpha, 167
Ulverston, 65, 69, 142, 148, 149, 151, 152, 169, 176, 186–7, 188, 190, 193, 194–5
Urswick, 69, 71

Vaccination, 76–7
Vale of St John, 126
Veterinary techniques, 81–6; *18*

Wakefield, John, 149
Walney Island, 71, 170
Walpole, Hugh, 27, 68
Warcop, 71
Wasdale Head, 69, 127, 137, 151; pl 101
Watermillock, 173
Weather lore, 124–6
Wedding customs, 67–8
West, Thomas, 65–6, 88, 151
Whinlatter Pass, 195
Whitewashed farmhouses, 27
Whooping-cough cures, 75–6, 78
Wife-sale, 68
Wiggs, 47
Wild cat hunting, 175

Wilson, John, 167
Windermere, 144, 149, 190, 199–200, 217
   ferry, 198, 199–200; pls 192, 193
   regatta, 188
Windermere (town), 198, 218
Winster valley, 120, 144
Woodland crafts, 141–8

Woolpack Inn, Eskdale, 118
Wordsworth, Dorothy, 194
Wordsworth, John, 195
Wordsworth, William, 27, 195, 199, 217
Wreay, 167
Wrestling, 189–91